Aikido - Moving On

by Alan Drysdale

Director, Enmei Dojo,
Godan, ASU

Spitz Publishing
Titusville, FL, USA

Also by the author:
Doing Aikido. An introduction to aikido for kyu rank students.

ISBN 0-9668244-1-5

For additional copies:

Aikido – Moving On	$20
Doing Aikido	$15

Send to: Alan Drysdale, 3436 Parkland St., Titusville, FL USA, 32796

Aikido - Moving On

by Alan Drysdale
Enmei Dojo

Foreword

This book takes the next step from where my previous book, "Doing Aikido", left off. It is intended for upper kyu ranks and new yudansha: to help people take the next step forward. How many people get a black belt then quit, thinking they know something about aikido? How many people keep practicing, but only polishing their techniques and not otherwise progressing? I hope this book will help show the way forward.

Once again, techniques are included to illustrate significant points rather than to teach how to do basic technique – something that is better learned hands-on in a dojo. However, the difference as I see it between a shodan and a more advanced aikidoka is not technique per se. Rather, it is the way you do the techniques.

I do think that as one achieves increasingly advanced rank, and particularly as one starts teaching, one should provide a good example for students to emulate. Regrettably, advanced rank in aikido does not always correlate with better human beings. Perhaps this is not surprising, given that a broad spectrum of the world's population has studied aikido: all sorts of personalities, all sorts of cultures, all sorts of goals. However, it is a pity that an art with the name "aikido" – the way of harmony and spirit – should be no less prone to politics than any other organization. I've not always been a good example either, but the important thing is to try, just as in the physical side of the art. Continually try to improve, and you will. As always, the way to progress is through practice, focused intentional practice.

Once again, I have generally used "he" as a personal pronoun in this book. This is not a slight to women. There are some women who have wonderful aikido. I just refuse to conform to mere political correctness. Too often, in an attempt to redress a wrong we create a bigger mess than before. The majority of aikidoka are, in fact, male, and there is no generally accepted alternative to the generic "he".

Disclaimer

Aikido is physical and strenuous, like any martial art. This book is for advanced students, not for beginners. Beginners should only practice at a reputable dojo under an experienced instructor. People may, of course, do whatever they wish. However, they should only practice what is described here in a sensible fashion and with appropriate respect for their ukes.

Acknowledgments

I'd like to recognize all the people that have helped me improve my aikido over the years, both by providing good and bad examples. I'd like to thank my teachers over the years, first in judo, then in aikido, and lately in karate. Along the way I've even had a few classes of ju jutsu, jodo, and iaido. I'd like to thank members of Aikido List, who greatly expanded my perspective on aikido and other arts, and even on life in general. I'd like to thank them for the stimulation they provided when I started to think I knew it all, particularly Chuck, Chuck, Dennis, George, Jun, Mike, and Philip.

I'd like to thank the people who helped with this book, directly or indirectly, particularly Anita, Gary, Hooker Sensei, Ikeda Sensei, Kelly, Kevin, Linden Sensei, Saotome Sensei, and all my students. Many of the changes in my aikido since I wrote "Doing Aikido" have resulted from studying with Saotome Sensei and Aikido Schools of Ueshiba.

Contents

Part 1: Introduction and Background

Aikido - what is it?

It is quite hard to define aikido. Webster defines it as "a Japanese art of self-defense employing locks and holds and utilizing the principle of nonresistance to cause an opponent's own momentum to work against him". This is a start, though it does not mention throws which are half the curriculum. More importantly, it does not address what is unique about aikido. The definition could apply to a number of ju jutsu styles.

For years I have not had a good definition – aikido was simply what I did – but it was rather unsatisfying to not be able to define it. Lately, I have been formulating some ideas that relate to both the technical and ethical content and the historical lineage.

I guess we could say that aikido is the study of aiki as it applies to a defensive martial art with a certain historical lineage and, in consequence, technical repertoire. While I understand there are some older styles of ju jutsu that were named aikido, modern aikido is derived from what was taught by Morihei Ueshiba, Aikido O Sensei, though there are usually other influences. My aikido does trace back to Ueshiba Sensei, through various of his students at first and second remove. Sometimes when I bow to the kamiza I wonder what he would think. I like to think that he would approve of what I call aikido but of course there is no way to tell.

Aikido is usually related to unarmed defenses against unarmed attacks or attacks with archaic weapons like swords and sticks. It has a distinct repertoire that mostly seems to be derived from Daito Ryu Ju Jutsu.

Aikido – Moving On

Then we need to define aiki. I think of aiki as blending with an attacker's energy so as to deal with the attack. In aikido, the goal is to lead to a more or less benign ending. Other arts also use the concept, sometimes with less benign goals. This "energy", which some folks call "ki" and some don't, has physical dimensions like momentum, force, and power. It has relational dimensions like timing and distance. But it also has important informational aspects, like intent. It is not anything supernatural, anything outside of the realm of science.

Aikido is tremendous fun. If you didn't think that, you probably would not do it for long, much less continue long enough to get a shodan. It is also strenuous mentally, physically, and spiritually, but we come away from practice reinvigorated, ready to continue the relentless opposition to entropy that is life*.

* Schroedinger, Erwin. “What is life?” Reprinted 1992, Cambridge University Press

Moving On

It is easy enough to get a shodan - first-degree black belt - in a martial art. It takes a reasonable amount of physical ability, perseverance, and lots of practice (two to twenty years depending on the person, the number of hours of practice in a week, the quality of instruction, the quality of ukes, the dojo, and the particular art). Many people stop there, either quitting entirely or not progressing further. It is a pity for a teacher to invest time and energy, to see a student go so far then to fall by the wayside. It is a pity for a student to invest a lot of effort then to stop at the point where so many new ideas open up; but everybody does have the right to make their own decisions.

Aikido can be tremendous fun, whether you are uke or nage

Shodan in aikido, as I see it, indicates that the student knows all of the common techniques, can do them competently from any of the common attacks, and can take any of the ukemi that would result from them. Perhaps he's gone a little beyond that and started to put it all together in a unique style.

To get beyond shodan in aikido, it isn't enough to do more of the same. Continued practice of techniques will make your techniques better and you can add new techniques to broaden your repertoire. Indeed, your techniques should improve, becoming more flowing and confident. However, to progress through nidan and sandan it is necessary to go beyond improving techniques. Techniques are just tools. Like any other tool you need to hone them, but it is also necessary to understand when and how to use each one, its strengths and weaknesses. Each technique should become developed to the point that it is taken for granted. This doesn't mean technique is unimportant. Quite the reverse: good technique is the foundation for everything else. But it is only the foundation, and Frank Lloyd Wright did not get to be a great architect by designing foundations.*

Given that you are a good technician, or at least working on the few technical shortcomings you still have, what is the next step? Technique is the

---

* Though he might have gone too far the other way. The foundation of Falling Waters recently needed to be reinforced.

"what" of aikido, the things you learned to reach shodan. The next step addresses the "how" and "when". Some of us are lucky enough to have a good school to practice in without having to run one. Then, this progression comes naturally. More often, pretty soon after reaching shodan, we find that we have to teach, or even run a dojo. Teaching is instructive to the teacher as well as to the students. Learning how to manage a class relates to managing multiple attacks, though usually without the same immediacy. Running a dojo has its own challenges also, and requires attention to a myriad of detail. This is one direction you might have to move towards.

Racking up frequent flyer miles

Not having consistently had the advantage of a good school to practice in, I've had to think about these issues and find my own way. "Moving On" is the result. It is more of an exploratory book than "Doing Aikido", because I am still working on the things I talk about here. Also, having visited more dojos and attended seminars across a wider range of styles, I've seen a wider range of teachings, and have not fitted them all into my world view as yet. This is more exciting a time for me than if things were all neatly in place, but it has made this book hard to write.

When I moved from England to the USA, I had the fortune – or maybe misfortune – of finding a style of aikido that was almost identical to what I had learned in England. Especially in the last few years, I have seen different styles, most of them good and all with something to offer. For whatever reason, I see more potentialities now, and am less prone to tell students that what they are doing is wrong. Plus it is far easier to de-motivate people than to motivate them.

If you don't have a good teacher and good dojo, you can still progress, though less rapidly. You will need to watch good technicians. Ideally this should be in the flesh, feeling techniques, maybe at seminars. Video is a useful substitute, especially with slow motion and repeated playback. However, you will also need ideas, as to where you should be going as well as what to do. Hopefully you will find some in this book that you can use.

Goals

To get somewhere, it's a good idea to know where you're going. Aikido is a "way", in which the process is as important as the destination, but failure to define goals is likely to result in you losing your way.

It isn't enough to have a goal to get away from something. That would be a negative sort of existence. You should be wanting to move towards something, and to want it with all your heart. You should want to make a difference in the world, to make it a better place.

Goals in Aikido

Why do we do aikido? What is our goal? Ask a dozen people and you will get a dozen answers. Generally self-defense and fitness are high on the list, particularly for people just starting. Aikido is certainly a martial art, though the emphasis on the martial aspect varies from school to school and style to style. It has the tools to be an effective martial art, and I believe it should be practiced as such. Because this approach involves strenuous activity, aikido is also effective both for getting fit and for keeping that way. However, excessive martial focus can lead to pushing too hard, to damaging your own body. This is not good for either your art or your fitness, and is likely to result in a shortage of people to work with. Aikido is inherently interactive, and therefore difficult to practice by yourself.

There seem to be medical benefits from practicing aikido, including improvement of conditions with a psychosomatic component. However, these benefits might accrue from any physical activity that was practiced regularly. One would also expect that an activity like aikido would benefit the body, particularly as bone density is enhanced by impact exercise. However, I'm not aware of any studies to support this supposition specifically for aikido.

Other aspects of aikido that are valuable to people in our stressful and materialistic society are mental and spiritual development. Indeed, Saotome Sensei, one of the best aikidoka in the world and an uchideshi of O Sensei, explicitly states this is important.[*] Aikido practice should include mental/spiritual aspects, developing practical benefits such as the apparently contradictory abilities to concentrate fiercely and to relax. Mu shin, which is a lack of conscious thought, is the ideal state of mind in combat. It is also ideal for many other stressful situations in everyday life.

There should be a balance among the various mental, physical, and spiritual aspects of the art. If the focus is too much on fitness or on the mental

[*] Saotome, Mitsugi (1989), "The Principles of Aikido". Shambhala

aspects, your art may not be too effective in a physical confrontation. If you are constantly ready for combat, it is hard to relax.

The importance of the sheer fun of throwing people and being thrown is often undervalued. If you don't enjoy practicing aikido for its own sake, you probably won't keep doing it. Fun is often underrated, both in its own right and as an incentive for people to work hard for years. We live in a stressful world, and most of the stresses in Western society are mental/emotional. The negative attitude we often have towards enjoyment is not the least of our problems. Enjoyment is a valuable antidote to stress, and I personally get a great deal of pleasure from working out, both as uke and as nage. It feels great to take a big guy and throw him across the room. It feels just as good to take such an impressive ukemi myself, bouncing back unhurt and ready to fly some more. In addition, the dojo community gives me a sense of family that I would not otherwise have, with my relatives spread as they are halfway across the world. While a martial art cannot be all fun, it is necessary to have elements of both enjoyment and satisfaction for students to come regularly to class.

Aikido involves both giving and receiving. You should develop an appreciation for uke's side of the technique, not just nage's side. There are several reasons for this. The obvious one is that you don't want to get broken by a technique, whether applied too enthusiastically or maliciously. Avoiding injury is a large part of what ukemi is for. Another reason is that ukemi is the key to counter-techniques (kaeshi waza) and free-flowing improvisation (jiyu waza). You want the people you work with to get better so that both of you can practice at a higher level of proficiency. They can't do that unless their ukemi improves. And, of course, half your time in class is being uke.

Looking at goals over a shorter timescale, what are we trying to achieve in each class? As a teacher, I want my students to take another step along their road. As a student, I want to understand a little bit more about a technique or principle. Nobody can remember every detail at once, but if you capture a little bit of knowledge during each class you will eventually become very good.

Other goals are possible. I could go through the class banging people about, especially when I'm teaching. However, this would be self-defeating: the class would dwindle. Eventually I'd be alone on the mat. Practical aspects aside, that sort of abuse isn't what aikido is about.

Keeping on Track: which way is up?

Cape Horn used to be a notorious graveyard of ships. This was because of the violent weather and the primitive technology of navigation. Ships might leave the coast of Africa and not see land for thousands of miles. If astronomical sightings were prevented by clouds or an error was made in reducing the sightings by hand, a ship could be hundreds of miles from where the captain thought she was.

In going through life, how do we avoid shipwreck? In doing aikido, how do we know we are following the right course to reach our goals? In life, our parents, our role models, other adults, and our peers influence us strongly. In aikido, our sensei, sempai, and peers similarly influence us. Bad parents can give somebody a start in life that they can struggle against but never quite overcome, and one wonders what such a person could have done with a better start. On the other hand, adversity makes character. In aikido, your initial dojo might be just as influential. We don't get to choose our parents, and I suspect that for most people their initial dojo selection is almost as constrained. How do we know that we are on the right course?

The metaphor of climbing a mountain is often used for martial arts. There are many roads to the top, there may be sub peaks that look good until you get to the top and see that you will have to go back down part of the way to reach the ultimate summit. If you take a wrong turn, you might get caught in a difficult place from which you have no hope of reaching the summit, and might just blunder off a cliff with disastrous consequences.

Fortunately, the metaphor is flawed. There is no one peak that we all hope to reach. In sports, perhaps the ultimate peak is an Olympic gold medal, or to win the Cup. Then what do you do with the rest of your life? In aikido, the goal is generally considered to be some form of synthesis of physical prowess and spiritual understanding. There is no single ultimate peak. Aikido can be a lifelong study. There may be quick and difficult ascents, or leisurely and rambling ones. There may be elevations from where we can see the terrain more clearly than others, but there is no indication that there is a reachable summit. There may be scree-covered slopes and cliffs, such as when a prominent teacher takes advantage of an underage student and becomes ostracized and possibly jailed. There may be cul de sacs, from where you can't progress without backtracking. Perhaps an example of this would be practicing incorrect movements, where the more we practice the harder it is to retrain our bodies.

Still, mountain climbing provides a metaphor that going up is good. What is the equivalent metric in aikido? It is not rank, nor time in the art. It is not rank, because rank does not translate from one organization to another and is not totally consistent even within organizations. It is not time in rank, because some people progress faster than others.

Most of us who have been in aikido for a while have some idea of what we are looking for, what we consider "good" aikido. But I doubt if there is widespread agreement as to what is considered good. Some organizations applaud powerful technique. Others applaud technical subtleties. Others applaud street effectiveness. Others applaud, at least to some extent, competitive effectiveness. The last one at least has the merit of being readily assessed, while the others are rather vague.

This is rather like life. We each get to define "up", and how to measure it, though with some external constraints due to our environment. In the case of everyday life, this is primarily the laws of where we live. In aikido, it is primarily the outlook of the organization which we are part of, though most organizations leave a lot of latitude for the advanced members. This is why I like the metaphor of sailing rather than the one of climbing a mountain: when sailing, you have a goal, you have charts and pilot books, and you have navigational instruments, and much of the challenge is to determine where you are and what direction to sail.

Fighting and Harmony

Is there a conflict between the idea of harmony (ai) and a martial (fighting) art? Some of the apparent conflict might be due to translating cultural ideas. Still, there is only a conflict between these ideas if the art is used in a way that disturbs rather than supports natural harmony. Is it harmonious to refuse to fight when being threatened, or when your loved ones are in danger? It is certainly unnatural to do. Rather, controlling the threat will restore the harmony that a troublemaker has disturbed. If you don't do so, you may not only be hurt personally, but this person will go on to threaten other people and disrupt harmony on a wider and wider scale. Be careful, however, that you are not the problem rather than the solution. Aikido is powerful, and must be used wisely.

If you are attacked, how much force are you justified in using to defend yourself? In the USA, though I am no lawyer, there seems to be a general right of reasonable self-defense. If you are frightened for your life, you can use whatever force seems reasonable. Though you might have to defend your actions in court, it is better to be "judged by twelve than carried by six".

What is "reasonable" is the minimum force sufficient to take care of the problem. Thus, you can justify more force when attacked with weapons, or by many or larger opponents. A woman can generally justify more force than a man in a given situation, because she is generally smaller.

My advice is to do whatever you feel is necessary, and if you feel this means using deadly force, then do so. But recognize that I am not a lawyer and that the rules differ in different places and times. It used to be that, in Florida, you were legally required to retreat if possible, even in your own home. This is apparently no longer required unless your attacker also lives there.*

I have often seen students who are practicing knife defenses taking the knife away and going through the motions of cutting their uke as they back away. To me, this is both counter to the spirit of aikido and legally indefensible. Once you have the knife the threat is controlled. To use the knife on uke at that point is to be as ugly as they are. (It is different if you should use the knife on uke *during* the take-away, but this could still be excessive use of force, depending on the situation.) Such behavior is even less appropriate in the dojo, where we are all moving towards a common goal and should respect each other.

Willingness to do what is necessary is often enough to resolve a problem without it becoming physical. Aikido principles of harmonizing with an attack

---

* "Questions and Answers pertaining to the use of deadly force for lawful self-defense". Pamphlet provided by the Florida Department of State, 1994 revision.

in order to resolve a problem can be applied to non-physical situations, if only because of the increased difficulty of intimidating an aikidoka.

What must absolutely be avoided is the misuse of the art, the abuse of techniques for ego gratification, money, or power. It is easy, but quite wrong, to look for an excuse to try out your art. This sort of behavior is not new: Yagyu Munenori* warned against it centuries ago. Starting fights and using excessive force will not only subject you to legal sanctions, but it is bad for the soul.

Spiritual Development

Will aikido make you a better person? Some people practice it for this reason. Others think spiritual development and aikido are unrelated.

I don't see how we can totally divorce one from the other. We become what we practice. The name "aikido" includes the word "spirit". I think that aikido can be used to make you a better person. It can also be practiced as a mostly physical art form – though even boxing and football have been encouraged as developing character. The choice is up to you, part of finding your own path in aikido and through life.

In my opinion, everybody has a spiritual side, and that aspect is often neglected in these days of MTV and instant gratification, to the detriment of both the individual and those around him. In terms of aikido, if you don't develop your spiritual side, how will you know where you want to go in life, or whether you are getting closer or further away?

Deciding where your path lies is very important and every individual should do it for themselves, rather than accepting what some other person wants them to become. We are never short of people telling us what to believe: family, friends, bosses, co-workers, car dealers, sales people, preachers, priests, government bureaucrats, ads on television, billboards and newspapers, and politicians. How many of these people are telling you what is really best for you? How can they know that? Some of them don't even know you. Not even your parents and lovers can see inside your head or heart. It's up to you.

However, there are two sides to this issue also. "No man is an island." We grow up in a society. We generally live in this social environment until we die, though some people do change cultures and cultures themselves change. Martial artists in the West, in particular, might be on the fringe of their societies. We should make our decisions with knowledge of this context.

Spiritual development sounds so serious. There is a common misperception in the West that it involves "mortification of the flesh". The Japanese have some misogi practices that also seem to be related to this idea. Meditating under a freezing waterfall isn't my idea of fun, but those who do that sort of thing say it is invigorating. I'm happy enough just going to class and working out. Call it an endorphin high or whatever. Almost always, I finish

---

* Yagyu Munenori. "The Book of Family Traditions on the Art of War" Translated 1993, Thomas Cleary. Barnes & Noble Books, New York.

class in a better mood than when I started and am reluctant to leave. Some of the best classes are ones where I don't have to teach, but where I find partners who are at a similar state of development and we go at it, attacking hard, wearing each other out to the point where we leave tired but happy. I believe that this physical discipline of doing aikido is itself a spiritual discipline, one that will make us better people because of the aikido dojo atmosphere.

Where does the dojo atmosphere come from? I'm sure it started with O Sensei, whatever mistranslations might have been made of what he said, as he was a deeply spiritual person. This spirituality evidently struck a chord with a lot of people, across all races and religions, and the international aikido community has absorbed, developed, and passed it on.

Struggling with Life

Even we ourselves may not know what we really want and need. Unless you have spent half a lifetime reflecting on where you are and where you want to be, you probably don't. Aikido will not make these choices for you (though it can provide some useful tools). Rather, that knowledge is crucial to deciding where you want to go with your aikido. Where do you want to practice? Who do you want to practice with? How do you want to practice?

Many people struggle all the time. If there is no enemy, they create one. If there is no resistance, they make some. In doing aikido, half the difficulties are ones we create ourselves: worrying about rank or refusing to test, using all our strength to throw somebody instead of just the right movement, not just relaxing and doing. It is the same in life. Some people work terribly hard and get nowhere because they fight themselves every step of the way.

Life is like aikido. There are openings where a little judicious effort has far reaching consequences. If we try too hard, we miss opportunities, get off balance and fall down. If we try too hard to attain a particular result, we often fail. Instead, we should just study what we need to know, decide what we want to do, and quietly move forward, polishing our souls as we go.

Relationships

There are a number of relationships within a dojo: to sensei, to sempai, to peers, and to kohei. There might be one sensei who teaches all the classes, or a number of sensei who teach different classes. Successful dojos are normally run by one person, though he may listen closely to what other people in the dojo say.

Your relationship with your sensei is usually a singular thing. You have one person you regard as your particular teacher, mentor, and leader. Your attitude towards your sensei should be one of uncritical acceptance, especially at first. This might seem to conflict with my general admonitions to think about what you are doing, and indeed this is not medieval Japan where if your sensei tells you to jump off a cliff you should promptly do so. But you should definitely give your sensei the benefit of the doubt. When you see contradictions, you should try to resolve them in his favor rather than using them to prove he is flawed. Criticism is something that seems to be inherent in Western society and will only slow you down if you have a good sensei. If you do not believe in your sensei, you need to find another one.

I firmly believe that your sensei should be both a technical and a spiritual leader. He should both teach you excellent technique and be an example for you to emulate inside and outside the dojo. This is especially important for dealing with young students. It is less important for more mature students, but bad behavior will influence even mature students to some extent.

Sensei means teacher, one who has gone before. It is used in Japan for schoolteachers, for example. Some dojos in the West apply it outside the dojo. I guess this is perfectly fine if that is what they want to do. I go by Alan or Dr. Drysdale outside the dojo. Respect is respect however it is shown. However, I must admit to having never had much of a sensei – student relationship. As I came through the kyu ranks we were discouraged from developing a "sensei complex", and becoming overly reverent towards our teachers. I moved out of town and ended up teaching as a new ikkyu, and from that point on was expected to teach in each of the dojos I joined.

A sempai is a student more advanced than yourself. A kohei is one less advanced. In Japan, I understand that it is based on seniority. In the West it is more often based on rank, especially as sometimes people will drop out for a year or two and then come back. In Japan, I understand that students will often pair up, so that each kohei has a sempai. This seems to be less emphasized in the West. However, it seems like a good idea to have sempai look out for and help kohei. In return the kohei should do the jobs like sweeping the mat and keeping the dojo clean.

Perhaps more important than hierarchy is respect. Respect should be shown to everybody, particularly in the dojo but also outside. In the dojo, it is important because we are trusting our health and even our life to our partner.

Perhaps the most important relationship is that with yourself. Are you unfailingly honest to yourself?

Finding a Teacher, then moving on

You can find aikido teachers in the Yellow Pages of most phone books, at least in the larger cities. Some are good. Some are not. Asking around in the community should eliminate the ones that are least qualified. Your feeling when you visit and talk with the sensei is another good indicator. Rank in an major aikido organization can indicate that the teacher is at least somewhat competent.

Finding a great teacher is the quickest way to become a good aikidoka. Some places, like the Bay Area around San Francisco, have many aikido teachers. Some places, particularly in rural areas, have none. There are as many styles of aikido as there are teachers. Some styles are immature, under development. Some are mature, strong, and vibrant. Some are senescent.

Some teachers are open to new ideas. Some have picked up erroneous ideas. In martial arts and probably all physical pursuits, people are exposed to crackpot ideas that were novel and innovative two hundred years ago. To become the master of all things, as Musashi said a good martial artist should strive to become, you must study. Root out the crazy ideas, the inconsistent ones, and build on the good ones in developing your personal style. This striving is not easy, but it is the only way to become a sound martial artist. I can tell you what I believe. I can try to convince you that I'm right. But you should weigh those and any other ideas and reject any found wanting.

This personal development is, to my mind, critical to becoming mature in martial arts or any other complex endeavor. It is not an easy path to take, because every time you disagree with other people they are likely to try to coerce or seduce you to a path that is not your own. It is especially difficult in a dojo with a strong hierarchy (though there are far worse sources of personal goals).

There is a time for uncritical acceptance. That time is from committing to study a martial art to shodan. Once you have reached shodan, you are still only a beginning student, but you must start taking responsibility for your future development. You should still respect your teachers. You should listen carefully to make sure you heard what was really said, rather than what you expected to hear. Then you should look to see how your body of knowledge fits together, and how each new piece fits into this corpus. Only then will you be able to continue to progress past where your teacher was able to take you, when the time comes for you to pick up the baton.

If you are lucky, you will have a teacher who can show you the way forward for a substantial part of your life. Great teachers have, however, not been that common in my experience. You might not find one that is ideal for you at a convenient location. I've traveled a lot of miles to train. Good technicians are not always good teachers, but poor technicians don't have anything to teach.

Even if you are lucky and you start with a superb teacher, and he or she leads you forward for years, we all die in the end. When your teacher dies you will have to either find a new teacher or move forward on your own. If your teacher can only help you for a few years before your ways part for whatever reason, then you have to start finding your own way sooner rather than later. I'm not sure which is more unfortunate; to never have a good teacher or to have one so great that you feel you can never surpass him.

A Book of Wind

This is a collection of miscellaneous thoughts about aikido in particular and martial arts in general. The title comes from Go Rin No Sho.

Aikido and Religion

Sometimes people see martial artists bowing, and think that aikido is a religion. I have heard of people refusing to have anything to do with martial arts because they have heard that they are related to Eastern philosophy and are therefore seen as a work of the devil. Some religions forbid their adherents to bow to an idol or icon, which they see in bowing to O Sensei's picture.

Bowing in martial arts is not particularly religious, though you can make it that if you wish.* It's a sign of respect. In the USA, we shake hands; in Japan, they bow. In so far as religion is about spirituality, there is, however, a link between aikido and religion: Aikido is, to some degree, a spiritual exercise, though non-denominational. O Sensei said that aikido is not a religion, and that people of any religion could practice it. Some people seem to practice aikido as a religion, but most don't. I certainly don't. As an analogy, you might consider working on a car. A car is for traveling, and we can use a car to travel, but working on the car to make it run better (tuning the engine, changing the oil, fixing the brakes, polishing the bodywork, chrome plating the engine, or whatever) is not, in itself, traveling. Thus, aikido can develop our spirituality of whatever flavor we choose, while not itself being a religion.

Having said that, aikido does have a set of ethics. O Sensei emphasized ethics: non-aggressive behavior, protection of natural harmony, and so on. However, as we come from different cultures and as we only have access to what he said by second or third hand, and often in translation, it is very risky to assume we know precisely what he meant. It is even more risky to assume that what worked for him will work for us in such a different society as the one we now find ourselves.

Everyone must make up their own mind about what they want to believe and how they want to practice. The bottom line in aikido is how you practice, and more practice is better than any amount of discussion of philosophy and religion. By practicing aikido correctly, you will develop spiritually.

Aikido and Spirituality

Aikido is profoundly spiritual. It even has the word "spirit" in its name. But spirit means many things to many people, and sometimes the meanings are contradictory. There are thirty-eight different kanji for "ki" in my guide to

---

* There is a stronger argument that clapping and bowing is religious, the clapping being a Shinto practice to wake up the spirits. However, most aikidoka who clap and bow do not seem to be practicing Shinto.

Japanese writing. I take the word "ki" in aikido to mean the sort of spirit displayed by a "spirited" horse, the "spirit" that moves people to do what they do. Hepburn* defines this particular reading of "ki" as "the spirit, temper, feeling, mind, heart, disposition, vapor, exhalation". "Kami", on the other hand, means "god", specifically a Shinto god, according to Hepburn. Of course, we do have to be careful with literal translations of technical jargon.

I see this spirit as being whatever it is that is beyond the conscious mind that moves us in our lives, like emotion but more profound. We can be strong or weak in spirit. We can develop more spiritual strength through suitable exercises. Spirituality can be good or bad, beneficial or detrimental. It is up to us to develop strong and beneficent spirits as we practice aikido.

Strengthening the spirit starts with going to class. When you don't feel like going, it is easy to justify why you should not go. You have to go to the trouble of getting there, getting dressed out, possibly in the chill and damp of winter or the heat and humidity of summer. Maybe you wonder if you're not starting to get sick. Maybe you're still stiff from the last practice. But progress, both physically and spiritually, results from consistent practice.

Just showing up is a good start, but not enough. You must also actively search for the way ahead, study each movement, and keep your spirit strong and focused. Each movement that you make with full intent and commitment means that you are improving. Each one you make half-heartedly, thinking of something else, not only fails to improve your aikido but takes it back a step. This does not mean that you have to do every technique violently, smashing your uke to the ground, but that you must focus 100% on some aspect of that technique. As a beginner, you might have to work on the gross details, like where your feet and hands go. As an advanced student, you might work on any of a number of aspects, including ma-ai, position, stance, extension, breathing, or all of them at once to make the technique flow better. Then you might need to back off and work on the hands and feet again. Study what works, and determine what is due to the artificiality of the practice environment.

Loose interpretation of the 2nd law of thermodynamics
– the easy way is usually the wrong way

In aikido, just as in the rest of our lives, there are temptations to misuse the power we develop and to take the easy road. Just as in the rest of our lives, we must resist temptations and instead use aikido honestly and for good ends. We must avoid beating up on beginners just because we can do it. We must avoid looking for excuses to try out our technique. The road, the "do" of aikido, is somewhat narrow and not easy to stay on.

---

* Hepburn, J. C. "A Japanese and English Dictionary with an English and Japanese Index". Tuttle, 1983. (Originally published in 1867.)

Advice

As we move up through the ranks, we will get all sorts of advice, both well meaning advice and advice from people who intend to confuse and confound us. Hopefully, most advice will contain at least a nugget of truth.

You should be grateful for the effort, but careful about the content. Some of the advice will be conflicting. Some of it might be correct, and that is easy to work towards, though perhaps not easy to achieve success in. Some of it might be right but you may misunderstand – human language is imperfect. Some of it might be passing on a misunderstanding the other person has, perhaps something he has been told and has failed to correct.

A common example is "don't use strength". I heard this all the time when I was growing up in the art. Like most misleading things, there is some truth in it. Aikido practice is not about straining and forcing techniques. That way, you'll damage joints and get a hernia. Aikido practice is about learning to effectively use what strength we have. Technique is about direction, angle, timing, efficiency, and making your entire body work to a single end. It does use muscles – the only other way to move your body is gravity and that only goes one way. When you hear people saying "don't use strength", sometimes they are putting you down, discouraging you from challenging them so that they can make the technique work and you can't. Sometimes they see you are doing things incorrectly, straining to make the technique work, and in the absence of more specific suggestions they latch onto "don't use strength".

Some advice might be correct in general, perhaps correct for your would-be mentor, yet wrong for you personally. A common cause of confusion is when somebody is attempting to advise a person of different body type. Even though people are all pretty much the same, big people do move differently than little people. You need to practice with and study all types, to see the differences due to physical or mental make-up.

When you hear advice, what do you do? It might be from somebody you can't ignore, or just somebody that you don't want to be rude to (and rudeness is far more common in society today than is justifiable). That is when you need to follow the way, your way. You should be polite, you should try their way, and often, even when they don't mean to be, people are actually helpful if you look at their suggestion in the right light, but ultimately *you* have to decide what you want to do.

Styles of Aikido

Aikido was largely developed from Daito Ryu. Reputedly (and I am taking this at second hand, not yet having had the opportunity to practice Daito Ryu), they have many techniques in common. Morihei Ueshiba, Aikido O Sensei, was a qualified teacher of Daito Ryu. He developed what he called aikido, and passed it on to a large number of students. Some of them went on to develop their own styles either early in Ueshiba's life or later. Shioda Sensei, for example, broke away early and with O Sensei's blessing. The style he developed, Yoshinkan Aikido, was and still is a somewhat rigorous and physical style. Kenji Tomiki held a high rank in judo before studying aikido. He founded Shodokan Aikido, a style that is something of a blend of aikido and judo. Another prominent offshoot was the Ki Society, formed when Koichi Tohei broke away from the Aikikai Hombu shortly after O Sensei's death. This style was a lot softer than Yoshinkan, perhaps because O Sensei did softer techniques as he got older. Tohei taught a less physical style and emphasized ki development, perhaps to be distinct from the Aikikai. Aikikai itself incorporates a variety of styles. Both the Hombu and Saito Sensei at Iwama say they teach what O Sensei taught, even though there are distinct differences in style.

All these styles of aikido derived from O Sensei. Personally, I think all of his students are correct when they say that they are teaching what O Sensei taught. I suspect that the differences that have emerged are the result of the different timeframes during which they studied with O Sensei, the degree to which they were his personal students, and the different personalities, backgrounds, and physiques of the students themselves.

Which is the best style? That depends on who you are, your personality, and your physique. I have tried to write this book to be somewhat in the middle, avoiding extremes. However, perhaps everybody thinks they are in the middle.

You could argue that as O Sensei developed aikido, all we have to do is to follow what he taught. This might be true, even though few people are built quite like him or have his temperament, education and upbringing. But O Sensei died in 1969, over thirty years ago. He cannot teach us personally. His students were taught by him, but they are not him either, and the transmission was certainly not perfect. It never is. All the shihans I have seen (perhaps a dozen) who were taught personally by O Sensei teach aikido differently from one another. Perhaps they saw things differently, missed things, invented things, and adapted things. And the same happens with us, as we learn our art.

If aikido is taken to be only what O Sensei taught, nothing more, it will die. He has died. His direct students are also either dead or getting old. They will all die. His students' students will also die. We will all die (though maybe not for a long time if research into molecular biology pans out). Each generation, the transmission is further weakened by the sheer difficulty of accurately passing an art from one person to another.

O Sensei's aikido was not fixed in form. It evolved through time. Whether it got better or worse as he got older depends on what you are looking for, and your opinion of what "better" and "worse" mean.

Should aikido continue to change? I think it must, or it will wither and die as the direct transmission weakens from being passed from one teacher to the next. The only way to keep aikido vigorous is to learn all we can from those teachers who we can study with, and to move beyond that. Clearly, there is plenty of opportunity for developing something less good than O Sensei's aikido, as few of us have the ability or determination to give as much to the art as O Sensei did. Every time somebody insists his way is the only way, and makes his students only learn that way, aikido is weakened. Every time anybody half learns a technique and thinks that is good enough, aikido is weakened.

But every time anybody searches hard for the truth, building on what his teachers gave him, looking for what the technique really is, without compromise, without settling for good enough, without making excuses for themselves or others, aikido is strengthened. We are all like the blind men and the elephant. We each see different parts of the elephant, different parts of what aikido is. By working together, comparing notes, sharing ideas, rigorously examining them, and looking for a constructive solution as to why one man thinks the elephant is a pillar and another thinks it is a rope, we can identify more of the whole beast, which is much more wonderful and powerful than its parts. What are the boundaries separating "aikido" from "not-aikido"? That is something we collectively decide, with some people having more influence than others.

The few people that have the ability and determination to take what is left of O Sensei's art and make it stronger will be conspicuous in both technique and ability to teach it. When you see a great teacher, follow him or her. Even better, become a great teacher.

Accepting that aikido has changed, is it a rigorous martial art that has been watered down by concern over ethics and lawsuits, or a more humane but still viable approach to self-defense? There has been lots of discussion of aikido, martial arts in general, and philosophy of life. At one extreme are the Daito Ryu and Yoshinkan stylists, who generally seem to think harder and more rigorous is better. At the other extreme is the Ki Society, where functionality has sometimes been relegated to second place after personal development. I think the middle road is generally the place to be. If you practice excessively hard it will be difficult to find people to practice with, and your career will be limited to a decade or two before you are too broken up to keep training. On the other hand, if you do not retain the martial aspect of the art, not only will your ability to defend yourself be minimal but the mental/spiritual benefits of martial training will be lost.

This is not to tell you that either hard or soft techniques are the way to go. It depends on the student, and some of the hardest falls are taken from "soft" stylists. If you can take an aggressive attack and use uke's strength and power to bring about his downfall, that is the essence of aikido. Rather, I am concerned about martial intent. Aikido should be practiced sensibly, with due regard for the safety of all concerned. But it should also be practiced so that the envelope is constantly enlarged, so that you can deal with harder, faster, and more diverse attacks from bigger and more aggressive ukes as you progress along your path.

Aikido – Moving On

Aikido and Other Martial Arts

A one-time student of mine, Steve Morone, used to quote a saying that went something like "the mountain doesn't scoff at the river because it is lowly and the river doesn't scoff at the mountain because it is fixed in place". Everybody likes to think their art is the best one. In reality, all arts have something to be said for them or they would not have been developed and would not still be around (and conversely, they all have deficiencies). Some are good for one personality, body style, or situation. Some are good for another. Still, there is only one basic type of human being, with variations. Thus, there is really only one martial art – and the types and styles we see around us are subsets of that martial art. Some of these subsets are broad and not very deep. Others are deep and not very wide in scope. Aikido emphasizes defense rather than offense. It emphasizes throwing and submission holds rather than atemi. But there are atemi in aikido, and aikido can be used preemptively. The limits are in our minds rather than in the arts.

However, the names we are familiar with do designate particular subsets that have a history. It really isn't honest to develop a new art – even if it is a very good art – and claim it is aikido, or karate, or some other established art. If you develop something new, give it a new name.

Nobody can say much that is significant about a martial art unless they have been exposed to it long enough to understand it. As a shodan is merely the first step in a martial art, there are not too many people that have been exposed sufficiently to more than one art to truly understand more than one. Indeed, most people who start training in a martial art do not even get to shodan. Certainly I know of people with honorary rank in various arts, but honorary degrees do not count in this instance.

Respect is an important part of any martial art. Thus, while it is perfectly reasonable to say that you like aikido better than any other art, it is not respectful to claim that other arts are inferior. This is particularly true as there are practitioners of any art who are extremely good at what they do, and those who have rank purely because they have persevered for many years and have made other contributions to the dojo. So if you compare a good aikidoka to a poor karateka, the aikidoka will look better. And vice versa.

Cross training is a perennial question. Some teachers forbid their students to cross train. Other people find cross training to be invaluable. I can understand both points of view. In my opinion, it comes down to cases. If a student cross-trains and brings back an attitude or does techniques that are incompatible with my class, I would ask them not to come any more. I do not accept that a teacher has the right to do any more than this. However, the student should listen very carefully to what his sensei says on the subject, and might need to find a different teacher if there is an irreconcilable difference in this or anything else.

I have found cross training is valuable in those technical areas where aikido is not as strong. Thus, most aikidoka who have never studied another art can't hit or kick effectively. Most aikidoka who have never fought competitively or in the street have an exaggerated impression of how easy it is to win a fight. Most aikidoka who have never been hit have an incorrect impression of the effect of strikes - and the impression might be that their atemi would be devastating, or that they are invulnerable to strikes from an attacker. Aikidoka are often weak on the ground (ne waza), and should avoid being pulled down. (However, remember that suwari waza is a form of ne waza.) Other arts often give a fresh perspective on aikido itself. My advice is to learn all you can about anything that appeals, but to temper it with working mostly on what is highest in priority to you. You need a core discipline. Presumably if you are reading this book, that core is aikido.

When I cross train, I compartmentalize to a large extent. Both aikido and karate, for example, have similar wrist locks. One nikkyo in aikido is the sixth tai ho jitsu in Yoshukai Karate. They are, however, done somewhat differently. You should do the technique the way the teacher shows it in class, of course, but if you learn both ways you know more than if you blend the two of them and try to make one way fit all cases.

One of the greatest opportunities for cross-fertilization between aikido and karate is in the attacks. Typical aikido and karate punches, for example, are very different. In this instance, the karate punch is generally better, though you still need to learn how to deal with a technically incorrect but possibly still powerful attack.

I read something ascribed to O Sensei that claimed that there were no kicks in aikido because kicks were ungentlemanly. I suspect this was a joke. More likely, the limited repertoire was a reflection of the importance of weapons training in his art. Practical problems are that the ukemi are difficult and knees are vulnerable to being wrenched. Also, kicks are more difficult than punches to do well, and most of us would have to practice to be adequate ukes. I believe we should work on defenses against kicks. I believe we should practice using kicks as atemi. I don't do so as much as I would like to, because my practice hours are limited.

My exposure to boxing is quite minimal, though is enough to see it is quite different in style from karate. There are a lot of people with some knowledge of boxing out there. Boxing punches are shorter and thrown more from the body. More work is done close in (perhaps because kicks are not allowed in boxing).

Judo was originally quite similar to aikido, though involving more grappling than does aikido, particularly ne waza (groundwork). Modern, Olympic, judo is quite different, being a competitive sport with extensive rules to limit injuries and make it exciting for spectators. There is something to be said for learning judo groundwork as a supplement to aikido, though you should be quite sure there is only one attacker before willingly going to the ground.

Judo chokes and strangles are also useful to know, if only to avoid falling victim to them. The principles of judo and aikido are much the same whether we are talking standing techniques or groundwork.

There are technical similarities between other martial arts and aikido. There is less commonality in attitudes, stances, and strategies, however.

Aikido in Daily Life

Aikido is not just about self defense. For most of us, the need for self defense is rare. I haven't been physically attacked since I was in college in Newcastle upon Tyne, more than thirty years ago. However, I have been in situations where I probably would have been but for my aikido: one for sure, and several other times when it looked likely. It is like a lottery: low probability of a high payoff. While the payoff of being able to defend yourself in a physical confrontation is large, a lot of time and energy is involved in learning aikido and remaining proficient. Is it worthwhile? It is to me, having grown up as something of a wimp. On the other hand, I don't play the Florida lottery.

Some of my students have used aikido extensively in their jobs as policemen or working security. It has been useful, giving them both an effective and a legally defensible art. One student was attacked by five people, and subdued them all without using his gun or other weapon. Another, after only six months in the art used it to arrest a larger man who attacked him.

In addition to providing self defense, aikido has kept me physically fit. Other ways of getting exercise have left me bored and I've quit doing them after a few days or weeks. Aikido has kept my attention for thirty years and counting, and is a good all-round exercise. However, I get less exercise as I practice less and teach more, and as my technique improves.

The biggest benefits have probably been in the way I feel about myself and how I relate to others. Not all of this can be attributed to practicing aikido. Certainly, I've grown older and experienced a lot to which I had to adapt. However, aikido has helped me deal with problems both at home and work. When unreasonable things have happened, it has helped me to deal with the real problem, rather than responding the first way that came to mind.

The principles of aikido such as keeping your center, entering when pulled, turning when pushed, using an attacker's energy, are all applicable to confrontations in everyday life, even non-physical ones. However, this is rather off the focus of this book and books on that topic are available, one of the first being "Aikido in Daily Life", by Koichi Tohei.

Perfection and Perfectibility

Lots of us are perfectionists. We want to be perfect, to do everything perfectly. This isn't a bad aspiration, so long as we realize it is only a goal and is unattainable.

Wind

We can look at perfection in two ways. The first is to be perfectly yourself. The second is to change your innermost self to more closely match some ideal.

Being yourself is interesting and has more character than symmetry, the unique perfection of a Japanese tea bowl. It merely involves doing what we should do. This is less easy than might be thought, and will only result in lack of caring for others if that is what is in our heart.

Trying to achieve some ideal can be dangerous. It requires that we work to change. It doesn't just happen. Apparently, most of us aren't happy with ourselves and desire to be seen as being more than we are. This desire is a weakness, even if we are not Zen Buddhists, but it is a necessary step towards changing ourselves if that is what we decide to do. When we are in this state we are easily perturbed, vulnerable, which is a long way from Musashi's "body of a rock". Wanting to be better than we are – better martial artists, better sportsmen, better writers, better lovers, or whatever – can be good in that it pushes us to learn new things, to actually improve our abilities, but it can also be a handicap if our wishes are unreasonable or if we are unwilling to pay the price. This can leave us in a sort of spiritual limbo, always yearning but never succeeding.

Perhaps something of a blend of these extremes is needed for us to become the best people we can be. We need to believe in ourselves, in our worth as a person, a human being, a martial artist, while working to become better. We must learn to trust ourselves. Some people act totally confident but are hiding a basic insecurity, constantly needing the approval of others to bolster their self-image. Others act totally the opposite, as if they are worthless. They rarely have enough confidence to find out what they are capable of. Most people appear to be somewhat in between, but few seem to have sufficient self-confidence to just do what should be done with neither wailing nor chest thumping. Most of us are neither as good as we'd like others to think, nor as bad as we fear we are.

Inability to see ourselves improving is particularly common in aikido, where we are mainly struggling with ourselves. There are no competitions, no trophies, and progress often seems slow and uncertain. To make it worse, we tend to start with a group of people, all of whom progress at similar rates. This can make it seem as if we are not progressing, unless we are sensible enough to look at the latest crop of beginners and realize that they are probably starting about where we started and that they really are not a bunch of physically incapable morons.

This might be a particular problem at shodan, when you have got a black belt, but your sensei corrects you as often as the new students. Of course, he is correcting you at a higher level of technique, but this perspective might get lost in the frustration. Occasionally, a teacher feels his status is threatened by his students, and actually tries to cut them down as they attain some rank. This is unfortunate, and there is probably no cure for it but to move on.

Persevering at aikido seems to be particularly difficult for somebody that is physically gifted. They are used to succeeding in physical pursuits, and often find that aikido is not as easy as it looks. They might do very well at first, then find they can no longer maintain their original rate of progress. The slower progress doesn't matter in the long term, but many of them can't seem to accept a slower pace and they quit.

The antidote to these spiritual problems is to practice. The harder you practice the more progress you will see, and the less energy you will have to criticize other people or worry about your own lack of progress. Mental focus is vital to developing a robust sense of personal worth that is critical to developing an imperturbable mind. Breathing exercises and other centering exercises will help tremendously, especially just sitting, breathing, letting your mind go quiet.

As in most things, a balance is good. We should neither be so driven to succeed at aikido that we leave no room for other things in our lives and risk burning out, nor should we be so complacent that we no longer strive to improve.

Part 2: About Aikido

We all bring our own perspective to whatever we do. As a "rocket scientist", I bring that perspective to my aikido (and, every action having an equal and opposite reaction, most likely aikido influences my work also).

A lot of aikido involves physical manipulation of the body. In fact, there is nothing in aikido that I have ever been able to find that is outside the laws of physics. This is not to say that I understand all that aikido can encompass, but that the supernatural has never been necessary to understand what I personally have seen.

Aikido involves mostly mechanics, static and dynamic, some biophysics and physiology about things like nerves, muscles and bones, and some psychology (which is a bit off the mainstream of physics, but again nothing supernatural). While good aikido can be done with an intuitive understanding of physics learned by trial and error, some theoretical understanding can help.

Physics of Aikido

A number of topics come to mind, and they are inter-related so that there is no obvious starting place. Aikido is about taking people's balance, both physically and mentally. To physically take their balance, you have to apply muscular force to move your own body and in so doing also moving uke's body, and you have to control your own balance to do this. Leverage is important. So is momentum.

Many people don't like to think of aikido as involving force, but some force has to be applied to uke's body to move it, and uke will generally resist if they can. The key is to apply force in such a way that we don't have to strain at it and uke's ability to resist is negligible.

Generation of Force in Aikido

In physical terms, you must apply a force to move a physical body. Force is not a pejorative term in physics, and is in fact the only way to physically move another body (or your own for that matter). It is, of course, possible to convince uke to supply the force to move his own body, and this is the basis of "no touch" throws. Taking the balance and atemi can do this. However, that is the topic of another section, and force is still needed even if uke supplies it.

The human body has only one way to generate force, and that is through muscular contraction. Even when we talk of extending our arm, this action is powered by muscles contracting in such a way that the set of bony levers that make up the skeleton of our arm unfolds and moves the hand away from the body.

We hardly ever pull in aikido, though some flexion movements are important. When we push, we have to push against something: every action has an equal and opposite reaction. Thus, if nage pushes uke, he also pushes himself back. If we had two people in the space station pushing each other, weightless, they would move apart. The same thing happens in the dojo unless we have something to push against. That something can be the ground (through our feet) or our body mass or momentum. When we push against the ground with our feet and at uke with our arms, the ground is so massive that it doesn't move measurably. We move, and uke moves. (Unless, of course, he is pushing the other way against the Earth.)

If we define pushing as using our arms in compression rather than tension, we can often figure out how to move uke with a push rather than a pull. These two ways of moving uke have different effects. Pulling would bring uke in towards us. Pushing would tend to move him out, around our center. In general, we can push more effectively than we can pull.

Muscular power depends on the size of the muscles and their inherent strength. Mechanical work is force times distance moved: thus a small strong movement might perform no more work than a weaker force operating over a longer distance, but a strong movement operating over a long distance performs the most work. Thus, if nage uses his arms to move uke it is generally ineffective. If he uses his whole body and pushes, it is more effective because he (a) uses his most powerful muscles (his legs and torso), (b) transmits his power through his arms in the strongest way (using them as pillars – see below), and (c) he can step forward and so exert power over a longer distance.

A fairly strong individual can bench press about his own weight. Thus, with a body weight of 140 lbs., I should be able to press 140 lbs. (In fact, I can't, but that isn't particularly important to this discussion.) My legs are much stronger than my arms. I can comfortably stand on one leg, so I should be able to support 280 lbs. on two legs – making my legs perhaps three times as strong as my arms. Thus, to maximize the force I can generate as nage, I should find a way to push through my legs. This is often described as pushing from your center. Of course, my legs are generally supporting my weight also, so my net force might be similar to my body weight.

There are lots of pushing exercises used in aikido. Ikkyo undo, for example, is a pushing exercise that uses the first movement of ikkyo. The student stands in hanmi and moves his hips forward as he raises his arms. A key is to connect to the ground and push with the whole body. This exercise can be done by pushing against another student. This gives both people something to push against, as well as providing an exercise in connecting to uke. However, the two participants should be careful not to make it an excuse for competing for the centerline.

Ikkyo Undo

Another useful exercise is to have somebody hold our belt from behind as we step forwards. The goal is not to see if we can pull him along, but to make sure we are moving by pushing our hips forwards against the resistance. The first time people try this, they tend to either step out with the legs and leave the hips behind, or to lean into the exercise. Instead, the torso should stay erect, and the legs should thrust them forwards. It is important that nage learn how to push in this way, directly from the ground.

Gravity

Gravity can also move uke's body. We might use gravity in a variety of ways. If we can take uke's balance, he will tend to fall under the influence of gravity. By manipulating where he is falling towards, we can steer him where we want him to go.

We spend most of our lives fighting against gravity, so we do get rather proficient at it. When uke grabs hold of our arm or when we have made a similar connection with uke's arm after a strike, we can hold up our arm ourselves or we can let uke hold our arm up. An arm is surprisingly heavy, and if we let uke carry that force, it can be that much force we don't need to supply. Sometimes when doing a technique, we find we are holding uke up. Instead, just let them go.

Also, if uke picks us up, generally we can make sure he cannot hold us up simply by relaxing, or by cantilevering our weight out from his body. Relaxing means that uke has to carry all our weight, and sticking our legs in front moves the center of gravity of the two of us forwards, making him step to recover his balance or drop us. (However, if uke is big enough, he will be able to hold us for a time.)

Thus gravity can be quite useful, but whenever we use our weight we have first to use our muscles to lift our body into position to do so.

Straight and Bent Pillars

Elephants don't stand with bent legs like grasshoppers or cockroaches. Instead, they have legs like pillars. Architectural columns are usually straight. In both cases, this is because straight compression members are stronger than bent ones. As our arm bends under compression, for example, the load on our extensor muscles will increase as the sine of the joint angle, approaching zero as the elbow angle approaches 0 or 180 degrees, with a maximum value at 90 degrees. Thus, in doing aikido, we should keep our legs and arms almost straight. Doing ikkyo with our arms straight instead of bent is stronger if uke should resist.

If we are pushing with our entire body, we should be lined up so that there is as straight a line as possible between the point of contact with our partner and the floor. This position only needs to be maintained, however, at the point of maximum load.

Straight legs become important in koshi nage. The more we bend our knees or spread our legs, the smaller the load we can carry. In addition, there is more risk of uke falling on our leg and damaging our knee if our feet are further apart than our hips. With our feet under our hips, we can easily throw an uke twice our weight. Of course, in koshi nage uke should fall over us not on top of us, but there is always some load, and we should be prepared for problems.

Balance and Kuzushi

Taking the balance is critical to aikido. You might not realize how critical it is until you see a beginner turning and almost falling over his own feet. Mechanically, when the center of gravity of a body moves so that it is no longer above that body's base area, the body falls over. If somebody is pushing it, when the resultant* of the forces of gravity and the push is in a direction that leads outside of the body's base area, it will tip and fall over, whether we are talking about a person or a statue. Thus, something tall and light with a narrow

---

* The resultant is the vector sum of two or more forces. For example, if two equal forces are acting at 60 degrees to each other, the resultant is halfway between them and 1.76 times the magnitude of either.

base is easy to push over. Something squat and heavy with a wide base is hard to push over.

Much of the mechanics of aikido, especially kihon, are about what it takes to push somebody over, which, in turn relates to the force needed, the best angle to apply it, and the effect of that push on nage.

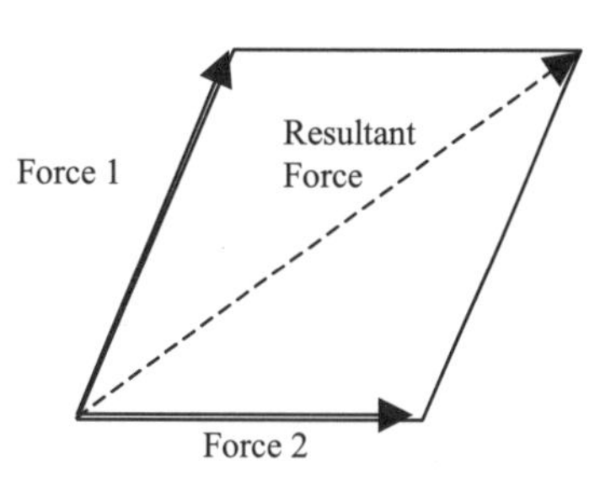

Parallelogram of Forces. The resultant is the vector sum of the two forces.

As long as the person's center of gravity remains above the base area delineated by drawing a line around his feet, the person will stay on his feet without having to move. A person can adjust where his weight is by changing the force on each foot or part of a foot. When the center of gravity moves from above that base area, the person must either move to a new position for which the center of gravity is once more over that base area, keep moving, or fall down.

back foot
Weak
Strong

Uke's balance is weakest to the sides

Drawing a box around uke's feet will show you where he is weakest. In general, he is strongest along the long axis of the box, along the line from one foot to the other, and the further apart the feet the harder it is to move him in that direction. He is weakest at ninety degrees to this line. However, uke's ability to resist will depend on where his center of gravity is within this box. If his weight is well forward, and if nage can extend uke a little more (so that his nose is in front of his toes) he can still be thrown forward, even though this is not normally the easiest direction.

Kamae. Weight can be forwards or back

So long as uke's center of gravity is over the box, he is stable. If you can catch him on the move this may make it easier or harder to take his balance. We move by putting our center of gravity outside the box, and then moving our feet to arrest our forward fall. A common foot technique in judo is to prevent this foot adjustment. Uke trips, and the throw is completed with an arm movement. In aikido, we might prevent the head moving to catch up with the feet (irimi nage) and, again, uke falls.

If we think of a person as being like a statue, quite rigid, we can calculate the force necessary to tip him over. To do this, we have to overcome the force of gravity holding him down, and this can be calculated by how we need to move his center of gravity to get it outside his box.

As we push him over, his center of gravity will rotate about the point of contact with the mat that is furthest from the force applied. As seen in the figure below, to tip the person over, we have to rotate the center of gravity around his back heel in the direction we are pushing. This point, the fulcrum, is marked with a triangle in the figure. For the example above, this would involve the center of gravity initially moving upwards at an angle of about 30 degrees. As the stance narrows or uke's weight moves backward, both the force required and the optimum angle will become smaller, but the center of gravity must first rise for him to fall over. Whoever is pushing must supply the force necessary to elevate uke's center of gravity by that amount. This force will never equal uke's weight unless we pick him up off both feet, and is often less than half as much.

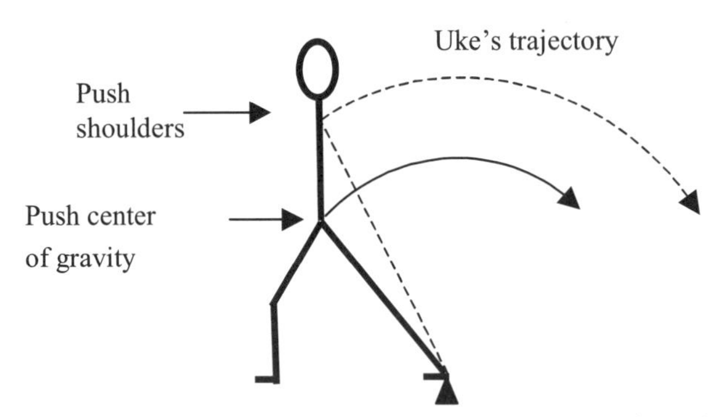

Mechanics of Balance – Standing. Uke's center of gravity will rotate about the furthest point of contact with the mat.

Typically, in a front stance perhaps 70% of the weight will be on the front foot, 30% on the back one. With a moderate stance, the feet separated by a third of the height (2 ft. for a 6 ft. person), a force of about 20% of the person's weight, horizontally, at shoulder height will push him back over. About 30% will be needed at their center of gravity. A force of about 5% will be needed to push them forwards in this position. A still smaller force will tip them sideways.

These values will vary with uke's posture and the position of his center of gravity. Thus, if his weight is back, his center of gravity is at the further edge of the base area, we can push him a little further, hardly needing to elevate his center of gravity, and gravity will do the rest. If he over-extends forwards, and relies on our force to prevent him from falling, he can require even more effort on our part to push him over one way, but if we see that and suddenly step away he will fall on his own.

As uke's center of gravity is moved, the effective base length (from the point on the mat under his center of gravity to the point of rotation) gets shorter, and he gets easier to move. Thus, once you get somebody moving, it gets easier and easier, quite apart from the effect of momentum.

A similar analysis will also apply to whoever is pushing. Thus, if two people of identical size and posture were to push each other at the same angle, neither of them would fall over. Their efforts would cancel each other out. Instead, we want to create a disparity in our favor.

The force necessary to push somebody over can be calculated. For a 200 lb. person (as used as an example in the rest of this chapter), with a center of gravity 3 ft. above the mat and a 2 ft. base (i.e. with his weight over the foot closest to the force), the necessary force will be 200 lbs. times the sine of the angle at which the center of gravity rises (34 degrees in this case). The necessary force will be about 111 lbs. However, we would only need to apply part of this force, as up to half of it is supported by uke's back foot. The proportion we do have to supply would be greatest if we push at uke's center, and least if we push at his head.

The angle at which we apply this force is important. If we push along the trajectory that uke's center of gravity will take as he tips over, the effort required will be the least, and the reaction to that force (being in the opposite direction and so partly down) will push our feet into the mat. This would make our two equal people no longer equal and nage has the advantage. If we push horizontally, instead, greater force (about 133 lbs.) will be needed, the balance being a compressive force pushing uke backwards, and the angle of reaction will be less favorable to us. (Two equal people will again be equal.) If we push at a greater angle than 34 degrees, the force will also be greater (up to 200 lbs., picking him up vertically from the mat), but the angle of reaction will be even more favorable to us, up to the point where the resultant force meets the mat ahead of our back heel. At this point, the force available will depend on our strength rather than on the mechanics of the situation. So we need to push up, in this instance, and the degree we can usefully push up depends on the depth of our respective postures and on how strong we are. (In the limit, whether we can push 200 lbs. vertically up over our head.)

As can be seen from the effect of the angle at which the force is applied, the shorter person has an advantage. If one of the people (uke) kneels, as in the figure below, his base area may be increased somewhat, the center of gravity is lowered, and a standing person pushing on his shoulders is now pushing downwards. The direction uke will rotate in tipping over is a steeper angle. Thus, much of nage's effort will be wasted and greater force must be applied to tip over the kneeling person. Generally, people will understand this intuitively and try to push more horizontally to improve the angle, but they cannot apply as much force as when uke is also standing. If uke feels his knees rising, and lightly touches the bottom of nage's arms or leans into the push, this will redirect the resultant force so that the direction is again within uke's base area, and the force on uke is one of compression rather than rotation, and he remains kneeling rather than being tipped over.

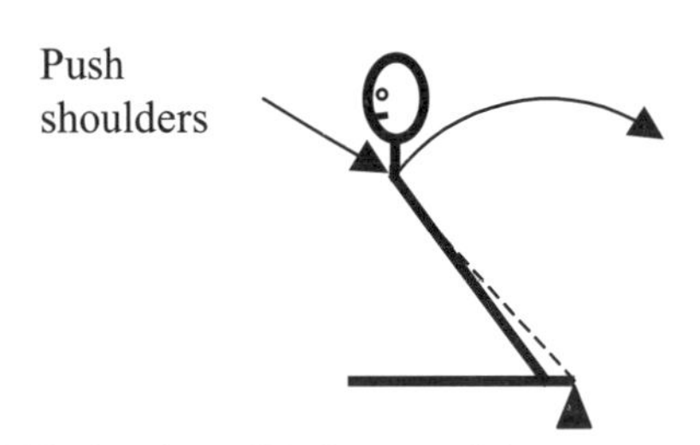

Mechanics of Balance - Seiza

If we assume uke's center of gravity in seiza is lowered to 12 inches, but the base length remains the same (knee to toes, rather than heel to opposite-foot toe), the force required will become many times as great, due to the different geometry. The optimum angle will also become greater, about 45 degrees, and again upwards. In this case, with nage pushing down, perhaps 500 lbs. of force is required, depending mostly on the angle at which nage is pushing compared to uke's geometry, and the angle is unfavorable for nage to push this hard. Even a 500 lb. nage would not be able to exert all of his 500 lbs. without standing on uke's shoulders. Of course, in reality I would not feel very comfortable with an Akebono pushing on my shoulders.

Angles do matter

If we look at kokyu dosa (suwari waza kokyu ho) instead, both uke and nage are in seiza and the angles are more nearly equal. The best direction to push uke over is back and up, perhaps at 45 degrees. If uke can keep nage's hands down to prevent an approximation to this direction, he can prevent being tipped over. To prevent being countered in this way, nage can offer his hands high, particularly if working with somebody bigger, stronger, or more advanced. Otherwise, nage must find a way to get his hands up so that he can push effectively.

Uke is only strong while he can bring his weight to bear, by keeping his arms substantially straight. Nage can avoid this by rotating his hands and curving them up so as to apply the force against uke's hands rather than along his arms. Then uke either lets go or lets his arms bend. At that point, nage continues to push, and uke's arms bend increasingly.

Once nage gets his hands up to chest high so that he can push at 45 degrees up and back, he should be able to readily tip uke over. If uke pushes hard at this point, he will most likely just push himself over.

These numbers, both for standing and seiza, are based on simple calculations of what it would take to move a rigid person. A real person can resist or go with the force. If he resists, he might push back harder than the stated force. In particular, if uke can find a position from which he, rather than nage, can push upwards, the total force can greatly exceed the 50 to 110 pounds force identified above, and the roles of nage and uke might reverse. But the horizontal component is still limited to this same amount, or he will push himself over. It is the angles that matter most.

Uke can resist more strongly by increasing his base dimension. Typically he can do this, when standing, by lengthening his posture. To the extent that his new posture increases the force necessary to tip him over, he will be able to resist more. Another way to increase resistance is to lean into the push. However, as I pointed out earlier, if uke leans excessively but then nage suddenly stops pushing, uke will fall over on his own. A good rule is to keep your nose and front knee behind your front toes.

If uke goes with nage's push, he will bend backwards, most likely at the waist. As he does so, his center of gravity will move in the direction of the push, reducing uke's effective base dimension and compromising his resistance. However, he may be able to change the direction in which nage can push. As he moves further, he will eventually fall over. Though the force might be less, the amount of work to bend uke to this extent might be greater than for making a stiff uke fall over. Some ukes are quite good at absorbing energy, at making nage work hard to throw them.

The amount of effort required does not depend on who does the pushing. Uke can push himself over quite as well as nage can. Thus, if we can cajole uke into doing the work while we transmit this force to the ground with minimum effort, uke will get tired sooner.

Posture does matter. If the horizontal distance from your heel to your center of gravity remains constant, the force you can exert or accept will remain constant. However, the center of gravity will move as you change posture. The strongest posture to the front appears to be with the front leg bent at the knee and the torso erect. The practical limit is with the knee over the toes. Beyond that point, it is a strain to hold position, and you are vulnerable to losing your balance forward.

It is useful to practice pushing uke off balance while he stands still, resisting passively rather than trying to recover. (This is the reverse of one of the ki tests, where the object is to center yourself and not be pushed over.) If you walk around uke and push smoothly and slowly at uke from different angles, you can feel which direction is most effective in taking uke's balance. You should look at different directions both in the plane parallel to the mat, and at the effects of different angles in the vertical plane. You should feel the effect of pushing at uke's center, and parallel to this direction but shifted sideways or up and down. You should try to relate this to the different aikido techniques.

Forcing vs. Steering

Aikido is generally not a case of one person manipulating a passive body. Rather, it involves applying force generated by one human body so that it interacts with another human body. If nage pushes back against uke, the two forces subtract from one another, and the stronger person wins. If they are evenly matched, most of their effort cancels out. However, this is a waste of effort, particularly for the smaller one, who will always lose in such a scenario. If, instead, nage uses the force at his disposal to steer the force generated by uke, either can win, even the weaker one.

The steering force can often be applied at the end of uke's arm, providing a lot of leverage (see below). If nage does this right, uke will find himself in an awkward position and unable to effectively push back.

These rather obvious points do identify several important issues. One is that uke must be providing a steerable force. Without this, nothing happens (but also there is not much nage needs to do). The second is that size is not the overriding issue, and either person can win. A third is that you don't want to resist uke's force, just to redirect it.

Of course, in real life, things are much more complicated. Uke might not give much force for nage to steer, and may in fact be actively attempting to prevent nage from steering him. This is a good reason not to indulge in a lot of competition, whether formal or informal. First, it is important to learn how to do the technique. Before that, it makes no sense for uke to try to stop you.

Levers and Techniques

Many techniques use levers. Thus, kote gaeshi, nikkyo, and sankyo involve using the hand as a lever to twist the forearm bones around each other and to generally lock up the body. Ikkyo irimi uses the forearm as a lever to twist the upper arm and thus lock up the shoulder and the rest of uke's body. Koshi nage uses nage's hips as a pivot point or fulcrum, and we then variously turn uke's body about this point by pushing on another part or we move the fulcrum by rotating our hips and let gravity take care of the rest.

Give me a fulcrum, and I'll move the world

I was taught in school that there are three types of levers. All of these are used in aikido, as shown in the figures below. Techniques are shown that use each of these types of lever. The first order lever is the most familiar one. This is exemplified here by the first part of an ude kimi nage where nage extends uke's arm across her body, inserts her arm in uke's armpit, plants her foot by uke's foot, and pivots her whole body and uke's body around these two points. Uke is forced to step forward. Uke's arm is generally about three times the distance from the shoulder to the centerline of his body, so uke experiences three times the force that nage applies.

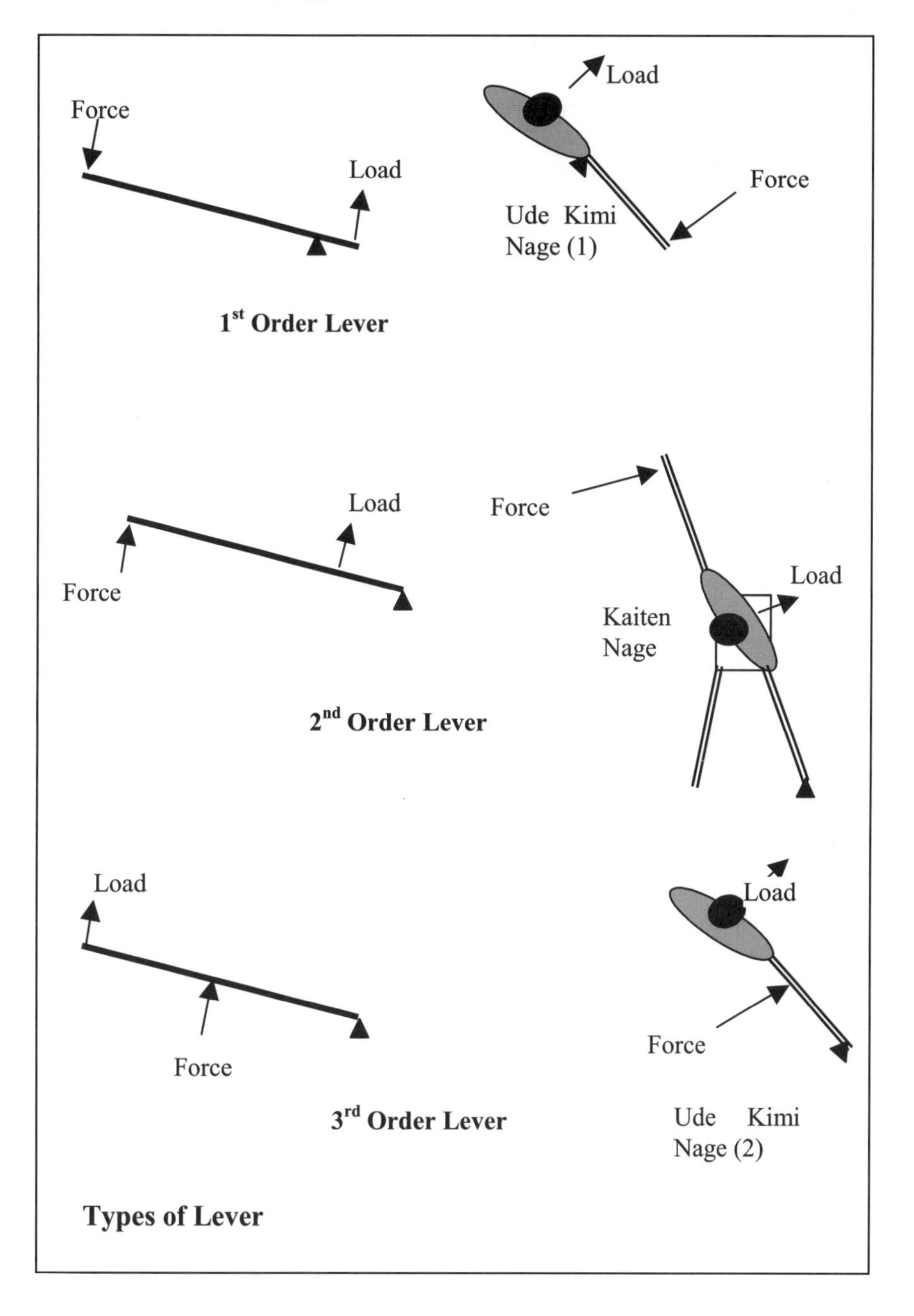

Types of Lever

First Order Lever. Uke's upper arm is the fulcrum (black arrow) as nage takes his balance by drawing uke's hand back.

Second Order Lever. Uke's foot is the fulcrum (white arrow) as nage throws.

The second order lever might be represented by kaiten nage irimi. Once uke is bent over at the waist and nage has elevated uke's arm to the vertical, force is applied to uke's wrist to push his body into a roll over the fulcrum of his foot. Again, the distance from the pivot point to the centerline is a fraction of that from the centerline to the wrist, giving perhaps a two to one force advantage.

Third Order Lever. Uke's hand is the fulcrum (white arrow) as nage throws by pressure near uke's elbow.

An example of a third order lever would be the final part of ude kimi nage when nage holds uke's hand down and steady, and then steps forward, driving uke's elbow forward, making uke step into a fall. This is considered a third order lever because the fulcrum is essentially fixed, and pressure is applied between the fulcrum and the load. Third order levers increase the velocity of the moving point rather than the force. In this case, the technique works because nage is applying the force to uke's straight arm, threatening his elbow if he resists, and forcing uke to step forwards faster and further than he intended because of the velocity ratio of the lever.

Static Application to Ikkyo

In practice, while these classifications are somewhat useful, the situation is more complicated in reality. If we look at a particular technique, perhaps kosa dori (ai hanmi katate tori) ikkyo irimi, we can see some applications of these simple principles in more detail. If nage is stronger than uke, or, more interestingly, if he gets into a position where he can apply more power, nage can execute a basic ikkyo by driving uke's elbow through the position of uke's head, forcing his head off that position and bending uke over. This movement will rotate uke's upper body away from nage and lock his shoulder so as to limit his ability to fight back (due to the awkward position of his body), including if he tries to punch nage with his free hand. We are using nage's forearm like a lever, at this point, to rotate the upper arm, twisting the shoulder. As the radius of the lever is at least half the length of uke's forearm, perhaps six to eight inches, and it is opposed by the shoulder joint with a radius of maybe two inches, nage has at least a three to one mechanical advantage. Every pound of force that nage applies has a three-pound effect on uke's shoulder joint. Thinking, instead, of uke's elbow as a fulcrum, there would be a twelve-inch lever and a somewhat smaller joint, giving perhaps a ten to one mechanical advantage. The actual movement is complex, and the effective leverage is probably between these two estimates.

Ikkyo Leverage. The fulcrum could be at the elbow or the wrist, and the effect is to rotate the arm at the shoulder joint.

Nage is also driving uke's arm forwards, up and over. In this motion, uke's arm is a lever with a length of perhaps 12 inches (shoulder to elbow) to 24 inches (to the wrist), and is again operating against uke's upper body, with a half-width of perhaps 9 inches. Thus, if uke is able to lock his shoulder, nage would be applying leverage of at least a two to one against any resistance uke can generate. In addition, nage will typically have his feet planted firmly and be using mostly his leg muscles to drive uke's arm up and over. Nage's arms will be transmitting the forces involved. However, the forces will mostly be transmitted lengthways along nage's arms, and structures are stronger when straight than when bent: the strength of nage's arms is generally not limiting.

Even a 100 lb. person will typically have leg muscles as strong as a 200 lb. person's arm, and two legs are involved. In executing the technique, nage's legs are doing what they do best, extending, while uke's shoulder is resisting rotation, which does not involve its strongest muscles. As discussed earlier, our hundred-pound nage can exert about 100 lbs. net force (using both legs) on uke.

Excepting Olympic gymnasts, few people can support their weight on extended arms (Maltese Cross). Thus, we can perhaps assume our 200 lb. uke can at most exert a downward force of 100 lbs. (half their body weight) per arm. In actuality, the force on this sort of ikkyo is mostly on the elbow (perhaps 85%, and 15% on the wrist). This makes things a bit better for uke, but the direction is forwards and the upper arm is rotating, so 100 lbs. is perhaps a good estimate of how much resistance a 200 lb. uke can generate.

Thus, nage might have 100 lbs. of force acting through a mechanical advantage of perhaps five (between three and ten), generating 500 lbs. of force. This is working against the 100 lbs. that uke can apply. Clearly uke's muscles will not avail him once nage gets into position.

Other things are involved, like strength of joints and torso muscles, and stance. As a rough measure, joints and muscles can take similar loads. So the joint might be able to take another 100 to 200 lbs. of load. But the conclusion seems to be that a 100 lb. nage should be able to apply ikkyo to a 200 lb. uke, which is indeed what is observed.

The difficulty with this analysis is whether uke will let nage get to this position and stand still to let him apply the technique. If uke is too strong for nage to initiate this form of ikkyo, which works fine when it works at all, then we are in the situation where uke and nage are pushing against each other. If, instead, nage turns a little, there is no longer a confrontation, and nage can again push through and upset uke. If nage turns one way (to his left, if the technique is right handed), we get perhaps an irimi nage or a figure-four arm lock. If nage turns the other way, everything proceeds as before.

If uke is still resisting, nage can do some more interesting things. Uke must have gripped rather strongly by this point. If nage cuts down through uke's wrist as if he held a sword, nage can apply a nikkyo that forces uke to bend over and nage can then proceed again as if for ikkyo. (See Figure 22 in "The Sword and Body", Page 187, below.)

This cutting movement is extremely powerful. Here, we have the whole length of nage's arm as the lever, and it is being applied to rotate uke's forearm bones around each other. So the mechanical advantage is now about 24 (the length of nage's arm) to 1.5 (the radius of uke's forearm). However, nage is now applying the technique with a downward, sword-cutting motion, rather than surging with his legs from the ground. If we apply the logic from above, our 100 lb. nage is only able to apply perhaps 50 lbs. force. But with the 16 to 1 mechanical advantage, we have a rotational and translational force on uke's forearm of about 800 lbs. Uke bends over, and ikkyo proceeds as before.

What makes uke bend over? Several things. The mechanical forces on his arm lock up his shoulder. Uke could perhaps hold himself upright. However, 800 lbs. of force will physically tip over a 200 lb. man-sized statue. If our 200 lb. uke has a center of gravity 3 ft. from the ground and his feet are separated by a distance of 2 ft., the most he can resist (with all 200 lbs. over one foot), will be about 60 lbs. As nage is pushing not at uke's center of gravity but at his shoulder, the force uke can resist with will be less, perhaps 40 lbs. If uke falls over at this point, we are happy. If not, he has to accommodate to the force and bend over, and we are still happy.

As uke bends over, the angles change. If nage is not careful, a 200 lb. uke should be able to pick up a 100 lb. nage. To pick up nage, uke needs to get close to nage and wrap an arm around nage's waist or thighs (aiki otoshi). Nage can prevent this by applying the force out from his body and on uke's arm rather than over uke's center. Nage can put his weight over uke's elbow and use that as a fulcrum, and pull up on uke's forearm. In this case, he can use his 50 lbs. to maintain the fulcrum and apply the strength of his legs against the forearm. The net force uke can apply results from both the 50 lbs. contributed by his weight, and the 100 lbs. contributed by his legs. This will still not be adequate with a 200 lb. uke if he can exert his strength. Thus, nage must ensure that he cannot, by keeping uke bent over (in the position we are warned against using to lift heavy boxes), and off balance.

Sometimes people will put a hand on uke's shoulder rather than on his elbow. This is probably too close to uke's canter, and uke can readily shift his weight and lift nage up. With the hand at the elbow instead, uke is put in the position of lifting nage at a distance, which is much harder to do.

So leverage is important, but nage should also have positioned himself and uke so that uke is almost off balance and unable to apply more than a fraction of his strength. If nage now pushes along uke's arm, like using a broom, nage can generate a lot more force than when pushing straight down. This might be sufficient to collapse uke, as he is bent over and pushing to stand up. If not, and he pushes back, nage can over-extend him in the new direction and lay uke on the mat. But this is getting off the subject of leverage.

Dynamics

So, some interesting aspects of ikkyo can be explained by simple static mechanics, as long as uke stands still and only passively resists. In reality, movement might well be involved through nage's timing so that uke is more effectively taken down. This is as much in the realm of psychology as mechanics, but dynamics, the physics of moving bodies, also applies.

Dynamics would be involved in two ways, both related to momentum. In the first way, you can use your body momentum to give an extra push, rather like storing up your muscular power in a spring. In the second, by manipulating uke, you use uke's momentum to throw him off balance.

Aikido – Moving On

In using his own momentum, nage can push through uke's resistance by being in motion in the right direction. This can be at the instant of contact or when resistance occurs later during the technique. This is very effective in some cases. The effect of momentum can be seen quite readily by bouncing up and down on the bathroom scale. It is easy to increase your weight dramatically, though there is a corresponding decrease shortly afterwards. Similarly, if you are moving during technique you can have much more power than you could generate statically, but if you mistime it you can be worse off. Thus, you can apply more power to ikkyo by starting in a stance with your weight on the back foot and move your weight forward as you make contact with uke's arm. This can easily double the force uke experiences.

Transfer of momentum depends on the type of interaction that occurs. If the collision is "elastic", both objects rebound each with half the total momentum. If the collision is "inelastic", the two objects stick together and move with the same total momentum. (That is to say, if the one object hits another of the same size, in one case they spring apart, each with half the original velocity, in the other case, they travel together at half the total original velocity.) In aikido, the type of collision is somewhere between these two types. Furthermore, we often limit recoil by planting our back foot, which makes our body seem much more massive with the earth as our pool cue.

When two bodies collide, the energy is shared equally, but the effects are not. The smaller body is more likely to suffer damage (as if a car and semi collide). Thus, we don't want to run into bigger people, but the more weight disparity we can mange e.g. by colliding with a smaller part of a person, the more we can deflect that member. Thus, we might initially want to deflect uke's arm, rather than his body: to attack his corners. Then we can build on this to affect his center.

From our previous analyses, we can see that the maximum static push that a nage can provide is about half his body weight: 50 lbs. for a 100 lb. person. Walking at 4 mph across the mat, he can smack into somebody his own size and they will both move at 2 mph, with no added effort on nage's part. However, for the maximum effect, he might want to add the force he can apply to his momentum, and get an even greater effect than either force or momentum alone.

When uke is moving fairly rapidly and we stop part of his body, his momentum makes him continue moving, often turning a linear motion into a circular one. Thus, we might check uke's leg, and trip him, his head and throw him in irimi nage, or his arm and throw him in kote gaeshi.

Momentum and inertia are also important when we move our own bodies. Turning in a bent posture is slow because the inertia is greater than if you are upright. (This is the same reason that an ice skater speeds up when she pulls in her arms and slows down when she spreads them to the sides.) Thus, to turn fast, we should keep our bodies erect. This also why we use hasso no kamae –

holding the jo vertically – to turn with a jo, and why we sometimes defend against a bokken attack by moving our hands rather than the tip of our sword.

In Yoshinkan Aikido, a pivot is made with a sweeping leg movement, keeping the back leg straight. This may introduce more momentum to the system and make it harder for uke to stop nage from moving, though I'm far from being knowledgeable in this style.

Dynamic Analysis of Shomen Uchi Ikkyo Irimi

Suppose uke strikes at nage with shomen uchi. As he does, his arm swings as a compound pendulum, the movement starting from uke's center and progressing like a whip to uke's shoulder, upper arm, forearm and then to his hand. The resulting energy is quite significant. If uke's movement is efficient, most of the energy generated by his body movement should appear in his blow.

If nage merely stands still, placing his arm to intercept uke's, protecting his head, and waits for uke's attack, uke will deliver a blow with most of his momentum behind it. Nage can deal with this strong blow by deflecting it, but then he cannot also step in and execute an ikkyo irimi. That would have to rely on a rather abrupt change of direction and using strength and position to deal with uke's momentum.

If, instead, nage moves forward and off line, he can connect with uke early, when uke's body is moving fastest and his momentum has not been transferred to his arm. Uke's hips will tend to keep moving forwards, while uke's arm and upper body are pushed back and rotated by nage. This has the effect of bending uke into the position we want him to be. Nage's movement can be as slight as nage shifting his weight from his back foot to his front foot, or he might step forwards with his front foot (particularly if nage is shorter than uke).

If we assume nage contributes a similar effort as uke does to his technique, moving in at about the same time, but remaining better coordinated (as his movement is not disrupted by uke), he has most of both his own and uke's momentum at his disposal. Twice the effort that uke was putting into hitting nage can rebound against him: with a strong attack and the right timing, shomen uchi ikkyo irimi can become a nose breaker, with uke being slapped down suddenly onto the mat.

Momentum Transfer

Momentum can be transferred in interesting ways when nage manipulates uke's and his own momentum to make a throw occur. In kote gaeshi, for example, applications of mechanics similar to those we have discussed above underlie the basic movements. However, changes occur when the technique is done on the move.

If uke attacks with mune tsuki, for example, his momentum is moving towards nage. Nage might escape to the side and redirect uke's movement around nage's body. Thus, uke goes from linear movement to circular movement. (This can involve some rather critical timing, as well as taking balance and making connection, especially if uke attacks with due care rather than merely rushing in, but here we are discussing what can happen rather than how to make it happen.)

Nage and uke originally have independent centers. As nage escapes, turning tenkan, he makes a connection to uke's body, and manipulates this connection to transfer momentum from himself to uke, and to make uke's center travel around his own.

The radius of this movement is initially between one and two arm-lengths (~ 3 ft.). If nage allows this movement to continue but pushes down, this brings uke closer to nage and so shortens the radius of uke's rotation. This shortening of the radius forces uke to rotate faster around nage (again, like a skater pulling in her arms). Nage also adds effort to the technique. Uke's feet are only moving at the speed he attacked with, so this acceleration moves uke's balance forward. Uke is forced to run faster to avoid falling over. As uke catches up, nage then changes the direction in which uke's arm is moving and uke's hips tend to over-run his shoulders, causing uke to lose his balance in the opposite direction. If nage redirects the technique up and into a small vertical circle, uke rotates in the air and lands on his back. This can be done with kote gaeshi applied to uke's wrist or, more spectacularly, open handed.

From this perspective, nage can do several things to make the throw more effective:

- Interrupt uke's motion as little as possible.
- Accelerate uke further by pushing in the same direction.
- Reduce uke's radius of rotation as much as possible.

For the first item, nage's movement should be to get off the line of attack and to do as little as possible to resist uke's movement. Besides the physical aspect, if nage can give uke the feeling that he is going to hit his target, uke might put more into the attack than he should (over committing).

In accelerating uke, the effect is cumulative, so if you keep pushing steadily, you will build up a large effect without straining. If nage already has momentum he can transfer this to uke through this push. Thus, in executing a tenkan movement to get out of the danger zone, nage is building up rotational momentum. He can transfer this to uke by pushing uke to go faster, while slowing his own movement.

In reducing the radius of rotation, the largest radius possible is a straight line (infinite radius). If uke and nage were point masses, the radius could be reduced to a very small size and the rotational velocity would then be very large. As it is, the smallest practical radius is limited by the size of our bodies. If we were to deal with rotating uke about a horizontal axis, which would be what happens when we perform irimi nage, the radius would be perhaps 3 ft. We could shorten the radius by working closer to his center of gravity, pushing at chest level. However, this prevents us using uke's full momentum, as the part of his body above the contact point would work against the rest of his body. Uke has less rotational inertia (resistance to movement) around the vertical axis of his body. A similar limit of about 3 ft. would be found working at the full length of uke's arm in a more or less horizontal circle. A smaller radius could be found by working at his elbow. The inertia of his forearm can then make it easier to connect to the rest of uke's body. In reducing the radius of rotation, nage should provide a fixed axis of rotation or even move against the direction uke is moving to maximize the effect.

Developing Power in Throwing

In aikido, we want to transmit power to uke for at least two reasons: to imbalance him, and to throw decisively. If we use too little power, we might not be able to effectively do the technique. If we use too much, we might break the connection between uke and nage.

As discussed earlier, there are two ways to provide power to uke: by transferring momentum and by using muscular power. Transferring momentum can be done by the way we move, so that by virtue of the movement itself nage loses momentum and uke gains it. We can also transfer momentum by muscular extension, nage using his momentum as a base to push against, in effect. This lets us push in directions we could not otherwise effectively use.

In either case, we have to modulate the power to what can be effectively used. If the throw is done using uke's grip (as in many kokyu nage techniques), we can only apply as much power as uke allows us to use. We can influence this, for example, by pushing towards uke's face, when uke holds on to keep our hand away from his face. If the throw is done using nage's grip, nage controls that to some extent but there are limits due to the strength of nage's grip on the particular part of uke he is holding. It is easier to grip a smaller person's forearm, for example, than a larger person's. When uke is sweating, it is more difficult to hold on to their forearm. So if the connection begins to fail, you might use a little less power and push for a longer time.

Another limitation is what might be called impedance matching. If a small uke tries to throw a large uke with a sudden movement, uke's body has no time to react, and the movement is ineffective. He has to apply force for a longer time to accelerate uke, or else he has to work on a smaller mass, just a part of uke's body that then affects the rest and allows him to accelerate it over a longer time. You might think that a large nage can toss a smaller uke around with impunity. There is some truth in this, but the large nage is limited (fortunately for uke) as to how much force he can apply by the lack of resistance and loss of connection.

In any situation, the effect depends not on the amount of force that nage puts into the technique, but on the net work (force x time) done. To effectively use our power, we must do a lot of things at once: take uke's balance, move our body into the right place to apply our power, move uke into the right place to receive it, establish the right posture, and manipulate uke into the posture we need them to be in for a particular technique. In doing all this, we need to apply the power smoothly and at the right rate and direction, often changing direction and power in a complex fashion. Sometimes the complexities get in our way, and we end up with a technique that is not very effective. In consequence, it is a good idea to practice merely transferring power.

To do so, we need to pick a technique that is simple enough that the complexities don't get in our way. We need a technique from which uke can easily survive the ukemi, even if they are not very experienced. A good one to start with is ushiro ryote tori (ushiro te kubi tori) kokyu nage, the one where uke grabs nage's arm ai hanmi, goes around behind nage and grabs the other arm, and is thrown in front of nage.

This exercise is perhaps a little artificial (or requires a naïve attacker). However, we don't want to worry about practicalities for now. All nage needs to worry about is learning to transfer energy to uke. Uke should move in smartly and grab one arm, and move as necessary to grab the other. Ideally, he should grab hard and hold on, though if uke is concerned about the ukemi he can let go at any time. Once you have good ukemi, it does feel cool to hold on and see how far nage can throw you.

Momentum Transfer – Ushiro Ryote Tori Kokyu Nage

Nage should move off line and lower his arm as uke grasps it. He should lower his center and grip the mat with his toes. This movement, strongly anchored to the mat, should accelerate uke, moving his balance forward and swinging him around the point of attachment, which nage controls. As uke moves round, nage should enter under the arm holding him, allowing his arm to rise but maintaining extension on uke's arm and keeping his own hand in front of his head (like for shiho nage). He should present his free arm to uke so that uke can readily grab that arm too, raising it so that it is in the best position for the next segment of the technique. As uke grabs nage's second arm, nage should step forward, maintaining the extension of both of his arms and cutting to the front, towards where uke is going. Nage should maintain his extension for a moment or two (zanshin) and not tail off the movement into the wrong direction. This exercise should project uke maybe 10 ft. forward, so that he can perform an easy front roll.

The whole time that there is physical contact, nage should be passing momentum to uke. Uke should feel a constant steady acceleration, leaving the ground just when his feet can't keep up with his body any more. There should be no time at which slackness develops in the connection between uke and nage. The connection should not be broken by use of too much force. Nage can throw uke down at his feet, or across the mat. As the goal is to develop nage's power without excessive stress on uke, nage should project uke out so that he can take a nice lazy roll at the end.

Nage should practice projecting uke strongly

Once the basic technique is working, nage can polish the various pieces. For example, nage can use one hand at a time, seeing how much momentum he can impart with the first hand grabbed, and then practicing by letting that one do very little and throwing strongly with the other hand. (The latter is much harder to do effectively.) Then he can put the two together and see if he can efficiently use both. Common problems are that nage loses his center, that he breaks the connection with uke, that uke is too afraid of the fall to hold on, and that the technique is disjointed.

It is difficult at first to keep your center, especially if uke runs at you, grabs an arm, and keeps on running past you with no attempt to grab the second arm. You can minimize this effect by moving off line and lowering your arm and center. Your hanmi at this time should set you up so that your strongest position (in line with your feet) is aligned to resist uke's pull. You might need to allow your arm to come in a little by lowering your elbow, but keep it in front of you.

If uke breaks loose, the first thing is to make sure you are not jerking him. There is a tendency to try to do this technique with your arms and upper body, and this becomes jerky, especially with some ukes. Instead, move smoothly using your whole body, accelerating uke's center with your own. If it is uke that is being jerky, you can use your arm and body as a shock absorber to some extent, as long as you maintain a strong position. Sometimes all that is needed is to wipe the sweat off your forearm so that uke can grip more strongly.

If uke is just not holding on strongly enough for this exercise, you can ask them to hold your arm more strongly. (This does not mean grab and pull.) However, there is likely to be a greater problem, in that uke doesn't want to fly too far and fast. Time and gentle encouragement should take care of that problem.

Getting the whole technique to fit together is not easy, and is the point of repeatedly practicing a throw. Sufficient practice with a good uke will make it smooth. As for any other technique, use relaxed extension, work from your center, blend with your uke, and don't worry if you don't get it at first. Simple as this exercise is, there are lots of things going on at once, and you have to make them all work together at some minimum speed. There is a redirection at the beginning of the technique, when uke grabs the first hand. After that, nage should be pushing pretty much in the same direction that uke is moving. You can change the direction uke is thrown in this technique, as in most techniques, but that is not the purpose of the exercise. Instead, just work on accelerating uke.

There are lots of other exercises that could be used to practice developing power (kokyu). The common practice of (gyaku hanmi) katate tori kokyu nage, where uke runs up, nage turns, and uke falls is not a good one for this because almost invariably it gets to be merely an exercise in ukemi, with uke running up and throwing himself. Kosa dori (ai hanmi katate tori) kokyu nage, particularly with an initial move to the outside, involves more control of uke's direction and momentum, and is better. Yokomen uchi irimi nage can be done this way, stepping off line (inside) to get a nice circular attack, cutting down that arm, stepping behind uke, taking his balance, and throwing. Katate tori kaiten nage tenkan works very nicely this way, both uchi and soto variations. Ikkyo ura is shorter, but can also be a nice flowing technique.

Ultimately, the feeling of providing momentum to uke that is developed by this exercise can be used in almost any technique. It does, however, make techniques very powerful and lower ranked people should be careful in applying powerful techniques to other lower ranked people, especially with techniques like shiho nage and kote gaeshi that can cause serious damage if misapplied.

Physics of Ukemi

When uke is thrown, he hits the ground with whatever energy he inadvertently contributed, plus what nage added, plus whatever contribution gravity added. The best way to dissipate this is to roll back to your feet, as then no single part of your body has to take the brunt of this force, and you use the force of the throw to get back up. If you are unable to roll, you should dissipate the force of impact by spreading it over the greatest area possible. This is particularly true if you fall on a hard surface, when you should take the shock on all the big muscles of your back, by landing half on your back and half on your side.

Slapping the mat transfers a lot of energy to the arm, as your arm is moved faster than your body and kinetic energy is mv^2. Thus, velocity of impact has more effect than the mass, and your arm is better able to take the shock than your torso or head.

How hard do we usually fall? Simply leveling out and dropping from the height of our center would let us hit the mat at about 9 mph. If we run, we can achieve a similar sort of velocity, so I'd guess that gravity probably accounts for half the energy of our impact, and uke and nage's combined efforts would account for the rest.

If the combined give of our body and the mat is about 2 inches, we would decelerate at about 18 g (18 times the force of gravity). Tests with rocket sleds in the 1950s and 60s showed that the human body can absorb accelerations as high as 40 g (with extensive bruising), so that sounds about right. Falling from 6 ft. would result in forces of about 36 g. My arm weighs maybe 10 lbs., and if I can hit the mat at three times the speed my body is falling, by slapping I can half the impact energy absorbed by my torso. Some of the benefit of slapping may also be related to the result of slapping on the rest of the body: which muscles are tensed, and how the shock is transmitted to the rest of the body. Perhaps the slap also converts the impact into a different motion. Certainly the arm hits first, and then presumably we roll down the arm until our torso hits, spreading the deceleration over a longer period of time.

Physics of Weapons

Weapons cause damage by impact or cutting. Punches, kicks, bokken and jo are impact weapons. Guns also generally cause injury by impact (hydrostatic shock), though bleeding might also be an issue. Knives, swords, arrows, and spears cut, mostly causing damage by loss of blood.

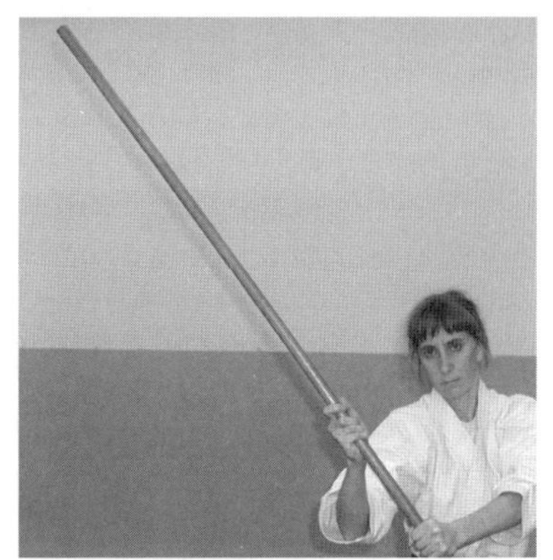

The tip of the jo is the most dangerous part due to mv^2

A strike (shomen, yokomen) with a jo or bokken might take several tenths of a second and travel something like 15 ft., so the tip velocity might be about 50 fps (35 mph). The weights of my jo and bokken are about 1.4 lbs., so the impact energy is something like 5,000 lb ft^2s^2. To stop the jo over a distance of only a foot (using the forearm) would involve a load of about 120 lbs. Clearly this could be dangerous (think of a 120 lb. weight resting on your arm), even though a jo is “just” a stick. Thus, to deal with such a strike you should move in close to uke, to where the weapon is not moving as fast, and preferably deal with it either early, before the full force is transferred to the weapon, or late, when the impetus has somewhat dissipated.

A tsuki with a jo can be looked at several ways. The end of a jo is something like a square inch in area. If a 200 lb. uke got all his weight behind it, the pressure would be about 200 psi. This does not sound like a lot, but I have been told that 7 lbs. of force is sufficient to break a collarbone. Driving out the jo like a spear will not achieve as high a tip velocity as swinging it. The travel time is not much shorter and the jo only travels perhaps 3 ft., so the speed might only be something like 20 fps (14 mph). If you get much of your mass behind the jo at impact, however, preventing recoil, the kinetic energy could be similar to the energy behind a yokomen strike. To support this assessment, I remember practicing with a jo using a brick wall as a target. To my surprise, I drove a brick lose. Clearly, it is not a good idea to try to block a tsuki, and better to get off line.

A jo is a lethal weapon and should be treated with respect

Aikido and Biology

Aikido is about the mind, the body, and the spirit, and especially how they all come together into an effective human being. Biologically, there is no distinction. The mind is what the brain does. The spirit is a bit more complex, but probably involves the brain and a variety of glands around the body. The brain itself is a complex part of the body that operates using chemistry and physics. We see different aspects of the body and label them. Some we label based on anatomy, like the biceps and triceps muscles, the humerus, or the heart and brain. Others we label based on function, like the mind and body. Yet in the end, these distinctions are based on somewhat primitive ideas about biology, and are as often obstructions to our understanding as they are aids.

The mind moves the body. We can trace the events, in some cases, from the thought to the muscle twitch. Even "involuntary" functions are often changed by our state of mind. For example, when we are nervous our hearts beat faster. If our mind is distracted or confused, our body is weak.

Conversely, the body also affects the mind. If we had no physical limitations, as perhaps in our dreams, we could walk through walls and fly like Peter Pan. In practice, if we try to do these things we bump into solid objects* or fall, and our body reminds us that some things we can imagine cannot be done in practice. If we are in pain, our mind is hard to engage on some other topic. More subtly, if our body is tired, our mind gets tired.

There are a number of aspects of biology that are particularly related to aikido. Some that come to mind are, not necessarily in order of importance:

- Breathing
- Hand-eye coordination and proprioception
- Learning
- Muscle physiology
- Pain, injury, and healing
- Physiology / adrenaline
- Reflexes and reaction time
- Sickness
- Social dominance

Breathing

The main role of breathing is to provide oxygen to the body and to get rid of carbon dioxide. We need air just as a car requires air as well as gas to make it run and a potato in the exhaust pipe will stop a car engine. We need oxygen to power our bodies. The metabolic machinery oxidizes food and produces ATP that powers muscle. We need to get rid of waste products like carbon dioxide. Breathing has some other functions also. It gets rid of heat. The muscles we use

---

* Which are nevertheless mostly empty space.

to breathe can help us exert some other muscles, though the idea of breathing out as we push may not be as important as some people think. Paying attention to breathing can help us meditate, but paying attention to a candle flame would probably work just as well.

Oriental and occidental mysticism both connect the spirit and life itself with breathing. Certainly we will not live long without breathing, but there is no evidence of any élan vitale (vital spirit), and books that claim there is such a thing are a hundred years out of date. Life, as best we can tell, is a wonderfully complex and fascinating chemical process, but no more or less than that.* Our spirit is a high level manifestation of our electrochemistry, not something supernatural that animates our bodies like the strings moving a puppet.

Deep breathing will help keep your lungs functioning well, whether a result of exercising, breathing exercises, meditation, or blowing the bagpipes. Smoking tobacco or other substances will impair function, though some individuals are more robust than others.

Hand-Eye Coordination and Proprioception

A certain degree of hand-eye coordination is necessary to do aikido. The eyes are often the main external sense organ used to determine how we respond. Hand-eye coordination is particularly important in dealing with blows, and ball games are excellent for developing hand-eye coordination in children. Still, we should not depend on our eyes to see what our hands or bodies are doing. Rather, we should go beyond this to know where the various pieces of our bodies are without looking, like a musician playing without looking at his hands. We can work at paying attention to our bodies. Just being aware helps us determine the correct moves. We can practice blindfolded to reduce our dependence on our eyes, and learn to feel our bodies and what they are telling us. (See also below, page 85.) Airlines often provide convenient blindfolds on long flights.

A step beyond awareness of our own bodies is to feel what uke is doing through the contact with our body. My first judo teacher used to toss me around holding my gi with two fingers. If we are struggling and straining to move uke, we can't feel what his reactions are. Thus, we should be relaxed even when extending.

Learning

We learn whether we want to or not. Repetition increases learning. Repeating correct motion is good, and builds up automatic responses of correct motion. Repeating incorrect motion also builds up automatic responses, but of

---

* However, life may not inevitably be tied to our sort of chemistry, and perhaps not even to chemistry at all.

incorrect motion. Thus, try not to repeat incorrect movements, because you will have to unlearn them to progress.

Prompt feedback improves the speed of learning. In rats, the optimum delay between stimulus and response is about 0.4 seconds. We are not rats, but we learn in similar ways. If feedback is delayed beyond a few minutes, it has virtually no effect on simple tasks. Consistent reinforcement for each correct movement will result in the fastest learning, but intermittent reinforcement results in greater retention of the learned response.* Thus, it is better to reinforce a beginner every time he makes a correct move, then to taper off the reinforcement as he improves.

Learning can occur as a result of both negative reinforcement of errors, and positive reinforcement of correct responses. However, the effects are not identical. Positive reinforcement increases creativity and willingness to try new things. Negative reinforcement reduces them. Fear tends to inhibit learning. If we are pre-occupied with surviving, we are not learning what we are doing, but may be learning that we should avoid coming to class.

Our brains are massively parallel computers (~ 10^8 channels) with rather slow clock speeds (~ 1 kHz). Thus, my brain is about 1000 times as powerful as the computer I'm writing this on, and has better software than provided by Microsoft. Our senses have a wide bandwidth. We absorb tremendous amounts of information – several million bits per second (about the capacity of an Ethernet cable). We feel perhaps ten times more information (proprioception) about our own bodies than we see of the outside world. However, we only consciously examine a trickle – a few bits per second – of this flood of raw information. Much neural processing is simply recoding and selective rejection of information. This is why it takes so long to learn to play the piano like a virtuoso or to develop competency in aikido. We have to learn how to do a lot of the processing at a subconscious level and reserve conscious decision making for critical issues. Otherwise, we will be confused and slow in our responses.

People learn in different ways. Some remember best when they feel things. Others when they see things, or when they hear things. The best way is to use all three modalities. Mental rehearsal helps. You might also practice aikido on your own, make notes, or even teach it. Context is often important. Just seeing a technique demonstrated by a different instructor might help.

In learning a technique, we go through several stages. You learn the gross body movements first: which foot goes where, how many steps, whether there is a hand change. Once you have those, you learn the fine body movements – which might be details like the angle of the hands or feet, maintaining extension, or where uke's and nage's balance should be. Finally, you practice until you can do them all simultaneously without thinking about any of them. At that point, a

---

* This is why gambling and fishing are so addictive.

technique is like a tool you own, and all you have to do is decide which tool to use, when, and what you want to do with it.

To facilitate learning, it helps to pay attention to the appropriate details. Thus, the first time we see a technique, we should remember the gross movements. As we become familiar with those movements, we should pay attention to the finer movements. As we become familiar with the technique in total, we need to see the gestalt, and to polish that. If we try to grasp it all at once, we will forget it all. On the other hand, if you need to do a technique in the street, don't think about which foot to put forward or how to grasp the attacker's hand, or you are likely to be unpleasantly surprised.

To change the way you do a particular technique, whether to improve the basics or to learn another way of doing a technique, you might have to go back, possibly all the way to the gross body movements. These are very different between Yoshinkan and Aikikai Aikido, for example. An experienced aikidoka will still generally learn faster than a beginner, because some of the basics will be the same, involving things like stance, balance, and extension.

An exception to experience making learning easier can occur when what is being learned conflicts with what has been learned before. This can happen, for example, when you visit a dojo where they practice a different style of aikido from what you are used to. This can be quite illuminating, with basic techniques becoming advanced techniques, and with different assumptions as to how uke should attack, how nage should respond, and what sort of ukemi to take.

Muscle Physiology

Muscles only pull. This is Biology 101, but not everybody has studied biology. As discussed earlier, the only way we can push is through the use of levers (our skeleton) that convert a muscle pull into a push.

Muscles get tired if used a lot, and then get bigger and stronger over time. We tend to think that muscle development is not a good idea in aikido, but in fact we develop the musculature of our bodies in unique ways. This is obvious in retrospect, if we think back to when we were beginners and our muscles hurt in strange places the next day. For example, the triceps and anconeus (a muscle on the outer aspect of the forearm near the elbow) muscles seem to become more developed in aikidoka.

Muscles can be stretched to make them longer. However, they only elongate in response to stretches that last for long periods of time - minutes. Quick stretches make the muscles contract. Thus, to strengthen your body, do fairly rapid stretches. To increase your range of motion, do very slow and sustained stretches.

Pain, Injury, and Healing

Pain is a warning that your body is about to get, or has already been injured. Heed it. If something hurts, it is generally a good idea to stop doing it.

You can damage your body yourself by excessive stretching, by incorrect warming up, or by trying too hard.

Muscles and joints can both be damaged by application of excessive force. It is good to tap early when a joint lock is being applied. Locks should always be applied slowly and in a controlled fashion, and the force removed back along the same path it was applied.

We do, however, need to make a distinction between discomfort and pain. If a technique hurts as long as the technique is applied, but the discomfort stops as soon as the technique is no longer being applied, this is good. Nage is doing the technique correctly. If the pain lasts longer than that, excessive force has been applied, and some degree of injury has been incurred.

If you do get injured, as we are doing a martial art it is good to have the ability to work through the pain. It might even be worth doing so occasionally to prove it to yourself. However, doing so increases the damage and, consequently, the time to recover.

It is easy to be macho and tough it out to the end of the class, because we often don't feel the full effects of an injury until later. Instead, you should stop working out immediately you get injured and apply cold, wrap the injured part, elevate it if possible, and, above all, rest. RICE - rest, ice, compression, and elevation. Anti-inflammatory drugs such as ibuprofen and aspirin might minimize swelling. However, there is some suggestion that the COX-2 inhibitors, a more recent class of anti-inflammatories, delay healing of sprains.

It is generally a good idea to seek medical attention unless the injury is trivial. Some injuries do not heal on their own. Joint damage in particular may need surgical intervention. Not all medical attention is of equal quality. A sports doctor is likely to know more than a typical family doctor about aikido injuries. The best thing is to have a sports doctor in your dojo who does not mind helping out. However, remember that medicine is his business, and you should go to his office and pay for his advice. That way, he will stay eager to help out in emergencies.

It might seem too obvious to mention, but do what your doctor tells you to do. If he says rest, then rest. If the physical therapist says exercise with a 5 lb. weight, don't use a 10 lb. one. If he says 15 reps, don't do 5 or 30.

Students are generally eager to get back on the mat. This is good, but you should not do so until you are healed. Working out with a half-healed injury is likely to result in further damage, and doing so repeatedly can turn an acute problem into a chronic one. Older students may be more easily hurt and take longer to heal.

Physiology/Adrenaline

We feel a rush of energy under stress, due to our body secreting hormones such as adrenaline. We move quicker, and have more strength. These changes are good in appropriate times, less good if always present. We might like the "rush", but to be constantly on edge would wear us out. This response is generally considered to be autonomic, to happen automatically. However, we can learn to trigger it at will.

Aerobic conditioning will allow us to last longer in any physical situation, whether practicing in class or in a fight. Like weight training, it is not part of aikido, but it can be a productive part of our regimen.

Our bodies are about 70% water. If we don't get enough water, we can die. With lesser degrees of dehydration, we run out of energy. We don't heal as well. Like voting, we should drink early and often when practicing, especially in hot climates. It is easier to stay hydrated than to recover from dehydration. Drinking plenty of liquids (non carbonated, non caffinated) is especially important if we are sick. We should drink at least four pints of water (four large glasses) a day, and twice that when exercising. One pint of water will dissipate about 260 kcal of heat. A heavy day's practice, as at a seminar, might burn as much as 4,000 kcal, two or three times the normal expenditure. If the excess heat is 2,500 kcal, that is only about half a pound of fat but it would require about ten pints of extra water (ten glasses) to eliminate this heat by perspiration. Usually, we don't drink enough and get somewhat dehydrated.

Reflexes and Reaction Time

Human reaction times vary from about a tenth of a second up to several seconds or even longer, and are very situation specific. We react most quickly when we don't need to think about what to do. Reaction times vary from person to person, but are always fastest for things we are familiar with. Thus, beginners will need more time to respond in aikido. Our reaction times slow down as we get older, but speed up as we get more experienced, which helps make up the deficit. In addition to our mental reaction time, big movements take more time than small movements due to the physics involved. (Like the thinking time and braking time in stopping a car.) Ma-ai is partly ensuring we have time to react.

Aikido generally requires us to move more than does, for example, just hitting somebody. Thus we need a greater ma-ai than in karate. We like to stay ahead of uke, and the key is to see what he is going to do, and even to control his actions by the openings (suki) we provide him. It is easy to do this with some people, but trained fighters have very little pre-motion (the little movements that indicate what they are going to do, and when), and may be too smart to respond to obvious suki that are offered.

There is another aspect to reaction time: uke's reaction to what we do. It is quite difficult to move an uke if we do it slowly enough to give him time to think. This is not to say we should hurry, just that we should move without thought ourselves.

Sometimes, on the other hand, we rush uke. Perhaps for kote gaeshi we are so eager to throw uke that we don't give him time to respond. This makes throwing more difficult to do than it needs to be, and might either hurt uke if we are strong enough, or have little effect if we are not. It is like bouncing a ball or pumping a swing: if our timing is just right, it takes little effort.

Sometimes we can initiate a response in uke that we then use in doing technique. A reflex is an automatic reaction to a stimulus. It is something that is innate, rather than learned, though some reflexes might be susceptible to some degree of modification through learning. When a doctor taps your knee with a rubber hammer and your leg kicks forward, that is a reflex.

A similar reflex occurs when a muscle is stretched quickly. It shortens. This seems to be the reason that (gyaku hanmi) katate tori kokyu nage works quite as well as it does. Thus, if somebody is holding your arm strongly and you move their arm to the point between their legs and a couple of feet out from their center, and quickly "bounce" their arm (like bouncing a basketball), they take a quite satisfying ukemi.

What I think is happening is that you are taking uke's balance to the edge of where he has to step or fall, and he tenses to prevent you going further. You make a quick movement and, as the flexor muscles in his arm are stretched, these muscles contract reflexively. As he is close to the edge of his balance, this contraction pulls him all the way off balance and makes him fly through the air. All nage has to do is to maintain his extension so that uke's effort throws uke, rather than pulling nage off balance. Usually, if you have to do a technique fast, it is because you don't fully understand it. In this case, however, there is a dynamic interaction between uke and nage that is time critical. You still don't have to hurry the technique, but you can't get the same effect moving slowly.

A similar effect seems to work for tsuki kokyu nage. If nage moves behind uke as he punches, she can grasp uke's shoulders and pull him over backwards to throw him down. As uke completes a punch, his body should be somewhat tense to transmit the power of the punch into the target. If at this moment nage quickly pushes uke's arm down and towards nage, the muscle stretch reflex will tend to make uke pull up and turn the other way. If nage pulls uke's rear shoulder back and down as this happens, uke will fall with much less effort on nage's part. The timing is again crucial. If nage is a little early or late, uke's arm and body may not be tense and the reflex will be small or nonexistent. If there is any appreciable gap between nage's two pushes, she won't get the advantage of uke's muscle twitch. One must immediately follow the other with a separation of about a tenth of a second.

A third case where stretch reflexes seem to be important is in doing kokyu ho. If uke grabs really tightly and it is difficult to move him, a compound movement, where nage moves one way then immediately moves in a different direction, will usually allow nage to get past uke's arms. In this case, nage needs to remain somewhat relaxed, but extended. When nage twitches one way, uke will tend to twitch the other way to stop him. If at that time nage is relaxed and also moving in that direction, nage's effort is amplified and he can perform the technique.

Sickness

Diseases are passed from person to person by physical contact, sharing bodily fluids, contamination of drinks or food, or by insect vectors. Disease transmission is resisted by a variety of mechanisms, including our immune system. Drinking plenty of fluids boosts the immune system. Moderate exercise is good for moderately sick people, making them feel better and boosting their immune systems, but if they come to the dojo when ill, they risk passing it on to the rest of us. We don't always know when we are infectious. Obviously, we should not cough or sneeze on our partners. What is less well known is that colds and flu are often transmitted by hand to hand contact, which we do a lot of in aikido. We can reduce the chance of catching or passing on these infections by washing our hands before and after practice, and by not touching our faces or eating or drinking without washing our hands first.

There is little chance of catching hepatitis, and less of catching AIDS, except by blood to blood transmission. Thus, if any blood is spilled, such as from a cut lip, it should be cleaned up at once with peroxide or bleach. The most likely concerns with insect-borne diseases in the US would be encephalitis from mosquito bites or Lyme disease from ticks. These would be most problematic outdoors, such as when practicing in a park. Use of a repellant and avoiding dawn and dusk would most likely provide adequate protection.

Social Dominance

In case social dominance seems rather far removed from martial arts, note that Musashi has a section in Go Rin no Sho titled "To Strive for Height". Another is "To Hold Down a Pillow" (not allowing your enemy's head to rise). In "To Know Collapse", he says, "You must utterly cut the enemy down so that he does not recover his position".* These are clearly related to social dominance.

Social dominance in aikido is evident in watching techniques being performed by many high-ranking teachers and in watching video of O Sensei. There is a social hierarchy in any dojo, typically with the highest ranked person at the top, and the rest of the hierarchy being more or less consistent with the rank order. This is both good and bad. It is good if the student learns that he has a place in the world, and feels confident if attacked. It is bad if this hierarchy is used to manipulate others and obtain, for example, sexual favors from the lower ranked members that they might not willingly offer.

---

* Harris translation, The Overlook Press, 1974.

Nage should always feel in charge. This feeling can be described as being centered, but it is a largely social phenomenon. It is a useful additional tool for controlling uke, though it should be backed up with good technical ability. This feeling is similar to what is observed when animals come into conflict with members of their own species. Animals are more aggressive and more successful in confrontations when defending their home territory. Two animals meeting for the first time will size up each other. They might then ignore one another, particularly on neutral territory or if there is no reason for conflict. They might fight, or they might display to see who looks most threatening. All higher animals, including man, have dominance relationships. People do all these things too. What many people forget is that it is perfectly okay in many situations to just walk away from a confrontation. You can even do this and gain social stature.

In martial arts, you must learn how to determine who you can successfully take on and who you can't, who has training and who hasn't, who is aggressive and who is just pretending, who is hiding aggression, how they will attack. If you can do these things without showing your own hand, so much the better. This is one reason not to wear colored belts in a dojo (besides the fact that rank and ability are not always consistent). As soon as you work with another person, even before that, you should get a strong feeling of how good they are relative to yourself. Learn to see their ability rather than looking at their belt or asking their rank. Learn to feel who is capable technically and who isn't from the way they grasp your wrist. Learn to feel who is in a good mood, who is nervous, who is injured, and who isn't.

Consider things from other people's position as well as your own. There is an interesting scene at the beginning of the movie the Seven Samurai, where two of the characters are discussing a thief barricaded in a hut holding a child hostage. The less experienced person feels that the thief is feeling secure. The other points out that in reality he is trapped and frightened.

One particular weakness of the whole martial arts setting is that some people become too awed by their teacher. This is understandable: the teacher is often older, stronger, more technically proficient, has more authority, more charisma, and so on. This is not all bad. A student does owe his teacher, at the very least, respect. However, it can get out of hand when students get exploited or become insincere ukes by being overly respectful of their teachers. An uke should learn to see what kind of attack the sensei is wanting. He should learn to see the opening (suki) he is being offered. He should be able to see how to attack. (Generally, this should be hard and fast, unless the sensei is trying to show something in detail and slow motion.)

Revisiting the Basics

What technical aspects should we be studying when we are practicing aikido? There are things that always need attention, including the mechanics of the technique, posture and stance (kamae), timing and distance (ma-ai), and mental attitude (zanshin). All of these are important, but the basic mechanics are the foundation of your art.

Strength

There are many kinds of strength in aikido. There is muscular strength, of course, but also strength of purpose (intent), balance (stability), technical ability, stamina, and so on.

Muscular Strength

Muscular strength is good – I sometimes wish I had more of it. It is the engine that powers your aikido, however well or poorly you use it. Both too much strength and too little can be problematical.

Too much strength tends to lead people into doing poor technique, largely because it gives them a shortcut to getting uke to fall down. Beginners think it is important to get uke down on the mat. That is true in the street, of course. You do want to throw your attacker onto the ground, immobilize him, or whatever. What we are looking for in the dojo, however, is to learn, to progress technically, and strength is possibly the single biggest obstacle to technical progress for the average (male) aikidoka. If they use their strength, they can make other similar-sized (or smaller) beginners fall down whether they are doing the techniques correctly or not. Such a person will find that most of their ukes will fall for them, but they have little control and it is all too easy to damage small people. When they come up against a larger attacker, their aikido does not work.

Too little strength can also be a problem, but mainly for beginners and when doing kihon. It is all too common for strong ukes to clamp down on smaller people and make technique difficult or impossible. This is not helpful to nage, particularly not for a beginner. However, if technique is done correctly and without unnatural constraints such as a class situation, five to ten pounds of force is usually adequate, and just about anybody can generate that. The ladies, most often being physically weaker, are forced to learn to do techniques correctly early on. If they don't do them approximately right, the techniques just don't work. Then as they practice, they often get physically stronger and this feeds naturally into their techniques.

Once a technique has been learned, strength is good. Properly applied, it lets you be more effective than a smaller, weaker person of the same technical ability. Learning how to apply it appropriately without letting it spoil the technique is like learning to drive: it is easier to learn on a car that does not have enough power to get you in trouble. As discussed earlier, strength should be applied sparingly, smoothly, appropriately, and in a direction that helps the technique to work.

If you are both one of the biggest and most technically proficient aikidoka in the school, you will need to be careful. A technique that others can safely do with all their power on you might be devastating to them if you apply it the same way.

Technical Strength

Technical strength is also an important basis for martial arts. In general, a martial artist uses technical ability to counterbalance deficiencies in numbers and size. Your techniques need to be so good that you don't need to think about them when you use them. This is addressed in later chapters.

Stamina

Good technique conserves energy and can help make sure the fight ends before you get tired, but good stamina is also useful, both so that you can train intensively and for actual use if you can't quite bring the confrontation to a conclusion. Stamina is important for any fighting art. If you get tired before the fight is over, you'll probably lose.

You can only get stamina from working out. It doesn't have to be aikido, but working out in aikido will also let you practice your technique at the same time. However, you should not always practice aikido hard and fast. It is also good to practice slower, working on the technical details, and maybe doing other forms of aerobic training for improving your stamina.

Intent

Intent is possibly the most important strength in martial arts. The need for it is mentioned in many texts, by many people from Musashi to Tesshu. Without it, you won't persevere long enough to become good. Without it, you won't have the courage to face a real attacker and not be cowed. With it, you can be destroyed (and nobody is invulnerable and nothing lasts for ever), but not beaten. One of the more significant benefits to everyday life of studying martial arts is the strength of mind and character that must be cultivated to succeed in something that takes years of strenuous effort. This is what makes a martial artist formidable, no matter how old and physically weak he becomes.

You must not be overawed, not by bigger or mean-looking opponents, not by insuperable odds, not by somebody claiming moral authority, not even by your sensei. This is not to say you should not respect your sensei, your uke, the other people in your dojo, or everybody else you come into contact with. You should give everybody their due respect, but you must not let them dominate you and take away your freedom of action, not for love, nor money, nor out of fear. And only you can give something like that away. It isn't something that anybody can take. You should have intent, but not aggressive intent. Your mind in doing aikido should be peaceful (Saotome Sensei).

Size

People come in different sizes, obviously. It is important to understand the implications of this, and is not as easy to put yourself in another's shoes as might be imagined. Smaller and bigger people move differently, and you are faced with different technical problems when throwing somebody bigger or smaller than yourself. I prefer to work with ukes who are 25 to 50% bigger than me. Smaller ukes are not enough challenge, and larger ukes can be difficult to throw cleanly with a desired technique.

110 lb. nage throwing a 220 lb. uke

A smaller person needs to pay more attention to the details. By moving correctly, they can use two legs against uke's finger and thumb, and have leverage working for them with perhaps a ten to one mechanical advantage.

However, things are not all advantageous to big people. Little people are, pound for pound, stronger than big people (Galileo's law of proportions). They break less easily when working with somebody their own size. They can move out of the way more quickly.

Some accommodation to different sizes is possible in doing technique. For example, sankyo can be done using uke's fingers if nage's hand is too small to take the standard sankyo. In irimi nage, it can be difficult to bring a strong uke's head to your shoulder. Nage moving his hand higher on uke's head (changing the leverage on his neck) can help overcome this. If uke is short, it can be difficult to do shiho nage or koshi nage, and nage might need to bend his knees more, at least at slow speed. Doing shiho nage at full speed, uke's feet will leave the ground anyway. Nage might even need to perform shiho nage as hanmi handachi (uke standing, nage kneeling). Some techniques are easier to do on a taller uke – shiho nage or sankyo, for example. Others are easier to do on a shorter uke, like kaiten nage or ikkyo.

Weight tends to have more effect than height, and the difficulty of a 100 lb. nage throwing a 200 lb. uke (a difference quite often seen) is about the same as for a 200 lb. nage throwing a 400 lb. uke (which is much rarer).

Being big and strong also carries responsibility. Just as the more advanced aikidoka should be careful of how they apply technique on less advanced ukes, so should big and strong aikidoka be careful of smaller lighter ones. You don't need to work as hard at cranking nikkyo or kote gaeshi on them as they have to on you. Sometimes barely doing anything, from your perspective, may be excruciating to them.

In summary, small people are mechanically able to move more quickly. Large people can absorb more energy. All in all, it is best to mostly learn with people of similar size, where possible, but to work out with everybody enough to understand the differences.

Relaxation and Extension

You should be relaxed in aikido. This relaxation is not the floppy total relaxation of when you are in bed sleeping. Rather, it is the limited, selective relaxation of when you are walking. Clearly, all your leg muscles are not totally relaxed when you're walking, because you don't fall down, but no unnecessary muscles should be contracted. They not only add to your fatigue themselves, but they work against the muscles that are needed and make them have to work harder. This selectively relaxed state using no unnecessary muscles is the same as what I refer to as "extension" elsewhere in the book.

In karate, the entire body is tensed momentarily when a kick or punch impacts the target (kime). This abrupt focus is not necessary for execution of technique in aikido. The transfer of energy is much more gradual. You should still be using your muscles efficiently, extending where necessary, and relaxing otherwise. That way, you are ready to move in a different direction if the need arises, to adjust as you take uke's balance and throw him. You should never need to exert all your strength. If you do, you did not correctly take uke's balance.

Fear is the biggest enemy of relaxation – perhaps fear of ukemi, fear of the attack (or attacker), fear of doing something wrong while sensei is watching. Fear of ukemi should go away as you become more proficient at falling. Fear of the attack should go away as you become more proficient at techniques. Fear of other people will be reduced by the knowledge that you can deal with anything they can throw at you – which is one reason aikido is so empowering to women. However, fear is, like happiness, a mental thing. Neither is primarily a consequence of the environment, but is our response to it. You should practice controlling fear by centering your mind as much as by practicing technique.

The ability to relax at will is quite important in the hectic world we live in. You can see tension in the faces and bodies of people all around. Worse, chronic tension can cause muscles to spasm, locking tight and causing long-term pain (often in apparently unrelated places), distorting the posture, and perhaps causing chronic disease and debilitation. Releasing this chronic tension is one way that acupuncture works. Consciously relaxing as you move around the mat will teach you how to reduce tension in everyday life. Learning to monitor your body to improve your aikido technique will alert you to chronic tension which you can then eliminate one way or another.

Centering

Centering is one of the most typical traits of aikido. Ron Meyer and Mark Reeder have written an interesting book on the subject.* When we move, we move from our center. When we turn, we turn about our center. When we do technique, we do it from our center, taking control of uke's center and taking it around our own. This is shown for example in this figure, where uke is trying to regain his balance but nage can turn more readily and keep control.

Nage must take uke's center

Uke, nage, and the technique all have centers. I am not talking metaphysics here, nor even talking about the mind (though that is related). I am talking about the center of mass of the physical system. This is the center of the body, generally two inches below the navel but depending on body type. Uke has control of his center as he attacks. Nage has control of his center. The center of a technique is initially at the point of contact between you and uke. As you take control of uke you take that center and move it. Perhaps you make it move around your center.

When you rotate your body, you should turn about your center. When you execute a technique, you should relate the center of the technique to your center. Like anything else, to get better, we must practice. Tai no henko (tenkan undo) is a practice for turning about your center. A tenkan escape from a tsuki involves a similar rotary movement. As you turn, moving about the mat during randori you must think, at first, about keeping your center. After a while, your body will do it without you thinking about it. (You should still think about it now and again, however, or you will get lax.)

This turning motion has a number of effects, if done correctly. It provides momentum for doing the technique. It tends to make a blow glance off rather

* "Center, The Power of Aikido" (2000). Frog, Berkeley.

than penetrate. It lets you see what is going on around you. Turning from the center provides a steady reference point in a moving world.

Connecting and Taking the Center

In order for nage to control uke, there must be a connection between the two of them. One of the things people mean when they talk about ki is this connection. You should feel this connectedness to uke from before contact, through the technique, until after the technique is over.

Any connection starts before physical contact is made, with awareness, with uke's intent. It is extremely important during early training for uke to attack strongly and on target, or the connection will be weak and easily distorted, and nage will not have something clear to work with. Uke must really try to grasp or hit nage, or there is nothing for nage to practice with. Nage, in turn, must move with the right timing or he will be unable to use the connection. Too late, and he's hit. Too early, and uke retargets and he's still hit. Between the two is a window of opportunity.

It is quite easy to learn enough about connectedness to mess up a beginner. It is easy to shut down somebody's technique by attacking poorly. This is frustrating for nage, and I really don't see what uke gets out of it. As the level of practice increases, uke should focus more on attacking and less about the connectedness, but should make a conscious effort not to mess up the technique by using what he knows about the attack or technique when practicing a particular technique. In free practice (jiyuwaza), of course, this sort of limitation should not constrain uke or nage.

Uke and nage often look symmetrical before or even at the start of a technique. However, nage should not feel this way. Nage should be extending energy from before the moment when contact is made. Otherwise, with a strong uke, nage will find it hard to move, and moving may even hurt his wrist if uke is gripping tightly and nage is not pushing out.

Being connected is particularly important if uke is bigger, stronger, there is more than one uke, or if they have weapons. This connection must be manipulated appropriately, with nage being strongly centered and his energy focused on uke's weakness (suki). Each instant, nage should have the advantage, and be moving towards greater and greater advantage until uke is fully controlled and either thrown or pinned.

It is pretty easy to connect with an attacker; all you have to do is wait for him to do it for you. However, then you are connecting on his terms, which will be disadvantageous to you. Instead, as he connects (mentally or physically), you should take control of the connection, and, through that, his center. Controlling the connection might mean that you move your hand a little as he grabs, so that he is jammed or extended a little, or moved off the line of attack. It might mean moving the target of a strike as he strikes, and perhaps substituting another target so that contact is made, but not in the way uke wishes. Physically controlling his center involves taking his balance. Mentally, it means taking his mind – establishing psychological dominance.

Connection can be felt most obviously with grabs. When a big strong uke grabs hold and locks down you know you're connected because you can't move in some directions. Yet even when you are held strongly, there are generally directions you can push through in order to perform a technique. If uke is bigger, use your entire body to attack uke's corners. If uke is stronger, blend with his power, push at an angle and undermine his position.

You can have too much connectedness or too little. By the way you move you can alter this connection. Movements to weaken or strengthen his grip can be quite similar, and hard to explain but easy to feel. The difference is the fulcrum of your movement and the force you exert relative to uke's body. These movements are not physically very different from just trying to twist away from uke, but the results are quite different. The movements do not need to be large to be effective.

You can reduce connectedness in a variety of ways. You can move either your center or your hand as uke grabs hold. Two inches of motion may be enough to prevent him clamping down effectively. You can change the relative position between him and you by moving off the centerline of the attack, up or down, or by moving closer or further away from uke. You can also reduce connectedness by rotating your arm so that uke's grip is weakened, either unrolling his fingers or by attacking his thumb. If you rotate your arm and roll it out along his thumb, using the distal part of the thumb as a fulcrum, this will attack his thumb. Similarly, if you roll it the other way, you can unwrap his fingers. You can also weaken uke's grip by attacking his thumb more directly, cocking your hand and lifting it like a sword.

Sometimes you need to increase the connection, encouraging uke to hold on so that you can break his balance despite a rather tentative grip. It is more difficult to strengthen the connection than to weaken it, but you can often do so by moving towards uke, pressing into his power, particularly by doing this in a threatening way. Pressing your arm into uke's grip will tend to encourage him to hold on, especially if the alternative is for him to give you a chance to punch him in the face. Rotating your arm to wrap uke's fingers around it will tend to strengthen his grip. As described above, you can also rotate your arm to weaken uke's grip. The details of how you rotate the arm determine whether it strengthens or weakens uke's grip. In particular, look at the fulcrum of your rotation within uke's grip.

With strikes, whether empty-handed or with a weapon, it is even more important for nage to control the connection rather than relying on uke to do so. After all, an attacker's intent is to hurt you with that connection. Nage needs to make the connection as he evades the impact, often with a redirection of uke's power. Aikido defenses against strikes are typically done with a sticky feeling, so that a connection is maintained. From a tsuki, for example, you might move your body off the line of attack, touching uke's arm with your palm and deflecting it, but more to make connection than to protect yourself from being hit. (The body movement should have done that.) With a yokomen strike, you might put an arm in the way of the strike so that the energy of the strike dissipates itself sliding along nage's forearm, and then maintaining the contact with light pressure in the direction you want to make his arm go.

A karateka or boxer is likely to pull back the arm as soon as the strike is completed (and probably whack at you with the other one at the same time). The connection can be made as the arm extends, as shown in this figure, pushing the arm forward, down, and across to encourage uke to overextend, possibly even taking the balance well enough to force uke to step to recover.

Taking the center: Nage is off the line of attack, and has made uke step forward by taking her balance with a touch on her extended arm.

A connection can be made as the arm is retracted also, going with the retraction and driving it in faster than uke expected as well as changing the direction, but then you have to deal with uke's next shot also.

The way to do this will depend on whether uke is retracting his arm to remove it from harm's way or (more critically) to provide power for a second strike with the other hand. If uke is just pulling back his arm, it is not hard to enter as it is retracted. If uke is punching left and right, it is a faster movement, and you have to enter deeply enough to make it hard for him to hit you. It might be easier to avoid the first strike and try to use the second or third one. Few people will keep throwing punches for long without a pause, and generally their punches will get less precise as the series continues.

Connection, whether from a grab or a blow, is like fishing. If you move the lure too quickly, the fish misses it. If you are too slow, the fish has time to spit it out. If you get the connection and jerk it, the line will break or the lure pulls out.

Once the connection is made, you can feel for someone's center, especially with a cooperative uke. Sometimes you have to move slowly and feel your way to get the idea of what you are trying to do, and you might need to work with a cooperative uke for a time to figure it out. Then, when you know what you are trying to do you can work up to where you can do the same thing with even a difficult uke.

If you push directly towards uke's center you should meet resistance. If you push at an angle to it, you should feel less resistance. The diameter of uke's center varies with what he is doing, and the stiffer he is, the larger diameter his center. This is rather like how Lord Rutherford found the structure of atoms, by

Controlling the connection to uke can be difficult, but is critical to technique

shooting smaller particles at them. The ones that came closest to the nucleus bounced back, while the more peripheral ones were deflected at smaller and smaller angles as the miss distance increased.

Finding uke's center is more difficult with an uncooperative uke. There are three ways uke can be difficult. One is by being stiff and strong. This can actually be good, as you have something concrete to work with, though sometimes he will just be too strong to move. Another is by giving you so little to work with that you can't do anything with him. This is a challenge to do some techniques with, but it is generally easy enough to overpower uke. When he feels this happening, generally he will respond and you can do something with that response. The third way is when uke moves to counter what you are doing. This is the basis of kaeshi waza, and can be a lot of fun to play with. It can, however, be quite frustrating when you are practicing a set technique.

Once you can feel uke's center, you can manipulate it. You can move it back and forwards, sideways, or rotate it. Generally, it will be difficult to move linearly. You push, and uke pushes back. It is easier to rotate it, up and down, left or right, while pressing on it to keep the connection. The contact with uke's center might change with time. You might get a response from uke and use that response to change his balance. This is particularly true with aggressive and strong ukes. Thus, if you push and uke pushes back, you can extend him as well as redirecting him. You might imagine uke's center as a ball repelling your hand. When you can control where uke's center goes, you have "captured" it. Then it is easy to do techniques (though, of course, you have to smoothly transition from kuzushi to executing the technique).

Generally, you want to work center to center: manipulating his center by moving yours. This is stronger than doing the same thing with your arms. Also, the rate of movement of your center and his is similar, so you are less likely to inadvertently lose the connection. You can move your arms to take up the slack, finding his center, then move your center to move his.

Control is a matter of position and balance

Mental and Physical Aspects of Connection

As stated above, generally an attack starts when visual contact is made. It might have started sooner than this if somebody is looking for you. It might start later than this if something (like bumping into him) happens to spark an attack after somebody already has visual contact with you. In any case, it is almost always long before physical contact is made. In the real world, it is important that nage be sensitive to this connection. Otherwise, he might get cold cocked.

You can call this connection ki no musubi (connecting ki), or you can think of it like the guidance system of a missile acquiring its target. The important thing is that it is there, and that it is initially non-physical. It is an informational phenomenon that is generally communicated non-verbally but apparent to both parties.

Even though the connection is non-physical, it is useful to think of it as something to be manipulated as if it is physical. You can draw somebody in or you can repel him using this connection. You can blend with their movement, or you can disrupt it. As uke approaches, nage can move to a greater or lesser extent so that at the point of contact, nage already has the advantage, as shown in the figure above.

This connection works two ways. Your attacker presumably feels some level of aggression towards you. (Why else would he be attacking?) This aggression builds up like a wave against your defenses. When you resist, this pressure can overwhelm you. Presumably he is the stronger, or you would not need aikido and he probably would not be attacking you. The connection will affect you particularly if you are poorly centered mentally. This can slow you

Connection is not dependent only on actual physical contact, but also on the threat of it

down and make you an easier target, less able to deal with their attack, like a rabbit "hypnotized" by a snake. On the other hand, if you don't let yourself get too strongly connected, you have a great deal of freedom of movement. Nothing constrains you physically. You might be able to defuse the situation with a smile and calm words.

The closer two people get, the stronger the connection becomes until physical contact is made. The contact might be sudden and short in duration, as with a single blow (possibly repeated, given the opportunity), or it might be continued for some time if the attacker grabs you. The physical connection is an attempt to act out the intent that is inherent in the mental connection, so they are parts of the same thing. In a sense, they are both physical, though one is a pattern of neuronal firing, the other is a muscular movement.

You can let the wave break over you and dash the power to one side (marubashi). You can turn, and let it roll on past (tenkan). You can enter past it, and let it be carried forward on its own momentum (irimi). Or you can step aside, draw it out, and let it over extend itself (ten shin). Any of these options work. If you do them too sedately, the attacker will adjust his attack, and the attack will still wash over you, though possibly a little reduced in amplitude. If you time it just right, the change in the target will confound the attacker, giving nage ample time to deal with the attack.

Doing this is quite easy in a dojo, where there is the tendency for uke to take the fall so that nage doesn't look bad, so uke doesn't look bad, and so that uke gets his turn to be nage. In a more realistic attack, the attacker has no intention of cooperating. The attacks are more sudden, more forceful, and more serious. On the one hand, the attack is harder to deal with. You don't have time to think about it. If you get hit, you are far more likely to get hurt. On the other hand, there is real intent and more energy to work with. When you do a technique the results are more evident.

Attacks in the dojo vary a lot. Some attacks in the dojo are realistic but not serious. Uke might attack as if with deadly intent, accurate, but slow enough to pull the shot. This is fine for learning the technique, but not for actually practicing doing it. Ultimately, a practice attack must be no different from a real one. Some dojo attacks are serious but not with intent to hurt, more like counting coup. Uke might come in slowly, but use the flexibility this gives him to hit nage, especially when he knows where nage is going to move. (One of the disadvantages of the way we normally practice.) Some are deadly serious, with intent to hurt, in the guise of practicing. Fortunately these are rare. Almost always, dealing with a real attack is easier than working in the dojo. There is usually less faking (whether benign or malignant) going on and the attacker usually doesn't know aikido.

Whatever the attack, it is easy to get caught up in the technical details, to focus on the minutiae that make it work. This is necessary up to a point. You do have to learn them. However, there is a tendency to keep on polishing the details. You should move on and also work on the use of the technique. You should work at a higher level of abstraction, playing the tune rather than the notes.

The first step is to simplify and shorten the defensive moves. The big elaborate defenses that you learn as beginners, stepping just so, using the arms just so, are fine as training tools. Essential even, because everything gets more abbreviated and shortened when you feel threatened. But as you progress you need to take out most of the movement and concentrate on the small part that actually matters.

Aikido – Moving On

Practicing Connection and Centering

A practice I like for this is to start well apart, 10 to 15 ft., and to both move, coming together as uke attacks. Then nage as well as uke is taking responsibility for the timing. At the most basic level, from, for example, shomen uchi, the initial center of the technique is at the point of contact. Nage needs to take control of this center, controlling uke, bringing him into a technique such as irimi nage or kote gaeshi, whirling them around nage's center, and then throwing them. He should also adjust his movement to control the timing.

Posture and Stance

Posture becomes more important the more you do aikido. In a famous picture of Musashi, he is "open on all four sides", which is to say that he can defend himself against an attack from any direction. Aikido is a moving art, though the movement can become quite small. Extreme, wide and strong, postures are sometimes used in the actual execution of technique, but only momentarily.

The classic aikido hanmi no kamae is a moderate defensive posture. It allows easy movement in any direction without strong commitment. During application of technique, nage's balance will generally be shifted forwards. Rarely, it will be shifted back or sideways. Generally, your kamae will be lined up with the direction of your force. Otherwise you will be vulnerable.

It is a triangular "half open" stance. The back foot is crosswise, almost 90 degrees to the front foot, which generally points towards uke. The stance is narrow. Aikido does not rely on nage's strength so much, so there is no need for the deep postures used during basic practice by karateka. Balance at rest is typically with seventy percent of nage's weight on the rear foot.* The arms and body should be oriented in the same direction as the kamae, though the degree of rotation of the torso varies from style to style. The knees should be not quite straight, but not noticeably bent either.

Kamae is more than just where your feet are. It includes your entire presence: your balance and spirit as well as your physical presence.

In comparison to aikido, a variety of stances are used in karate. Some of these, we use in aikido also, though I've never been in a class where they were pointed out as formal stances. Whatever kamae you use, you must remain relaxed and ready to move as desired without pre-motion.

In Yoshukai Karate the direction of movement is generally forwards, towards the opponent, often moving circularly around him to herd him where you want him to go, but keeping your natural weapons lined up on him. (He is,

---

* In Yoshinkan Aikido, the weight is on the front foot at most if not all times. In other styles, a weight shift is used to generate momentum, so the starting posture is generally with the weight back.

of course, trying to do the same to you, which inevitably brings the two of you into conflict.) In aikido, you want to be constantly moving, but in a different fashion, avoiding conflict, trying to connect to and line up with the attacker's power and force rather than against it.

It is important to keep your trunk upright, at least until the throw itself. If you are bent over, you will be slower and weaker than if you are standing erect. You are weak, because being doubled over results in questionable balance and because stress is taken by the back instead of the legs. This is, in fact, the weak position you want to make uke assume, for example when you do kaiten nage or ikkyo to them.

I generally stand with my hands fairly low (gedan). This encourages uke to attack high, where we practice most. In aikido we generally keep our fingers relaxed and somewhat spread. This does present a target for an attacker. If somebody grabs our fingers and twists, it is difficult for us to do technique.

We mostly work on mats, nice flat practice areas. However, in the street things are not as benign. There are obstacles to run into and trip over. Vegetation, curbs, and pipes can catch our feet. Sand, mud, or snow will slow us down. Learning how to feel with your feet is important, because during a confrontation you can't afford to look down at them. In a dojo, noticing people around you, loose mats, gaps between mats, wet patches on the surface of a plastic mat, the walls, and edges of the mat are all important both for safety and your general training. It is important to feel what you are standing on, and to adjust your technique accordingly. You should move with your legs relaxed so that you don't fall if you trip on something. Instead, you adjust.

Generally, martial artists are cautioned not to look at their opponent's eyes, but rather to look broadly at the center of his chest. There is a reason for this, as your opponent might be able to intimidate you and, if you are fixating on his eyes or the knife in his hand, you might miss a little movement of the foot that indicates he is about to kick you. On the other hand, not looking at somebody's face in everyday life can be interpreted as shiftiness or an insult. In some cultures, looking at somebody's eyes can be seen as challenging. As an everyday example, in our culture, if a man has a confrontation with a woman and looks at her at chest level it will be perceived as an insult. Misinterpretations can precipitate an attack that could be avoided. Eye contact is too complex for simple rules and should be considered in the same light as extending a hand – it could be seen as good or bad. It is more important to cultivate an undaunted and open spirit than to conform to a standard.

Whatever you do, almost always your kamae should point where you want your strength to be. Generally, this is towards uke. However, to enter past uke (irimi), that is where your kamae should be pointed. When you intercept uke's arm wide of his body, as in yokomen uchi, your kamae should point there. When you throw, your kamae should generally point to where uke will land or, occasionally, the opposite way. When you do a technique like ikkyo tenkan or kote gaeshi that involves taking uke around your center, your hands should always be in front of your body, rather than off to the side, and your kamae should come into alignment with them.

Posture in Throwing

In basic technique, nage's back foot should be planted firmly in a position and at an angle that allows him to exert all of the strength of his back leg in throwing uke, ending with full leg extension. His front leg should be under his body, the knee as far forward as the big toe but not beyond that. The force of the throw should be transmitted efficiently along nage's body, which requires nage's upper torso to be inclined slightly towards uke, otherwise much of the effort will be wasted by flexure of the torso, possibly hurting nage's lower back. Certainly, nage should never lean back as he throws forward. Nor should he lean forward excessively: nage's nose should never be in front of his toes. The ideal position is an adequate forward shift of the balance for throwing powerfully, but conservative enough that even if uke should hold on and try to take nage with him, nage can prevent it happening.

In performing a throw, it is acceptable and often necessary to widen the stance to get more power. However, this should not be overdone, as an extended stance makes the legs, particularly the knees, more vulnerable to other people falling on them. The stance should not be wide for throws like koshi nage or aiki otoshi where uke could fall on nage's leg and damage nage's knee. Instead, having both feet under his body will give nage more strength, as well as being safer.

Once a throw is over, nage should return to correct kamae, without excessive distance between his feet and with good balance and the torso and head upright, generally by drawing the back foot forward. Nage should look impressive. In freestyle and similar exercises, nage should continue moving throughout the entire throw, and before and after it. However, at maximum force, the foot should be planted momentarily to transmit the force to the ground. It is possible to throw uke without being in this position, particularly if his balance has been taken correctly, but it is not desirable as uke might prove to be harder to throw than expected.

Correct posture in throwing can be developed during practice with the sword, especially tanren uchi: solitary practice of striking with a bokken. When you do this practice you don't have an uke to concern yourself about, so it is easier to work on your posture. At the moment of impact, you should be in a somewhat wide hanmi, with the weight rather more forwards than in the basic position. Your back leg should be braced on the ground. Your arms should be almost straight, and there should be a feeling of great power developed from the entire body. When you can cut strongly in tanren uchi, with correct posture, this will also be the posture you should use on the mat for the moment of the throw. You should hold this posture for a moment (zanshin), then recover your normal kamae.

Atemi

An atemi is a strike at uke. It can be forceful or not. With an atemi, I generally want to elicit an automatic reaction. I might want to hit somebody to create an opening or otherwise distract them, rather than intending the blow to damage them as I might want with a karate mindset.

Speed is important. If an atemi is too slow, uke might well not react to it or might block it. If it is too fast, you will probably hit uke, and while they might then react, they will have a bloody nose and possibly a bloody attitude.

The normal reaction to an atemi is to flinch away from the strike. However, some experienced fighters will flinch forward. They have trained themselves to take a hit so that they can get in and do greater damage in return. Like much of aikido, there is no fixed formula. Rather, you do what makes most people flinch and work with the result. There is rarely a total lack of response, and if you are connecting well with uke, you can use the resulting movement whether forwards or backwards.

Ki and Related Thoughts

The one sure thing about "ki" is that it is hard to find two people that see it as the same thing. To some, it is everything. To others it doesn't exist. In the past, I've gone from a believer to a skeptic, and at this point am somewhere in the middle. I haven't found the term very useful, however, because it means so many different things to different people that you're never sure what, if anything, you are actually communicating.

Whether you believe in ki or not, there are "ki exercises" that are useful, especially for macho males. It can also be useful for the practitioner to imagine "ki", particularly "extending ki" when a technique is not flowing well. I have seen no great insights resulting from ki that cannot be better explained by using more specific terminology. However, the term may be useful to encourage the student to think beyond what can be verbally communicated, and there is a lot about aikido which cannot. This is particularly true when talking to a class; it is generally easier to communicate one-on-one with somebody of similar background and experience. Nevertheless, I think it is important to make the effort to communicate aikido at a verbal level, because understanding at a logical level is a key to our own progress as well as to educating others, even if it makes the subject seem less exotic.

Ki as used in aikido seems to have elements of anatomy, physiology, physics, psychology, and even religion. "Ki" is a common word in the Japanese language. It also has many homophones – words that are pronounced the same way, even though they are written differently and mean different things. Thus, it is easy to mistranslate a phrase that includes the word ki, especially from spoken Japanese or romanji. "Aikido" means the way of harmony and spirit, and "ki musubi" (uniting spirit) explains pretty well the thought of blending with an attacker so as to control and defeat the attack.

As discussed earlier, the word "spirit" in "aikido" is not the same word used for supernatural spirits or ghosts (kami). Thus, while "Aikido no Kami" might be translated as "the spirit of the way of harmony and spirit", the two spirits are different sorts.

Nobody has ever claimed, as far as I am aware, they could measure ki. This is perfectly reasonable if ki is an informational concept, as implied above. We may be able to extend this concept of ki to more aspects of aikido where ki is sometimes invoked. At the least, it gives us a more concrete definition to discuss, and might bring the two views of aikido closer.

Playing music is a useful analogy. The first things you learn in playing a melody are the notes. Once you know the notes, you can string them together, but you don't have a tune until you get the notes the right length, and the emphasis right, until, in fact, you make the passage a single piece of music rather than a sequence of notes. Thus, the details in aikido of how to move, where to put your feet, how to manipulate your hands to make uke do what you want, all those are like musical notes. They are related to aikido, but they soon fail to be very exciting in themselves. With practice, you figure out how to make the moves work together, and not just the physical moves but all of the interplay between uke and nage on both the physical and psychological levels. Furthermore, you stop thinking in terms of the details of the technique and think of the overall interaction between uke and nage.

This concept does have some use elsewhere in this book. A technique begins before physical contact occurs, and continues after it is terminated. We use information acquired during this pre-contact phase, for example, to blend with the attack. We can say that we are manipulating ki, or we can say we are manipulating the information flow to and from our partner, manipulating his ideas, changing his mindset, using information about the attack, using information about how the technique is proceeding. Different people prefer different imagery.

Ki Exercises

There are a number of exercises to develop ki and ki extension. While there is an element of showmanship involved, this is not inappropriate up to a point. These exercises are useful even if you prefer to use the terms "centering" and "extension" rather than "ki". Carol Shifflett has written a couple of excellent books on this topic.*

The Unbendable Arm. There is a distinct way in aikido of keeping the arm extended that is different from what most people in the West do if merely told to keep the arm straight. Anatomically, the extensors are mostly contracted and the

---

* "Ki in Aikido" (1997) and "Aikido, Exercises for Teaching and Training" (1999). Round Earth Publishing, Merrifield, Virginia.

flexors are mostly relaxed. However, there are aspects of posture and balance involved also, particularly when the unbendable arm is used in performing a technique.

To practice the unbendable arm, rest your wrist on your partner's shoulder and stiffen your arm. Have him try to bend it by using steady pressure* in the direction that the elbow normally bends. This should not be too difficult. Now try relaxing and reaching out beyond his shoulder. Don't think of pushing back against his force, just keep your arm extended. Your arm should feel like your legs do when you are standing but relaxed. Your partner should find it harder to bend your arm than before, while you use less effort.

The unbendable arm shows us a different way to use our muscles

Our goal is to learn how to use our muscles efficiently, using only those that are necessary for the movement we want to do. Usually, especially when told to resist, people also tense the flexors, which then fight the extensors and help your partner bend your arm, which is not what is intended. This feeling of extension and the muscle patterns that are involved are used in many techniques. For example, when we are doing kaiten nage or ikkyo, and uke is bent over, we should not be using our strength to keep them bent over, but rather using our extension to load much of our body weight onto them, making it harder for them to straighten up as well as manipulating their balance.

Weight Underside. This involves using the weight of the arm while settling the body to provide a solid foundation for the technique. We as humans are constantly subject to the effects of gravity and have postural reflexes to counteract them. I see this exercise as being largely to practice letting go these reflexes, and using gravity to help us rather than letting our reflexes help uke.

* He must not jerk your arm as this can damage your elbow.

To practice this, extend your arm and have uke feel how heavy it is. Now have uke touch the top of your arm and think about that part of your arm. Have uke feel its weight once more. It should be lighter. Now have uke touch the bottom of your arm and concentrate your mind there. It should now feel heavy.

Clearly in these two cases, the mass of your arm is no different. When thinking weight up, we are taking part of the weight of the arm with our own muscles. When we think weight underside, we are allowing gravity to make the arm heavy, or even helping it fall.

This feeling of a heavy arm should be used in a technique such as sokumen irimi nage, when we lay an arm across uke's face and press down. This approach works much better than thinking of pushing uke down, perhaps by involving more of nage's body and getting a gravity assist.

Extending Ki. This is variously expressed as having a positive mental attitude, and developing the feeling of constantly pouring ki out from your body to the universe. Obviously, a positive mental attitude is a good thing, yet one that a surprising number of people do not have. It can be cultivated, and if thinking of an outpouring of ki allows somebody to develop such an attitude, it is beneficial.

There may be a mechanical aspect of this also. If uke is resisting a technique, and we extend past his power, this generally works better than directly opposing his strength. Thus, if we meet resistance with ikkyo, extending beyond that resistance will usually succeed in redirecting uke's strength, and allowing the technique to work.

Centering. I see this as using the hara, or physical center of the body, as a reference point. Many Westerners, if asked where their "self" resides, will point to their head. There are good physiological and anatomical reasons to do so, but this is not a satisfactory reference point for physical activity involving six degree-of-freedom movement (rotation or translation about any of the three axes of the body), as in aikido. The hara appears to be useful as a mental point of reference, possibly from being more protected and stable than the head.

If we are faced with a big and dangerous attacker, the worst thing we can do is to think about how mean he looks. Rather, if we think of our hara and deal with what comes, it puts a more comfortable distance between him and us.

Mu Shin

"No mind" is a common concept in martial arts, being discussed for example by Musashi in the Book of the Void*. He makes an explicit distinction between being in a vacant state and mu shin, and stresses that it only comes from practice, correct practice. To me, he is clearly talking about "over-learned" behavior, when you know a technique so well that you don't need to think about it in order to do it. This is like learning to play a musical instrument. First you learn how to play the notes on that instrument, then the notes for the tune, and

* The fifth and last book (section) of "Go Rin No Sho".

finally you forget about the instrument, your fingers, and the notes of the tune, and play the tune from the heart.

This also relates to the mental aspects of aikido. If you think about all of the details of a technique, you will be too slow and tentative in its execution. You must learn techniques so well that you don't need to think about them any more, so that when you are executing (rather than learning) them, you will do so flawlessly, with precision, and subconsciously, even adjusting on the fly as is necessary in a particular instance.

We progress through a number of stages as we learn aikido. As beginners, we are pleased if we can remember how to walk through a technique correctly with a cooperative uke, putting the hands and feet approximately where they belong. Later we will be pleased to "really" do the technique – applying it so that uke has to go with it at least some of the time, and the frequency of this rises until we generally succeed in throwing uke. The next step is to do this without thinking about it – mu shin. As Musashi stressed, this is the fruit of a lot of practice. When it works, it will be without thought, without effort. You may not even know what you've done, but there uke will be on the floor.

Situation Control

Attack when they are unprepared; make your move when they don't expect it.

Sun Tzu

Situation control is one of the most important aspects of aikido. The best way to win a fight is before the fight starts. Ideally you should pre-empt any physical confrontation. Once the fight starts, it isn't easy to stop it, luck has a hand in the affair, and even if you win you are likely to get banged up.

In a less physical context, seeing a problem starting and heading it off or diffusing it is better than meeting it head on. Arguments rarely change anybody's mind; they just create grudges.

Awareness, Perception, and Acting On It

Awareness means knowing what is going on around you, what the threats are. Perception is the process of actively seeing, actively looking for, the threats and knowing what your options are. Acting on this information is crucial. Otherwise, the rest is futile.

People don't see what is happening mostly because they get preoccupied by something other than what they are doing: perhaps work, a sick child, plans for a wild night, or the argument they had the previous day. On the mat, perhaps they are thinking about how they could have done the last technique better. Zen teachings emphasize living in the present. Sure, it is useful to plan for the future. You can learn from the past. But don't be immersed in either the past or the future.

You should practice awareness at all times, both on the mat and in everyday life. You should be ready to deal with an attack at any time. At the end of a technique, don't just drop uke's arm and turn away. Release his arm in a controlled fashion and move away without giving him a suki (unless you want him to immediately attack again), or make him move away from you. On the other hand, don't continue to focus on a technique once it is over.

Awareness is often a problem in a multiple attack situation, with nage forgetting or not noticing that an uke is behind him while he fiddles with a technique that isn't working. Or nage might end up trapped in a corner just because he doesn't notice where he is going. Multiple attack practice often degenerates into ukes taking turns in being thrown. This is still useful training for beginners, but doesn't relate to situation awareness.

Awareness involves both attitude and position. Nage must develop a habit of awareness, and also of moving about the mat to change his viewpoint, constantly turning to check his back and never staying in one place. Through practicing in this way, he will develop improved situation awareness (and better ability in freestyle).

Two good practices for training nage to remain aware and avoid this sort of situation are having ukes tap nage (lightly – just to remind him you are there) on the back if they get the opportunity, and blindfolded practice.

Blindfolded practice is excellent both for maintaining a good center and for awareness. Airlines often provide convenient blindfolds on long flights. Nage should be blindfolded, and ukes should take care to keep both themselves and nage clear of obstacles such as the walls. Only grabs should be allowed. If nage has a good pattern of freestyle movement and listens to his senses, he will be able to handle quite fast attacks. I have heard claims that nage can sense and evade blows coming when blindfolded. I am skeptical of this, though you can often sense an uke coming towards you, even blindfolded.

Awareness is a problem in aikido in another way: we generally practice knowing what attack is coming and what technique is to be done. This is good for studying the details of how to do a particular technique, in fact it should totally eliminate the tendency to make a competition of the exercise, but outside the dojo there is no sense (except maybe to startle an attacker and make him die laughing) in saying, "attack shomen uchi" or "start again please". You must learn to see what uke is doing, and what he is going to do. This can be quite dramatic. About 20 years ago at a seminar in Tennessee, and again a few years ago in Sarasota, the attack was tsuki and we were practicing quite placidly when I knew that my uke was really going to try to hit me. Both times they did try. (And both times the technique worked even better than when we were working more sedately. There's nothing like commitment to make a technique work well.) You must study to develop this knowledge of what uke is going to do even before he knows. It isn't too hard when an attacker is not hiding his intent, but sometimes they will fool you.

Competition, whether in those styles of aikido that do it, in judo, karate, or even some sports, is good for developing this awareness. However, competition also teaches blindness to things outside the rules of the particular game you are playing. Atemi and leg locks are not allowed in Olympic judo. Kicks and grappling are not allowed in Western boxing.

Awareness should also be practiced outside the dojo, all the time. How do you develop this awareness? The first thing to do is to consciously pay attention to your surroundings. Children do this all the time, fascinated by the moon, the stars, a flower. As we grow up, we forget how to do it, because we have too much on our minds to smell the roses. Make a point of enjoying seeing the sun shining through the leaves on the trees, hearing the birds singing, and feeling the warmth of the sun on your face. Develop a habit of monitoring what you are feeling, what you are thinking, what you are doing. Most of the time, this will be enjoyable – then it is effortless. When things become unpleasant, it is all too easy to shut things out and to stop paying attention. This is a mistake. You should still pay attention and think of how you can ameliorate the unpleasantness. Perhaps the solution is as simple as just letting it go – walking away and leaving it behind. When you walk into a room, develop the habit of noticing who else is there, where they are, and where you can't see. It is always good to keep track of people in your vicinity. When we had a student planning to leave for boot camp with the Marines, we looked for opportunities to attack him from behind. He got very sensitive to where people were, which did, apparently, help during his training.

When you have developed the habit of living in the present, you will have taught yourself to be aware, in a martial arts sense as well as in everyday life. However, as Tohei Sensei says in "Aikido in Daily Life", it is easy to go from doing it all the time, to not doing it at all. You must be constantly vigilant, or you will get lazy and, perhaps, become a statistic. Not only is practicing awareness outside the dojo more realistic than dojo practice, but it might save your life. Apart from avoiding being surprised by people or dogs and not being run over by a car, there are many hazards in modern life. Certain places such as bars are particularly dangerous, especially to people on their own (and should be avoided). The majority of people seem to wander about in a daze, but it is easy to over-react and become paranoid when you see everything that goes on around you. Being aware of it makes you better able to avoid problems, but initially you might see far more to concern you than you might expect.

Perceiving what a situation means is the next step. Here, we might be talking about interpreting a developing situation on the street, or determining what an attacker is going to do. In the street, any change from what is normal should attract your interest, but what does it mean? On a smaller scale, you can tell much of what an attacker is going to do by watching his body. The stance of an attacker limits his options. Weight on a foot means he can't kick freely with that foot unless he first removes his weight. A short stance is good for kicking. A long and wide stance is good for punching. People generally make adjustments to their posture before hitting. These adjustments might be quite small with a trained fighter, or quite large for somebody that is more aggressive than skilled. People generally make the same preparatory movements time after time. People are often tense in a confrontation, and have to relax to move or hit. Sometimes they will look at their target before hitting. Of course, somebody with enough skill will try to make you think they are going to attack one way and attack a different way.

It is vital to react appropriately. Time and time again in real life, people see trouble and still walk into it. Part of the reason is just lack of perception. They see it but don't recognize it. The other part is not responding sensibly. Hunches might well mean that your subconscious mind – that processes thousands of times more data than your conscious mind, though less logically – has picked up on a threat it can't define but doesn't like. Pausc and think about whether it isn't right. If you see a group of strangers in an otherwise empty parking lot, do you really want to go towards your car and possibly get attacked?

To summarize, be aware, look for the meaning behind things that attract your attention, and respond without concern for looking dumb.

Rules

Human beings are social animals. As such, we live in a maze of rules. We may think that laws are a particularly nasty invention of civilized man, but there have always been rules. Primitive societies are just as hemmed about by restrictions – taboos – as we are. I don't advocate breaking rules for the sake of it, but it is important to see them for what they are and not let them get in the way of successfully harmonizing with the problems life can throw at us.

Besides federal and state laws, we have peer pressure, rules at work, housing association bylaws, and so on. There are rules in aikido too, things like don't hurt your uke, work with everybody in class, throw towards the edge of the mat, don't strain. There are rules in play in conflicts out in the street also. This is likely to cause a problem if you are attacked and, for example, expect fair play. Your attacker is likely to have a different set of rules, and part of the problem might just be those differing expectations of the two parties.

In general, women get grabbed and men get hit. A woman might have a guy put a "friendly" arm around her shoulders or grab her arm. In a typical bar fight, from what I've been told, you are likely to be attacked unexpectedly. The attacker might be verbally abusive then turn to walk away. Just as you are relaxing, thinking the problem has gone away, he might turn back and swing a terrific roundhouse at your head. More directly, he might walk up and push you, then take a swing at you while you are off balance. In either case, don't think of squaring off and fighting fairly. He might have a friend who is coming up behind you. Just take care of the immediate problem, and leave. Don't hang around for another beer, joking with the others in the bar. He might come back with a gun or a couple of friends.

Position

Position is related to awareness. All locations on the mat are pretty much the same, unless the mat is uneven, except for the edges and corners. You should avoid these obstacles and other students. In the dojo, one of the commonest faults seen in randori is nage getting trapped against a wall or in a corner. You might feel safer with your back to the wall, but it is a dangerous place to be, because aikido is movement.

Awareness of position off the mat means knowing where the fire exits are in a hotel, where the doors are in a bar. Not all locations are equally benign. Items like doors can be both a threat and an opportunity. A threat could come through the doorway, or you could exit away from trouble that way. Outside, the position of the sun can be important. Generally, of course, you should avoid standing with the sun in your face.

Positional advantage can be cultural. The Japanese think that there is advantage in a room in being at the kamiza (high point). Westerners might feel similarly about religious objects or safety barricades. Certainly we feel more secure in our own homes, while an invader will feel less secure. While there may be no objective reality to these sorts of beliefs, they can still be important because of the way people react, both ourselves and others.

Position is relative. If there are no other people to be considered, most places are about as good. Once an attacker is present, position becomes important not just in respect to the surroundings, but in respect to him. If he is unarmed (and you won't know that until it is too late), there is little cause to worry until he approaches a physical ma-ai. Once he comes within ma-ai, you must do something to deter him or you are surrendering the advantage to him. With two or more people, you do not want to be surrounded by them, and certainly not with any of them within your ma-ai.

Suki: finding one and exploiting it

A suki is an opening, an opportunity in time and space to do a technique. Either nage or uke can be open for a technique. (In fact, the separation of roles into nage and uke is artificial, a training tool.) What looks like a suki can be real, or it can be an attempt to lure you into providing a suki for the other person. If you attempt to do a technique where no suki exists, you might make one, you might find one, but more likely you will find it difficult or impossible to do the technique except on an overly cooperative uke.

If you are facing a master, there should be no opening, no opportunity to attack except for what he wants to give you. If you do see one, you might wonder if it is really there or if it is merely an invitation to disaster, but don't let reputation overawe you. It is important to learn to see suki, to see whether it is real or not. If there is a suki, you must move smartly to exploit it, because real openings generally do not last long. This movement must be without thought, mu shin. If you wait to think about the opportunity, it will be gone. If there is no suki (which would probably mean that uke was not attacking), nage probably can't successfully do a technique. However, if you do something anyway you can sometimes make visible a suki that was hidden. Aikido is a defensive art. However, O Sensei himself said that 90% of aikido is atemi. Thus, while the intent of the art is defensive, you can be quite proactive in executing defensive strategy.

Nage must, then, find or create a suki and use this to increasingly tilt things in his favor until he has full control of uke to immobilize or throw him. You can offer a suki, and draw uke into a trap. This is often used in aikido. A classic case is to move just a little too close while exposing yourself to mune-tsuki. This triggers a particular attack from uke on your timing, making it easier for you to deal with it. The move may have to be quite subtle, and often people exaggerate the movement, either through lack of understanding or lack of practice.

Sometimes it works the other way, and nage inadvertently creates a suki on himself, opens himself up, by incorrect positioning during the execution of a technique. For example, when you do shiho-nage, do you leave yourself open to a strike to your ribs by uke? If you do, you need to change your technique to be more technically correct. It is impossible to be totally secure in real life, but if it is easy for uke to do this atemi, you need to adjust your technique.

Most people start to find suki by trial and error. They find that a technique works some of the time on some ukes. They may try to understand why it works, and realize that they are using suki – though often not at a conscious level. This is not necessarily bad, because a suki is generally a fleeting thing that can only be used at a subconscious level. However, to improve, you need to bring the idea up to your conscious mind and work on it, while reverting to the subconscious mind for actual use.

Suki depends on position, timing, and mindset. By moving as uke strikes, for example, you are no longer where he thought you were, and you might have an opening from your new position. By changing the timing on uke, you might similarly create an opportunity. By doing something unexpected, you might create a suki.

If you show that you see a suki, uke will almost always close it. You must exploit it the moment it opens up, without a pause or any warning movements to telegraph your intent to uke, like water flowing into a hole. The opening is there and you use it. Warning movements (pre-motion, telegraphing) are themselves a sort of suki. They provide a warning as to what is going to move, and when to expect it. If you see such an intention movement, you are ahead of the game. As nage, examine your techniques to see what intention movements, what "pre-motion", you have that tells uke what to expect. Relaxing will often minimize pre-motion

Kokyu ho is an exercise for, among other things, suki. It's fun to do. After the young bulls wear themselves out, we can use it to practice looking for suki. The idea of looking for a hole into which water can insinuate itself is very appropriate for this situation, and the results can be surprising. Sometimes a strong uke will collapse with little effort on nage's part.

It doesn't matter how you find suki, just whether you can use it. There are people that use tremendous muscular power to do a technique, then say how good this feels. It might feel good, but it is inefficient, wasteful, and poor aikido. Just because I have money in the bank doesn't mean I have to spend it all. (But neither should I be reluctant to do so at need.)

Distance

Fighting distance or ma-ai is the distance at which two people are just too far to be hit without uke or nage appreciably moving their bodies, as shown in the next figure. This is generally two arms' length. To hit you from ma-ai, your opponent has to move in, in which case he is no longer at ma-ai. If you are closer than ma-ai, your opponent can hit you without you having time to respond. Some martial arts focus on in-fighting, where everything is within ma-ai. There the weapons of choice are the short-range ones like elbows, knees, and the head. Even the body can be used for an atemi. This is not the way to do aikido, and you should control ma-ai, rather than allowing your opponent to control it.

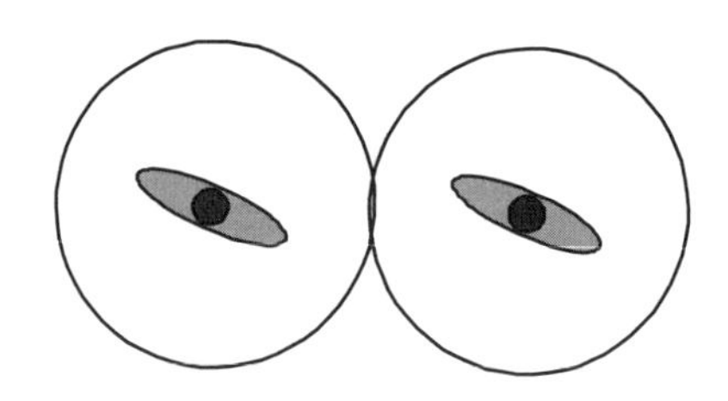

Two people at ma-ai.
They are far enough apart (about two arm lengths) that uke cannot reach nage before he can react. Nage can move to maintain the distance or do a technique to take control of uke as he moves in.

Ma-ai is not necessarily symmetrical and, as shown in the figure below, depends on what weapons are being used, whether we are talking about the body's natural weapons or artificial ones. An uke can attack from 50% further away by kicking than by punching. A jo (4 ft. staff) has a longer reach than a bokken (wooden sword). Thus, the elbow is a short-range weapon (about 1 ft.), and a bo is a longer-range weapon (about 6 ft., depending on how it is being used). Arguably, the range should not be defined as a circle, as it is impossible to punch at some angles and weak at others, but aite will most likely turn as necessary in order to attack, so it is shown that way. Some weapons, like a knife, are one-handed, and the ma-ai is further on one side of uke's body (shifting when he changes hands). Others are two handed, and the ma-ai is about the same to either side. For nage's side of ma-ai, generally nage will be empty handed in aikido, in which case his range will be about the same as shown above for the fist. Thus ma-ai for empty-handed techniques will be about 5 ft. for two average sized people. However, for kumi tachi, the ma-ai will be about 8 ft. (two sword lengths), for kumi jo, about 10 ft., and for jo tori about 7 ft. Thus, we can experiment with a wide range of ma-ai by using different weapons.

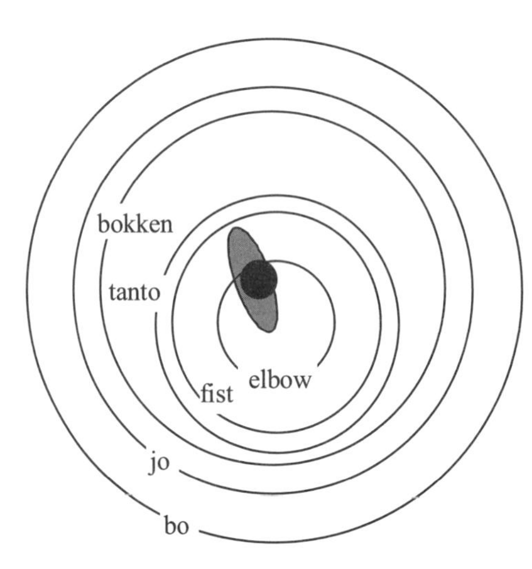

Ma-ai and reach of weapons – right side

Ma-ai might also depend on how the weapon is being used. The range for choku tsuki with a jo is perhaps 3 ft. You can get another foot or so by reaching further at the risk of weakening your position, as in the thirty-one point jo kata. A normal shomen or yokomen uchi has a range of about 3 ft. also, but toma katate uchi, a strike made by stepping forward and swinging the jo with one hand, might have a range of 8 ft. (Ma-ai would be about 10 ft.)

As I said earlier, ma-ai is not necessarily symmetrical. It may be shorter when uke is attacking empty handed and nage has a jo than when uke has the jo and nage must enter in on it to throw.

Ma-ai varies with body size, particularly with reach (length of limbs). Thus, arm reach commonly (5th percentile female to 95th percentile male) varies from about 24 to 30 inches, with much greater differences sometimes being found. Thus, ma-ai for a punch could vary from less than 4 ft. to more than 5 ft. As two inches makes the difference between a punch barely touching the skin and breaking ribs, twelve inches is a quite large difference.

The range of a kick is about 3 ft. (ma-ai perhaps 5 ft.). However, kicks often involve rotation of the hips, change of posture, and even jumping forward as they are delivered, which can extend the range of a kick to at least 6 ft. (ma-ai perhaps 8 ft.). These longer movements can actually be easier to deal with as the uke is traveling further (more response time) and has less maneuverability. Where they involve greater exertion, it might be easier to see the start of the movement (pre-motion).

Thus ma-ai varies with the particular uke and nage, their skill level, how uke plans to attack and whether he has any weapons. Considering ma-ai to be a time rather than a distance (see below) may make all this a little more manageable. The whole idea of ma-ai is to have time to respond.

Ma-ai can be manipulated. At the circus, if the lion tamer wants the lion to advance, he will move towards the animal. If he wants it to back away, he moves away. The key to making this work is the distance. Lions have a ma-ai also, and they will attack whenever a threat gets within this distance, and are likely to move away if the threat is outside ma-ai but too close for comfort. People may show a similar response. In karate, we are taught to attack the moment our opponent crosses the line. In aikido, we can similarly trigger uke's attack by crossing the line. This ability to trigger uke's attack makes uke more predictable.

Everybody has a personal ma-ai. In social situations this is the distance within which you begin to feel somebody is uncomfortably close, when they "invade your space". In western society this is commonly about 3 ft. It increases when you are nervous – like talking to your boss. It gets smaller with somebody you find sexually attractive, vanishing with intimacy. I knew a guy in England who always tried to get closer to people than was usual, and John would always be edging closer and people he was talking with would be backing away. Social ma-ai can be a problem with people of differing backgrounds, particularly from very different cultures.

Aikido – Moving On

If an opponent moves within your ma-ai you have two choices: to move away, so regaining ma-ai, or doing a technique. This can be a problem in a "social" situation. If you deck somebody just for moving within your ma-ai you will have a legal problem, maybe even if you control him nicely and don't hurt him. Instead, put your hand out (without touching him) so that it is between the two of you and ask him to stay back. If he grabs your hand or knocks it down so that he can take a swing at you, then he has started the assault and you can defend yourself. Plus you have made a suki that would not have been there otherwise, and limited his likely options, like Musashi's "moving the shadow".

Ma-ai should not be too close

You have to get within your opponent's ma-ai to do a technique. Generally, this is not a problem, because he is attacking and therefore invading your ma-ai (and moving you to within his own), but you need to recognize that in this space either of you can hit the other with little time to react. Thus, within ma-ai, you should be moving, keeping his attention with atemi, keeping him off balance so as to prevent a powerful attack, and getting rid of or controlling him with technique.

Timing

In a sense, timing is as much a part of ma-ai as is distance, but there is more to timing than just ma-ai. There is, as Musashi said, timing in everything. For martial arts, there are three main types of timing: sen no sen, sen sen no sen, and go no sen. Sen no sen is what might be called "normal" timing, when we move as uke attacks. Sen sen no sen is an "early" timing, attacking as uke attacks but a little earlier, forestalling him. Go no sen is a "late" timing, when we let uke attack, and then as his focus dissipates, take charge decisively. I like using shomen uchi irimi nage to teach these different timings, though just about any technique can be used.

We must be able to see uke's timing and be unaffected by it. Timing is not just speed (fast or slow), but also earlier or later relative to what uke is doing. As with a car engine, the timing might change as the speed and load varies.

Kumi jo and kumi tachi are excellent for practicing timing, particularly where an attack is evaded and a simultaneous counter strike is made. If a reactive timing is used, two aites can trade blows for a long time. If, however, nage merely evades the attack, he can counter attack a fraction of a second earlier, with more chance of success. This type of timing, to attack as uke attacks, is the essence of aikido.

Every situation, every pair of uke and nage, every instance, has its own timing. A big uke takes more time to react. It takes more time to throw somebody in kote gaeshi, moving perhaps a couple of hundred pounds, than to put nikkyo on their wrist. A stiff uke takes more time to respond than a flexible one because more mass has to be moved at a time. Timing is partly physical, partly mental. It takes time for an uke to respond to an atemi or for nage to move out of the way of uke's punch. A strong nage can drive uke to move faster, though this is less easy and less effective than you might think. A large part of the time involved in studying aikido comes down to understanding how different people react in different situations.

If you mistime your technique, it can not only be hard to take uke's balance, but the actual throw is harder to do. As an analogy, if you want to push a car, running at it and driving your shoulder into it might not be the best way for either you or the car.

Generally, in aikido we respond to uke's movement, even very early in the evolution of his attack. We also make uke react to us in ways other than by triggering his attack. For example, in kokyu ho, especially if uke is trying hard to stop you, you can get past his strength and open a suki by twitching your arms, making a small movement that uke interprets as the start of a bigger movement. As he reacts, working hard to stop the movement he thought you were about to do, you can slip past his strength and throw him over. This sort of timing is not always good. I remember seeing somebody cut on the hand with a knife during a shodan test when he and uke got into a reactive timing mode that neither of them was controlling.

Atemi is often used in aikido to elicit a reaction from uke. For example, as he attacks, a quick slap to the face will often make him jerk out of the way, thus losing his balance or even falling. The timing to get this reaction is different from what we would use to merely hit him.

Flow

Thus, the connection – ki no musubi – does not start when the technique starts, nor finish when the technique finishes. Rather, nage "flows" uke through the technique from the first (non-physical) connection to the conscious breaking of the connection, making the technique a single act. Every glitch, every discontinuity is an opportunity for uke to take hold of and stop the technique or even reverse it. Aesthetics and efficiency tend to run together. Good technique looks beautiful and works well. It should feel natural, like a stream running downhill.

Technique should flow naturally from one point to another, from the start to the finish.

State of Mind

> "It is sickness to be obsessed with winning. It is sickness to be obsessed with using martial arts. It is sickness to be obsessed with putting forth all one has learned. It is sickness to be obsessed with offense, and it is also sickness to be obsessed with defense. It is also sickness to be obsessed with getting rid of sickness. To fix the mind obsessively is considered sickness. Since all these various sicknesses are in the mind, the thing is to tune the mind by getting rid of such afflictions."
>
> Yagyu Munenori, "The Book of Family Traditions on the Art of War". Translated by Thomas Cleary. Barnes & Noble Books, New York. 1993.

As mentioned earlier, fear and happiness are states of mind. There is no direct relationship between the outside world and the state of our mind. We sense the outside world and our brain interprets what we see. Once, in Newcastle, I was walking past a dimly lit graveyard late at night. As I passed the gate I "saw" a supernaturally tall dark figure looking over the wall at me. A moment later, after my heart settled down, I realized it was only a gravestone with an urn-shaped finial, but in the second this took, my state of mind went from startled to scared to amused. Yet the world hadn't changed. Even my sensory input had changed very little.

Few people like getting hit. But getting hit is generally less bad than the fear of it. You can learn to deal with it. In fact, when the adrenaline is flowing, you barely realize it has happened. Similarly, nikkyo hurt really badly the first time somebody put it on hard. As I got used to it, it didn't hurt nearly as much. Part of this was conditioning, but part was knowing what was coming. As we get used to things like that, we learn to separate trivial, temporary discomfort from the pain of an injury. We can even learn to continue when injured, though it is foolish to do that without good reason.

In aikido, the state of mind should always be indomitable – Musashi's "body of a rock". The feeling should be that even if you are beaten into a pulp, even if you are killed in the most painful way imaginable, you will never give in. You always seek to turn the table on your opponent, and if that is impossible at least you retain control of your mind and never give in.

There are movements in aikido when you appear to back away from uke, to give ground. But these are ways to get what you really want – a detour rather than a retreat.* You might move back, but never with a feeling of giving up. You always remain strong mentally and emotionally. Tenkan is a movement

---

* One characteristic of intelligence in animals is the ability to move away from a desired goal in order to achieve it. Chimpanzees can do it, but most dogs can't.

that avoids uke's power, but only so that you can more effectively take control of him. Even as you turn away from uke, you go where ***you*** want to go in order to accomplish ***your*** goals. This firmness of purpose is reflected in the extension of your arms. You always maintain it. Slacken the intent in your mind or the extension of your power through your body, and you risk being trampled into the ground.

On the other hand, we can easily get too attached to particular outcomes. We might want uke to move in a certain way. We may want to do a particular technique. During training, this may be desirable. We want our students to learn the entire repertoire of techniques not just the ones they like. But we should be flexible. Sometimes the best way to achieve our aims is to give up the unimportant ones.

Intent

Intent is discernible by an attacker. If you have the greater intent, an attacker will generally back off. This works even with animals. Few dogs will attack if you face them with a sincere intent to rip out their guts. However, it is difficult to maintain intent in the face of overwhelming odds, or even just a bigger person. That is why you must practice. Intent is like anything else in this world, subject to manipulation. At times you might want your intent to be obvious. At other times you might wish to hide it until there is a better opportunity, as did the Forty Seven Ronin*.

The intent of an atemi is more significant than any damage it could do.

In the dojo, we look for harmony. The carrying out of intent might need to be softened a little. We have to make allowances for people with less skill or who are injured or physically less capable, so that we'll have people to practice with. Otherwise the dojo will wither away. In real life, we want to have time to do the things that we consider important, and not to be constantly fighting. Thus, we may accept some things that are less than perfect. However, we don't compromise on things that are important to us.

In the dojo we take turns in being the boss, being nage, expressing our intent. In real life, if everybody expressed their intent all the time, there would

* Though this approach was criticized by some of their contemporaries.

be a holocaust, people fighting all the time. To live in a civilization, we need to balance our demands on others and their demands on us. We need to have reasonable expectations. Otherwise, the incidents of road rage and the like would escalate a thousand fold. Thus, we should have the willpower to do what must be done, and the wisdom to use this ability carefully and sparingly. Just because you have a .44 magnum doesn't mean you should shoot everything you don't like.

Ultimately, everybody dies. Even if medical science was to extend our lives by a hundred years, that is still only a moment in the fifteen-billion-year lifetime of the universe. I don't know what happens after I'm dead – I expect nothing does – but I plan on dying with the same intent I am living, difficult as I expect this to be.

Reality

Sometimes people ask if aikido 'works', if it is 'real'. Aikido is real and it does work, but not every aikidoka can do aikido effectively. It depends on your school, on your training partners, and, most of all, on yourself. It is easy to soften the intent and just have fun without practicing sincerely, but if you practice rigorously and study hard to develop technically correct aikido, it will work. It will be as real as you make it.

Some people think that aikido should focus more on conflict resolution and spiritual development rather than on physical conflict. Some go so far as to say that they would not hurt somebody even to protect themselves or their loved ones. I respect their right to that opinion, even though I don't agree with it. The physical form of aikido can act as a form of meditation, and that can also be a reason to practice aikido. Again, I respect this position, though I don't agree that this is a major reason to practice aikido.

I think that aikido is a valid martial art with a defensive ethic that was designed to be used to resolve physical conflict, even if that involved pre-emptive action. If we don't make our aikido somewhat realistic, it loses this aspect, and much of its value. More and more we in Western countries live in a sanitized environment. There is something beneficial in practicing close to the edge, where somebody attacks you in a way that could seriously hurt you, yet you take care of the problem and move on. Other people get some of the same benefits by jumping out of planes.

Attitude

The state of mind is possibly the most important factor in regard to reality. If you are always looking for reality, you will find it. Aikido will not, however, nor will anything else, make you invulnerable. There was a reason the samurai respected the readiness to die. If you live your life with that sort of readiness to die, life, including having fun, becomes much more significant.

Aikido – Moving On

Perseverance

When attacked, you might start off all right, but when your opponent doesn't fall down like ukes do in the dojo, or when he gets up madder than ever, you could get disheartened. Most real fights continue until the first bone is broken (often in the hand or face), but a fight can last for some time. You will probably get hit. You might get hurt badly. In some situations you must keep on until you win or you will end up in hospital or the morgue. More fights are lost by one participant giving up hope than by serious damage being done before that point. Historically, in battles, most people are killed while running away.

Readiness

If you are not always ready, you might become a statistic. O Sensei challenged his students to catch him off guard and, as far as I know, none succeeded. However, it is hard to always be ready. Certainly, most people are not. A martial artist gets mugged. People say: well he should have defended himself. They are right. You should school yourself to be always alert, always ready, always centered. To me, this is the essence of being a martial artist. I don't always succeed, perfection is hard to achieve, but I succeed more often than I used to.

For aikido, this readiness should not be aggressive, as aggression creates aggression. You should be as ready to smile as to deal with an attack.

Willingness

One of the students in a woman's self defense class I taught, whose ex-husband had tried to drown her, said, "Oh, I could never hurt anybody". Perhaps this is a little extreme, but this sort of attitude is not uncommon. Pacifism is a choice you can make, but then should you be in a martial arts class? Aikido is philosophically opposed to hurting people, at least from what O Sensei is quoted as having said. Certainly it gives you the opportunity to minimize the damage. But when attacked you should take care of the problem.

Willingness to execute technique is crucial for effectiveness. Your atemi should be technically correct, and that means you should hit what you intend to hit, which is often the attacker's nose. In the dojo, your uke should have no doubt about your commitment to hit him. (Just as nage should have no doubt that uke intends to hit him.) Of course, you would rather that uke move, so that he doesn't get a bloody nose, and you can pull your atemi (particularly with a beginner) when it is apparent that he isn't going to move. But the bottom line should be that if an attacker doesn't move you hit him. Most atemi are not very serious blows. They are typically intended to make uke move rather than to finish the conflict. However, they are a serious part of the technique and if you do not hit at uke correctly, on target and with intent, your technique will be compromised. A similar failure on the street, and you will risk serious injury.

Mind

Breathing and Meditation

Breathing exercises and meditation can help you develop the steadfast spirit you need for aikido. Meditation can become a way of life. I'm too impatient to do serious meditation, but there are lots of schools out there. Aikido itself can become a meditation, especially with an uke that doesn't chatter.

There are lots of ways to do breathing and meditation. I generally practice breathing either standing or in seiza by lowering the arms and breathing out as I push forwards, breathing in as I raise and spread the arms to expand the rib cage to the maximum possible extent, and then lowering the arms while holding my breath. I hold the breath for half a minute or so, then repeat the cycle. This exercise somewhat counteracts the sedentary nature of our lives, making sure your lungs get fully utilized.

As I breathe, I think about breathing. This settles the mind, not that there is anything particularly important about the details of breathing itself. (Though not breathing would be a reason for concern.) What is important is to not let the everyday concerns that we all have take over the mind as they usually do.

After a dozen or so deep breaths, I sit and allow my body to breathe by itself. I try to sit vertically, so that it takes the minimum effort to stay upright. I think of my center. When I hear distracting noises, like the kids out on the mall, I accept the distractions and let them go. Getting annoyed would be holding on to them, letting myself be distracted for a longer time.

Sitting breathing is a good way for me to end a class. In this world of TVs and cell phones everywhere, it is good sometimes to let your mind rest, to let your spirit settle. You can get so frenetic that it is difficult to let things go.

Meditating can help you find your center

Tempo

Tempo: the pace of a musical piece or passage

Aikido techniques must flow, and aikido, like music or dance, has temporal form. The movement in a technique is like dance in having a pattern both in space and time. There is a rhythm, an ordered recurrent alternation of weak and strong notes, to a technique, a pattern of how it flows, but the tune is usually rather short. Like in dancing, tempo, extension and strength can vary from time to time within a technique, and from technique to technique. Atemi is almost like an accent, a stress on a note that has to nevertheless fit into the whole. These temporal aspects can vary, but are vital to making the technique effective. A particular technique has a recognizable structure, both a recognizable pattern of movement, and a tempo that varies within the technique. However, there should always be irregularity, an unpredictability, in a martial art.

Beginners tend to throw with an uneven tempo. They move in fits and starts: slowing down to think, then speeding up on the bits they know. This can be quite devastating to uke if nage gets out of hand and uke's ukemi is less than it needs to be. But at the same time it can be ineffective, the energy provided jointly by uke and nage being dissipated in conflict. Beginners should strive for an even tempo, one slow enough that they can maintain it.

A problem is that nage might not even realize what he is doing: he may feel that he is doing the technique at an even speed because his mind is working at a constant pace – hurrying to catch up. The pace reflects how much thinking that nage is doing from moment to moment. Thus, nage might move slower when he has to change hands, or forget about extension when he pays attention to his feet. Music, western and at least some eastern, is divided into bars of equal length. Sometimes there are few notes per bar, sometimes many. Whatever the number, you have to fit them in and keep the bars the same length. Similarly, in aikido, you have to pay attention to the rhythms of your own and uke's bodies, to how they play a duet, and fit all the detailed

Shakuhachi music is divided into bars, and if there are a lot of notes in a bar your fingers just have to move faster.

movements that make up the technique into the time available.

Techniques often have distinctive timing for nage to discover and work towards. Thus, ikkyo irimi (omote) might be a three-count technique. Katate tori kaiten nage might have a four-count timing. This is not to say that techniques should be separated into steps. (The Arthur Murray School of Aikido?) However, each part must be given its due and neither hurried nor allowed to lag. Uke and nage must come into the correct relative position and "energy state" for the next part, and nage must orchestrate the various parts so that they fit smoothly together and flow one into another.

Once a technique can be done smoothly, nage should start consciously manipulating the tempo, feeling how changes in it affect uke. A couple of guidelines are to speed up through the pieces where uke is most likely to resist, and not to move so fast through one part that it messes you up for the next. This is particularly apparent when nage takes uke's balance really well, but then loses the flow because he has to pause to change hands. Always look ahead to the next movement and set yourself up for doing it correctly.

Most techniques speed up as you progress through them. In Western music this would be called accelerando. Aikido is often seen as being circular, but this movement should not be a steady state that goes on forever, round and round. Rather, nage should, in general, accelerate uke as the technique progresses, and finish crisply. From, for example, kata tori, nage may strike at uke's head, using the rhythm of his atemi to encourage uke to push through hard with his blocking hand. He may give ground in such a way that uke falls forward into nage's lead, and then change the lead so that uke never quite manages to catch up. If nage pushes back too long, uke will stop moving. If nage does not push long enough to make uke push back, uke will not lose his balance. Ideally, nage can draw uke out, making him fall into a "hole" that nage has opened for him, falling into the technique.

Thus, for kata tori irimi nage, nage leads uke out and round. As uke falters, recovering his balance, nage may turn to get outside of uke's arm, and lead uke round the other way. As uke recovers once more, nage enters and throws him to the ground. Nage's rhythm may be fast to strike (preventing uke from striking first), slow to let uke build up some force, and then moderately quick to draw out (over-extend) uke. The turn isn't particularly fast at first, then faster again to draw uke around, then slow as he recovers and pulls back, then fast as you enter and throw. However, the whole technique must remain cohesive, flowing from one segment to another rather than breaking into the separate segments described.

Another example could be katate ryote tori (ryote tori) tenchi nage irimi. A common way to do this is for nage to meet uke and drive his hands round uke's power, so that nage gets into a position almost behind uke, with uke off balance and unable to resist the throw. This is a two-part technique: nage meets uke and enters to the side (zigs), putting his feet together to protect his groin, then drives in behind uke and throws (zags). Now if nage gives uke the idea that he is going to meet uke in this way, then speeds up to meet uke a fraction of a second earlier, what is the effect on uke? Uke isn't ready to resist. His timing is off, his feet are in the wrong place, and he is weak. Nage, of course, knew what he was doing, and is even stronger than usual because he has taken a slightly longer step than usual, and throws uke more easily.

There is a counterpart to this, when nage makes a slower and smaller move, so that uke has to overextend to get his hands on nage. This, however, is not as easy to do as what was described above unless uke is attacking strongly.

Katate Ryote Tori Tenchi Nage

A third example is ikkyo irimi. Whether from shomen uchi or kata tori, the basic technique is difficult to do slowly on anybody who is bigger or stronger. It is a lot easier if nage controls the timing. While it is not generally practiced as such, ikkyo irimi is a very aggressive move. Nage might even initiate by striking at uke's face, forcing uke to protect his face, at which time nage does ikkyo on the defending hand. Nage must then enter as he strikes. If he waits too long, it becomes a contest of strength, which, win or lose, is not aikido.

If this entry does not work or is late, uke will try to force nage's attacking arm down to either do his own technique or to open the way for a strike. When nage feels pressure he can push back, not to win by strength, but to encourage uke to push harder. Then he draws back in tenshin (with a quarter – J – step), drawing out uke as described above for irimi nage. This undermines uke's strength momentarily, and sets up nage for a different direction. Nage then steps in and completes the ikkyo before uke has a chance to regain his kamae.

Nage should not give away too much. He must not compromise his posture, or he will have to recover and do a totally different technique. The feeling should be strong, then falter (but in reality nage merely turns), then be strong again. As always, the mind should stay strong with not even the slightest feeling of withdrawing, but rather of just changing what is being grasped. However, there is a modulation of the degree of extension. The initial movement should be with strong extension; the second entrance should also be with strong extension.

If uke is really strong and nage cannot hold him back, then rather than going back to the initial technique (ikkyo), we might find that kote gaeshi works better. In this case, the second extension is in a direction that is even more different, with a turn of maybe 180 degrees rather than 15. The rhythm is a little different also, with a more flowing extension, flowing until uke is on the floor. It can even change into a complete tenkan. Changing height can also work well, even just settling the center a couple of inches.

Training

Training in aikido involves going to a dojo and practicing. This might seem too obvious to be worth stating, but if you don't work out you're not training. If you are teaching you are not training, at least not in the same way. You should learn something from teaching, but it still isn't the same as normal training. The only practice you get during teaching is when you actually throw people about, and that is a much shorter fraction of the class than if you are practicing. Furthermore, your uke is probably not trying to hit you as hard as he would if you were practicing together. He is helping you demonstrate to the class.

In particular, talking is not training. Some talking may be good, possibly a quick exchange to make sure you both agree on what you are supposed to be doing if there is some uncertainty, but training is something that involves your whole body, mind, and spirit. Some people like kuchi waza way too much.

You must have the right attitude towards training. You should practice hard physically, mentally, and spiritually. This does not mean that you have to push yourself beyond your capabilities, until a misstep results in injury or you have a heart attack on the mat. It does mean pushing yourself hard enough that you are tired at the end of the class. All three of these aspects are important. You should be working physically hard enough to build up your aerobic fitness and muscular strength. At the same time, you should be searching mentally for the way forward with the intensity of a Zen student attacking a koan. You should be pushing yourself to do the things you are afraid of, to learn not to flinch, to take the breakfalls that you hate, developing a robust spirit.

Physical Improvement

You might start aikido as a wimp or a "perfect" physical specimen of humanity. Most of us start in between. Even if you are "perfect", this will be according to some standard that may have little to do with aikido, and you will need to condition yourself. Aikido, like any other activity, uses some muscles you typically do not exercise. You will develop a strong grip and strong extensor muscles. You will also become more flexible, particularly in the wrists and arms. Typically, weight lifters are quite stiff. This can't be good for their joints, and they are amazingly sensitive to techniques like nikkyo and sankyo.

You might rationalize that a fight lasts for a few seconds, so you don't need any significant aerobic capacity. That might be true in most cases, but when it lasts longer you will need aerobic capacity. Furthermore, if you don't have stamina, you won't be able to train hard and you will progress more slowly.

How much is enough? If you get tired and run out of breath more easily than the other members of the dojo or compared to other people of similar rank at seminars, you should think about doing something about it. I don't jog or do the Nordic Track to improve my stamina, but I work hard on the mat and rarely run out of breath before my partners.

While practice should be physically demanding, it is not a good idea to let many little injuries accumulate. Over time, too much stress on the body will break it down. Tendonitis can result from too much stress on the wrist, for example. Injuries like this are often the result of inadequate warm-up before class, inadequate care being taken with ukemi, and too macho an attitude. Hard as it is to take time off, you need to give yourself time to heal, especially as you get older.

Warming up and stretching are not the same. Warming up should get your body ready for a workout, like warming up your car on a cold day. Stretching, on the other hand, increasing your flexibility, generally should not be done at the beginning of an exercise period. Rather, it should be done at the end, when you are fully warmed up.

Stretches should be slow and steady. Bouncing is generally bad, especially for muscles in your back. You should not stretch so much it hurts. Don't look for immediate results. Stretch as far as is comfortable and hold that for fifteen or thirty seconds. Relax and stretch a bit more and hold that. Let go, relax, and try again. Stretching should be done routinely, rather than being done energetically for a week or two, hurting yourself, then stopping for a couple of months to recover.

Ukemi should become something you love doing. If you hold back, trying to avoid taking a fall, you will get hurt, either because your nage seriously misjudged your ability to fall, or by the slow accumulation of minor damage. Not only will you get injured, but you are cheating your aite by resisting unduly. Finally, you are missing out on a lot of the fun in aikido. It is every bit as exhilarating to take a big fall and bounce back from the mat as it is to execute such a throw.

Of course, by the time you get up to shodan level, you should be physically fit, but it doesn't hurt to take the time to think about whether you really are. Did you make a big effort to get fit for your last test? You should be planning for the long haul now. For always being at that level.

Mental Improvement

You should not just wait for enlightenment to come. You must actively seek it. This does not mean that you should be vocal about it, always asking questions in class about what the sensei means. It certainly does not mean that you should always try to prove that your sensei is illogical and wrong. Rather, you should search for how your sensei can be right. How can what you are taught be fit into your world view? How can the opinions of different teachers be reconciled? For example, some teachers will talk about "ki", and how you should always "extend ki". Others abhor any use of the word. The point is not to challenge the teacher, but to understand what he is trying to communicate. To see how it can fit, rather than judging that it must be wrong because of your preconceptions. Aikido is big enough for different opinions. If you learn two different ways of doing ikkyo, for example, surely this is better than one way. Also, it gives you something to study, to find the principle underlying both ways. Einstein's theory of relativity did not invalidate Newton's physics. It extended it to a wider range of applicability.

Of course, learning two ways will take longer. This is the price you pay to get a broader body of knowledge. There is no hurry to learning aikido. It is the journey that is important, not the destination. We all end up the same way – dead – and there is no rush to get that way.

The mind is a wonderful thing. You can passively absorb knowledge, and the subconscious will work away at it, making sense of it as best it can. The trouble with this is that it is a slow process, and not necessarily logical. Even in Zen, students are exhorted to actively seek enlightenment. I encourage students to ask questions, of me and of themselves.

The mind is like the body in that if you do not actively use it every day it will waste away. Conversely, you can develop it, but this does take time and effort. There are no shortcuts, though there are long ways around. In the case of the body, you might have bad habits acquired over years and they won't go away overnight. Neither do the bad habits of the mind. In both cases, a good school can help you develop.

The martial arts ideal of "mu shin" does not mean that you don't think, that you go through life like a zombie. It means that you have reached the point where you understand what is happening, and can trust your (trained) subconscious to take care of the details. To reach this sort of "emptiness", you must train and train until your aikido is as natural as walking, and you no longer have to think about the minutiae. This frees up your mind to work on the more subtle aspects of the art.

Spiritual Improvement

I have struggled with the idea of spirituality since I was a teenager beginning to question religious ideas that I'd been force-fed as I grew up. I no longer believe in the idea of a god, personal or otherwise. The only concept I have for something godlike – in the sense of being all powerful, all knowing, and always present – is the universe itself, and I have no intention of worshiping that. If, when I die, I find I was wrong, I'll change my mind.

But there is something beyond the logical mind. What makes people good or bad? What makes people successful or failures? What makes one student keep going – even though he is not progressing any faster than his peer group – until he gets one black belt, and then another, and still keeps on going like the Energizer Bunny?

This other thing, this attitude, is what I think is spirit, an aspect of the "ki" of "aikido". It is determination, dedication, concentration, focus, and motivation: including all those things and more. It is an approach to life, and this development of the spirit is what I think is most beneficial to most people about studying martial arts.

I didn't come to these conclusions lightly. I worried for years that if there was no god, why were we here? Why should we try hard? Why strive to succeed at anything when we'll be dead all too soon? I guess inertia from my upbringing kept me going while I wrestled with the problem. I'm still not sure where the soul-searching has got me, though I can see the signs of it in the things I will and will not do.

Most people seem to be content to have other people answer these difficult questions for them: their parents, their teachers, their spouses, their sensei, their preacher, community pressure. Other people are suspicious of prepackaged products, and look for their own way. To me, this is better, though many seem to get lost, taking an easy way, getting too much into drugs, alcohol, or power to know what they are doing or why.

Martial arts, even aikido, may not give you answers. You can do martial arts for years just following your sensei, and that is perfectly all right until he dies or becomes no longer your sensei in some other way. That isn't the way I chose, it isn't my sort of martial arts, and isn't the life I want to lead. But wherever you, personally, are going, martial arts can increase your ability to focus, to think objectively. If you push hard enough it may lead you to a personal answer. Most people do not push it far enough or hard enough to find their own unique answer, either in life or in aikido.

I see strong parallels between martial arts and life. I think that the journey through life is its own meaning, that we all die in the end and all that matters then is what we leave behind. What survives death? Our students, our children, and our ideas.

Mat Aikido

On the mat, we have to look out for each other. We have to try to hit each other, and not hold grudges or try to get even when we get hit. We have to practice sincerely, or our art will not be effective when we need it (which is one of the main purposes of training in a martial art) and we will also lose out on many of the collateral benefits.

Sincerity in training is not a license to hit beginners as hard as we can or smash them to the ground so that their training is "realistic". This interpretation would be exploitative and sadistic. Sincerity really means that we attack as accurately as we can, but with a manageable force and speed, always pushing our kohei (juniors), but pushing moderately so that they can succeed by working hard. We know so much more than a total beginner that it is easy for even a low kyu rank to mess up a beginner's technique, or, worse, to mess up the beginner.

On the other hand, we should respect our sempai enough to push them, though again, not unreasonably. But they must be the judges of what is too much. If a sempai says hit me harder, you should hit him harder, and not hold back out of fear that he will slam you down harder than you can take, which of course he should not do. When he says "hit me harder", you should not be concerned for his safety or your safety. You should have faith in him, and he should merit this faith, particularly with regard to not trashing his uke.

We often know less than we think we do. Everybody is different, and the way to learn the technique is not the same for everybody. Ideally, we'd only need to see something done correctly once and pick it up immediately. Instead, people learn one part of a technique one day and another part another. And we all progress at different rates. Don't be so sure of your approach that you force your kohei to wear your shoes. Concentrate on attacking correctly, and take a nice ukemi to protect your body. It is the sensei's job to correct your training partners if they're wrong. The only time uke should correct what nage is doing is when nage is hopelessly lost. I see so many ukes talking and instructing when they should just be attacking correctly and taking good ukemi. Worse, I see people putting their own spin on what is being taught, sometimes even doing something very different, and shutting down their kohei if the kohei don't do what they are told is the right way. This is both rude and counterproductive. Instead, just practice. Attack honestly. Take ukemi reasonably. Be generous.

At the initial stage, a beginner should not worry about whether aikido works. He should just learn the moves, learn how to take ukemi. As a student progresses, he will want to see if techniques work. They do, and you will find that out soonest by not worrying about it. Start struggling and technique goes out of the window. Focus on doing exactly what sensei is teaching. Imitate the gross movements first, and then work on the fine movements. Work on the gross movements first, because they are the foundation for the fine movements and are easier to learn, plus they are less situation-specific.

By the time they are approaching shodan, students can usefully start to think about effectiveness. They should start to attack harder and harder as uke (with a nage of similar or higher rank). They should start to throw harder and harder (again, with an uke of similar or higher ability). But they should still be careful. This is when a lot of injuries happen. Uke should still be thinking about attacking, not about countering the technique. Once the technique starts, uke should be thinking about ukemi, not about criticizing nage. Nage should be thinking about doing the technique correctly and decisively, but still being careful with his uke. This is partly for selfish reasons: without an uke, how can we learn?

Above shodan, working with similar-rank ukes, you should be pushing still harder. The attacks should generally be full power, but still controlled. Techniques should also be executed at something approaching full power, but still carefully. Some techniques can be done so hard that uke might not be able to take the force, especially when nage is bigger. However, for similar sized, similar rank people at this level, you should be able to pretty much cut loose. (Though still looking out for other people on the mat.)

You will still need to slow down when there is a problem with your technique. You cannot even identify the problem at full speed unless you have video with slow motion capability at hand. You should slow the technique down, develop a solution, practice it, and build back up to full speed with the improved technique.

The ideal way to practice (above shodan, with similar rank uke and nage) is probably to do the first couple of repetitions full bore. You won't get any rehearsal in the street. It has to work first time. Then slow down to work on the problems and improve the basics.

Injuries

Aikido is relatively safe and free from injuries. However, there is a risk of injury no matter what we do in life. The risk is only moderately increased by practicing aikido in a sensible fashion. (And risks of some other undesirable events such as being hurt falling, being mugged, or having a heart attack are reduced.) When an uke attacks us, it is to give us a chance to learn, to practice. It is both ungrateful and irresponsible to hurt (damage) him in return. We should work as hard as uke can handle, but not so hard that we hurt him. It is better to err on the side of caution. Similarly, we can hurt ourselves, mainly by using too much muscle to force a technique to work when we just don't have it right (particularly when demonstrating, teaching, or testing).

We have to consider who we are working with. Smaller people need to be handled differently from bigger people. Smaller people can be hurt if you use too much force just because you have the muscle to make the technique work that way. You may not even realize how close they are to being injured until something snaps. Big people can be hurt also, mainly by exceeding their ability to fall safely and by nage moving too fast for their ukemi.

If you do get injured, you should not keep working out. Neither should you just disappear for a few weeks to let it heal. You should tell your sensei what happened, who was involved, and that you can't practice for however long the doctor says. You should still come to class. If you can't work out, you should watch. You can learn that way (mitori geiko), and you won't have as much problem motivating yourself to get back on the mat when you are healed. You should still work out if you can do that without aggravating the injury. For example, you might still be able to do most techniques, or perhaps just do the weapons classes. If your wrist is hurt, you might want to wear something on your wrist. That makes it easier for nage to remember that you are hurt, and which wrist is hurt.

You should study ukemi to see how yours can be improved to avoid a repetition of the injury. I do know of aikidoka that had to quit because of chronic injuries due to them having poor ukemi and holding back when being thrown, taking a lot of strain on their joints and "toughing it out". Wrists seem to be particularly susceptible to this, especially from kote gaeshi. Ukemi should be good enough to allow nage to crank hard on the wrist without uke sustaining injury. If the wrist hurts for more than a few seconds after a technique is applied, uke was holding back too much. Don't rely on nage being kind. He should be, but you should not rely on it.

There is a smaller but still significant risk of injury from "flying" – throwing yourself when the technique does not justify it. Besides being unfair to nage, telling him he has the technique when he does not, you can set yourself up on a trajectory that nage is not expecting and is not ready for. With some techniques, such as shiho nage, this is quite dangerous for uke, especially if nage hasn't the sense to ease up. My second sensei, Mr. Ron Russell, had his elbow broken as an ikkyu when the person he was taking falls for threw him in an unexpected direction.

The sensei should keep track of injuries. If a certain person is causing an undue number of them, he needs to be counseled. If the problem is particularly noticeable and persistent, the person should be told he is no longer welcome in the dojo. Failure to do this will not only drive away other people, but the sensei could be legally liable. O Sensei was explicit about not teaching aikido to people of poor moral character.

If the problem is related to a particular technique rather than to a person, action should still be taken. The problem might be in the way the technique is done, in the way it is taught, or in the way ukemi is taught. Ukemi is the part of aikido that is probably most critical to the success of a school, and the least taught. Some techniques do involve difficult ukemi. You can drop them from the curriculum or modify them to make them safer, as O Sensei did with some Daito Ryu techniques in evolving aikido. But there is still a risk to any member of one dojo practicing with someone from a different school simply because different schools make different assumptions. My feeling is that every black belt should be competent at ukemi from any commonly taught technique.

Pick Out the LZ

As you and your uke get better and throw harder, it becomes increasingly incumbent on nage to watch where he is throwing uke. If the technique is done correctly, uke cannot stop the technique and will have to go with it. Long ukes require more space to fall than short ones. Advanced ukes will generally see when they are heading for trouble and at least pull in their legs to shorten the distance, but nage should not rely on that, especially as it might cause uke to take a heavier fall.

There are several things nage can do if somebody is taking up the mat space towards which he wants to throw. He can turn and throw uke where there is room, he can ease off so that uke can take an easier (and smaller) fall, he can slow down to give the other person time to scramble out of the way, or he can stop. Picking a different spot and throwing uke there is the best option, and many if not all techniques allow you to do that if you see the problem early enough. The idea is even embodied in the name shiho nage. This name means four (all) directions throw – and you can pick a direction by appropriate hip movement at the appropriate time. It is generally not a good idea to attempt to radically alter uke's trajectory late in the throw. This can lead to major damage to his arm. In any case, it is important for nage to realize that it is his responsibility not to throw his uke onto or into another person. At least one aikidoka has become paralyzed by having another person thrown on top of her. Being aware is as important in aikido as anywhere else.

As uke you will have a little latitude, most times, about where you land, but wherever you land you should not lie on the mat where you were thrown. Rather, bounce back off the mat and back into kamae, facing nage. This continuation of the technique is uke's zanshin, with all that implies for connectivity and mindset.

Realism in Practicing

I probably answered this above, but to restate it, you must learn to deal with realistic attacks: fast, full-speed attacks, and you must learn to do it without injuries to yourself or uke. This doesn't happen instantaneously. You need to work up to that level. Accidents may still happen, though hopefully of a minor nature. Even when you are really advanced, you don't have to work only at full speed. You might slow down because you are working with a beginner. You might need to slow down to study technical detail, to look at different options.

Realism does mean there will be variations. (However, if you want to play with variations, you should do it on your own time, not in a formal class – unless that is what is being taught.) It means that nage will probably not know exactly what uke will do. But it also means that nage must take charge, and only give uke the openings (suki) that he wants uke to see. Realism means that uke can attack with any dirty trick in the book (or out of it). You should not let uke attack freely, however. You should confine, control, and confound him from before he is even within range.

Unpopular People

Every dojo has people everybody wants to work with, and people others avoid working with. You should work with everybody. I am generally not concerned about political correctness, and that is not the reason for this advice. It is part of the discipline to work with everybody: not excluding anybody, not avoiding people, nor seeking out people. There are a variety of reasons for this. One is that if we kicked out all the unpopular people, the dojo would be even smaller than it is, and I've never heard of a dojo that had as many students as they wanted. Furthermore, if one unpopular person is driven away, another takes his place as the outcast.

A more important reason is that everybody has something that you can learn from him. The big guys are challenging ukes because of their size. The little ones are challenging because of *their* size. Stiff ukes pose a different technical challenge from the flexible or limp ones. The muscle-bound are hard to move physically but are vulnerable to having their balance broken by correct movement on nage's part. The agile are hard to confine and control, but are generally less strong. The lame are excellent for studying balance, how to take kuzushi, and how not to take so much that they fall before you can complete the technique. Finally, the few that can't give you anything of a technical challenge are important for you to work with because you need to learn to control both your techniques and your mind.

There is an exception: if somebody repeatedly or intentionally hurts you when you are uke for him, politely decline to work with him again. Now to clarify this, I'm not talking about minor discomfort. I'm talking about injuries that take days to heal. There is no excuse for people intentionally damaging each other. It shows a deplorable lack of control and is not tolerated in my dojo. However, often, improving your ukemi will take care of this problem too.

You can refuse to work with somebody, though as I said earlier, this should not be done lightly. If somebody is taking it too close to the edge every time, or has a dirty gi, bad breath, long toenails, or whatever, you can just politely decline to work with him. Even after you have started working with somebody, you can bow and decline to continue working with him. This is perfectly correct etiquette, though is not in the spirit of training. After all, if somebody frightens you on the mat, in a controlled situation, how are you going to face a real threat on the street? Instead, it should spur you on to greater achievements.

Competition

O Sensei reputedly said that there is no competition in aikido. However, there are styles of aikido that do have competition. Tomiki Aikido is something of a mix of aikido and judo, and has competition. From what I've heard, the competition includes both direct sparring and judging on style. Informal competition is common even in other styles, with students vying to progress faster than each other. You could even say that testing is a sort of competition, and for that reason some dojos do not have testing as such, though there is still the comparison of the students to some standard.

Competition is inevitable, at some level, simply because we are all human and somewhat that way inclined. Competition can be useful in a number of ways: giving people motivation, giving people the opportunity to see what works and what doesn't. Unfortunately, if we are to have formal competition, we need to have rules to minimize the risk of injury, and weight classes, and so on. These rules become ingrained, automatic, and that could be dangerous to you in the street. Even Kenji Tomiki supposedly de-emphasized competition, particularly later in life, saying it was mostly designed to draw kids into aikido.

Over-emphasis on competition is certainly deleterious. Since it became an Olympic sport back in the 60s, most judo has evolved to focus only on competition, and has largely dropped techniques which, however useful they may be in the street, are not useful or are banned in competition. Many styles of karate have focused solely on competition, with a greater focus on high kicks which, while spectacular, are not very practical outside the dojo.

Competition is dangerous and a waste of time for new students. Until students know a range of techniques to a high enough standard to use them effectively, good enough control to minimize injuries, and have good enough ukemi to survive heavy falls, any competition will end up being decided by strength and whatever the students knew before starting aikido.

To my mind, the main reason to allow a small amount of competition in the dojo is that in the street, the attacker will not be thinking of cooperating. Thus, we do need to have a feel for doing our techniques on uncooperative ukes.

A way to introduce an element of this into training is perhaps to teach a technique, teach a counter to it, and then let the class struggle a little to see whether the original technique, the counter, or some other option works best. However, such competition should be supervised and contained. Nage should endeavor not to buy into the competitive mindset, and to simply control the flow of the technique.

Ways to Practice

Practicing can vary from very basic practice (kihon), to free-flowing aikido (ki no nagare). It can vary from doing strictly what the instructor tells you, to free style techniques that come from who knows where. It can involve exercises – tai sabaki, ukemi, ki exercises. It can involve complete techniques or studying particular parts of techniques. In any case, the goal should be the development of techniques that flow smoothly and strongly, any hesitation giving your aite an opening to counter your technique.

Tai Sabaki and Aiki Taiso

These "body movements" are a way to train your body in moving correctly. Generally, you want to move from the hips, with your arms extended.

The head moves the hands, the hips move the feet.
O Sensei

You need to be aware of the difference between tsugi ashi – following foot, where you slide the front foot forward then follow it with the back foot, or slide the back foot back and follow it with the front foot, but always keeping the same foot leading – and ayumi ashi, when the feet alternate as in normal walking. You need to be able to move freely in any direction without thought. You need to be able to turn freely without losing your center.

Some aiki taiso such as ikkyo undo and tenkan undo relate to opening movements. Some such as ude fune undo (rowing exercise) relate to throwing. Practicing these movements develops your muscles and the way you use them, what some people call muscle memory.

Aikido – Moving On

Kihon

One person's kihon is another's variation. However, kihon in general are basic techniques. They should be practiced slowly with consistent attention to detail. Otherwise, you will develop sloppy techniques. Lower-ranked people in the dojo might generally fall down for you because you are a black belt, so you'll think it is all right to do it that way. But one day, somebody will clamp down on your wrist and stop you dead. With strong kihon, your technique may not look flashy, but you will always have a sound fallback position.

Kihon can be frustrating, especially at first. There is no opportunity to camouflage technical errors by using speed and momentum. But there is the opportunity to use excessive strength as either uke or nage. It is all too easy for a big strong uke to clamp down on nage and stop them dead. At first, while learning a new technique, just ask them to ease off. Later, you should use the opportunity to feel for the suki necessary to do the technique, for the right position of the hips and hands. When you can't drive through, are your legs in the right position, lined up with your power? Are you pushing into uke's power, or towards where uke is mechanically weak?

A lot can be gained in practicing kihon by slowing down even more than usual. Then you can feel where a technique is problematical. You can feel where you are using a lot of strength, when you are in a poor position, when you are unbalanced.

During kihon, uke must play his part. Poor ukes cause most problems with kihon. Uke should not actively counter by moving to a different position as nage slowly applies kihon technique. For example, when doing ikkyo irimi, uke can become quite difficult just by stepping as nage pushes. This is perfectly reasonable in jiyu waza, but frustrating in kihon. The slower you do the move, the more impossible it can get. Uke should not resist unduly. Nor, on the other hand, should he fall down whether nage is doing something close to a technique or not. In particular, uke should go where nage pushes him, and not fall in some other direction. Uke and nage should work together to perfect kihon.

Jiyu Waza

Jiyu waza is performing free-flowing techniques in a free-form situation – pretty much the opposite of (but based on) kihon. As you are attacked, you flow, you take balance, you apply technique. Uke might attempt to counter you, depending on the groundrules you are working to. They might even succeed. That will teach you where the technique can be lost, where you need to improve your kihon.

The key to doing good aikido in jiyu waza is to move freely, not letting uke hold you down: he can have hold of your arm, but must not be allowed to control your body, your center, and especially not your mind. A certain level of technical ability is beneficial, so that you can think about the strategic situation rather than how to do a particular technique. However, so long as you know several techniques, you will be able to do jiyu waza. Jiyu waza is not the time to learn basic techniques.

A starting point might be to avoid attacks: just move so that uke is not quite able to get a firm hold of you. It is better to give each uke the suki you want them to see, not blatant, but enough to encourage them to do what you want. Move constantly. When you stop moving, you will be trapped, particularly when more than one uke is attacking. Use the mat, moving to open spaces, avoiding becoming trapped in corners or against the edge of the mat. Constantly turn as you perform techniques and between techniques to see who is behind you. Change the level of the openings, from high to low, by lowering or raising your hands, and use the initial position of your hands to initiate the technique. Many techniques can be started both by lowering your arms from a high position, and by raising them from a low one.

It is quite difficult to continually avoid being caught just by evading the attacks, even at a reasonable speed. Furthermore, running away is the wrong mindset. You should control the mat. Throwing an attacker is quite effective in clearing a space, particularly with techniques like irimi nage tenkan and kote gaeshi, that allow nage to take uke around his body. Generally, you do not want to do an immobilization when attacked by several people as while you are dealing with one, the others would then pile on top of you. Some immobilizations such as sankyo and ikkyo can, however, be used effectively as throws or to clear a space.

Jiyu waza should not become an exercise in strength. When nage comes to an impasse because uke is too strong, it is generally because of a technical error. For example, nage might try to do a particular technique when uke is coming from an angle that does not lend itself to this particular technique. When stopped in one way, move, change direction. Thus, if an ikkyo is blocked, a second attempt by cutting down at a different angle might work. If you can't push up to do ikkyo, perhaps you can push down and do kote gaeshi.

Often, nage loses the advantage (sente) because he loses control over the flow of the technique. For example, nage might turn, getting uke going well, then falter. This disrupts the flow and gives uke an excellent opportunity to stop nage or even counter. The pause may be because nage has to think about where to go next. For more advanced aikidoka it could be from too much practicing of kihon, which can build these pauses into a technique. An appropriate mix of kihon and jiyuwaza will provide both a sound technical base and develop a flowing style.

Nage should develop a habit of varying the techniques. It is no use to do the same technique over and over again, because in a real situation even the dumbest attacker will eventually realize what is going to happen next and will stop you or, worse, counter you. However, with beginners it is more important that they keep moving rather than worrying unduly about doing all of the techniques they know.

Aikido – Moving On

The jiyu waza might be a continuing set of attacks by one or more ukes, or it might be a series of techniques and counter techniques (see later section). In either case, the principles should be the same, with attention being paid to correct movement, position, and techniques.

Jiyu waza is necessary to counter the tendency to focus on one thing whether it is working or not. We typically practice a set technique from a set attack. This is a good way to refine our technique, but we have to go beyond this. Rather than only having one technique in mind, we should learn to look for openings, to flow, to move according to the rhythm of the interaction between uke and nage, while controlling that rhythm. This free flowing of technique is real aikido. The rest is just practicing for it.

Attacks

For us to practice a defensive art, we need to learn to attack. This is a little paradoxical, and some people reject the notion, but their aikido will suffer for it. Even more important, we might need to protect a third party, like a child. This might require that we attack an attacker. Most people do not learn good attacks in aikido. Nevertheless, we do need to develop sound punching and kicking abilities.

Especially at first, it is important that uke give his nage something to practice with. Generally, this means that uke should keep pushing or pulling, should work at maintaining the connection with nage. This will also result in improved ukemi.

Anita - hanmi handachi kokyu nage

Aikido, Men, and Women

Aikido can work for almost anybody. However, men and women do tend to be different in size, strength, and attitude. These differences are not absolute: there are small, weak, timid men, and large, strong, aggressive women, but, on average, women are smaller, weaker and less aggressive than men.

Two things I often see particularly annoy me. One is people who slam their ukes around like they are just pieces of meat. Typically, the people who do this are larger than their ukes, and their attitude is that the smaller people just have to take it. There is some justification for this attitude if the smaller person is the nage, as attackers on the street come in all sizes. There is much less justification for it with a small uke.

The other thing that annoys me is when I see people being difficult ukes. There is a time and a place for this, of course, but when nage is having difficulty in throwing uke, that is not the time. All you will do is frustrate nage. Learning aikido is a cooperative venture, not a competition. When you stop nage throwing you in this way, all you are doing is being annoying. Typically, this occurs when nage is learning a new technique or a new way of doing a technique from what they are used to. Typically it is done by larger, higher-ranked aikidoka. This is not in the spirit of aikido, and there is no value in it.

I can stop most people from throwing me. All I need to do is to attack with a little less commitment, and start to shut down the technique before nage has a chance. This sort of attitude has no relevance to aikido, however. People in the street do not attack holding back. Nor is nage restricted to one technique, known in advance. Mat aikido is just a way to practice. It is a way to learn aikido; it is not aikido itself. Students need to encourage their partners to learn, no matter what their size or ability.

Attitude is also different between men and women, between small and large people. More guys than women are quite happy to bang people around, even if they get banged around themselves. Aikido is mellower than most martial arts. We practice blending and harmonizing rather than confrontation, making aikido ideal for smaller people.

It can be quite difficult for a woman who has never been in a fight in her life to be forceful, whether physically or mentally. (Which comes to the same thing in the end.) It is quite scary for anybody the first time somebody comes at you with a stick (jo or bokken) and tries to whack you on the head – I remember the first time somebody swung a bokken at my head almost thirty years ago in the Reading University gym. It is doubly scary for women. Ultimately, there is nothing for it but to stand there and do technique, but there is no reason to expect women to be as naturally inclined to do so as guys – and not many 200 lb. guys would willingly stand there and let a 400 lb. gorilla take a swing at them, yet that is comparable to a 100 lb. woman being attacked by a 200 lb. guy.

Women and men are vulnerable in different places. Just as guys are protective about their crotch, so women are protective of their breasts. Breasts can get hit, grabbed, and knelt on in the dojo by accident, and the guys should think of this in the context of their being hit, grabbed, or knelt on in the groin. In either case, if there is a problem, protective equipment is available and should be used.

This all comes back to why we are doing aikido. I hope that everybody reading this book has the perspective that we are all doing aikido to learn, rather than to be bullies. Thus, as long as we are considerate of our ukes, there should be no problems whether we are men or women, large or small, strong or not so strong.

Part 3: Techniques

Advanced Techniques

There are lots of techniques. I've never counted them but there must be at least a thousand. Each basic technique has variations: irimi, tenkan (omote, ura), some in between, different ways to get into the technique – particularly for different attacks – different ways to complete the technique. No matter how long you study, there will be new techniques to master. Visit a new school, study under a different teacher, and there will be new ones, or at least ways of doing them that you've never seen before. It isn't important how many there are, and I doubt if anybody knows them all.

What is important is that we keep searching. We should try different ways before we settle on how we want to do a technique, and even then keep looking. Consider why one sensei does it differently from another. Is it body style or mental style that makes the difference? Is it historical, that his teacher did it that way? (Even though we all trace our lineage back to O Sensei.) Any technique provides opportunities to deal with an attacker. Any attack provides the attacker opportunities to deal with you. Your "investment style" might be high risk or low risk. You might like to take risks in exposing yourself to attack (a wide suki) in order to get a better shot at your opponent, or you might play conservatively. You might do one thing on one day and another on another day. You might be strong and like using your strength, or you might be physically weak and not have that option. However you play the game, there are opportunities and liabilities.

If we really study technique, we will come to understand some of them rather than taking them for granted. I've heard it said that by shodan we should have one technique we do really well, by nidan, two, and so on. (So by ninth dan we should do most of the major techniques really well.) We should know how many steps are required to complete the technique, what the posture should be at each step, and how to transition from one to the other. Generally, beginners take too many steps, and the fewer the steps used the better. But don't go to the other extreme of planting yourself and trying to move uke with strength alone.

Students always want to get to the flashy techniques. We get bored doing basic techniques, if only because we don't understand the kihon well enough to work on improving how we do it. But basic techniques are not just the first ones to learn; they are the foundation for the flashy ones. We might be able to do a flashy technique on a cooperative uke without good basics, but we will not be able to do it reliably on an uncooperative one, or even a different cooperative uke that wasn't like the first one.

Of the different ways to do each technique, Saito Sensei talks about basic (kotai or kihon), moving or flexible (jutai), and flowing (ki no nagare) techniques. As we progress, we should improve in all three ways.

With basic techniques, uke and nage are standing still. What is important is learning the mechanics of the technique. Which foot goes where, at what point and how you change the hand position, and so on. How you move off line. How you take uke's balance. As uke, how you take the fall. Kihon is also our fallback mode. When we intend to move before uke grasps our wrist but mess up and he clamps down, we are back to the basics. If we never learned how to disengage uke's grip as it turns our hand purple, we are stuck.

Some people dislike the discipline of kihon, rationalizing that they can always do something. This is often true, but to achieve mu shin we must have excellent technique, to be able to do virtually any technique impeccably without rehearsal or hesitation. We get this command of the basic building blocks of aikido by studying kihon.

Doing technique from movement is much the same as kihon. There is no major difference from basic, static technique (particularly with a good uke). However, start your movement about when uke starts his. Be just a little off line as he completes his attack. Move your hand just a little so that he doesn't quite get to settle but does still catch your arm. The result should be that the technique looks the same, but that uke is much easier to move. His attack should not change. He should still come in intending to grasp your wrist (or whatever the attack is), but it should be easier to move him. As we progress, the necessary amount of movement gets smaller and smaller.

Ki no nagare is the same thing as moving technique, but more exaggerated. Now you want to draw uke out and blend with him. Ideally, it should be effortless, as if uke isn't even there, yet the technique should work itself. This is what Musashi meant in the Book of the Void. It is, as he says, based on practice, lots of practice, and is not void – empty – in the sense of lack of knowledge. Rather, it is empty in the sense of being ego-less, without logical thought, without the intervention of the conscious mind.

Ki no nagare is easier to do with a committed attack by uke. This does not mean that uke falls down for you, just that he attacks without thinking of the last time he attacked, nor of the technique you are going to do, nor of the ukemi. This is easy enough for a lot of techniques, but harder when the ukemi is difficult. There is a nice koshi nage from shomen uchi, where nage enters as uke strikes, and throws him almost without contact. However, it is quite difficult for uke to attack correctly a second time for this technique, which makes it hard to practice.

Kihon is basic and should be practiced most often. As a guide, aim to do a technique ten times static for every time with movement, and ten with movement for every flowing technique. If you are doing ki no nagare technique and there is a problem, immediately default back to moving technique. If there is a problem with moving technique, default to static. However, it is also important to begin doing flowing techniques early in your aikido career. Otherwise, you may become too stiff and mechanical.

There are good, bad, and ugly techniques. Good techniques are ones that work effectively and reliably (which implies that you have practiced them a lot and believe in them). Bad and ugly techniques are ones that are ineffective. Typically, they are the ones that you haven't practiced enough to "own" them yet. Very often, all it takes to make them part of you is more practice, though there may be technical errors that need to be corrected.

Generally, if it looks good it is good, but pretty techniques are not always effective. They are like bright shiny lures – they just might be more effective in trapping students rather than for practical application. Pretty techniques and techniques you like are all very well. However, aikido is a martial art, and you shouldn't waste much time on ineffective techniques just because they are fun to do and make you look good. Still, effectiveness does tend to look beautiful.

Ukemi

The most important class of technique to learn in order to progress in aikido is ukemi. Ukemi is whatever uke does to protect himself, whether a high fall, a roll, or just tapping out when a technique hurts. Most importantly, it is movement to protect uke's body from injury. Thus it includes moving your head back when nage strikes, so that he does not have to bloody your nose to make a technique effective. More generally, uke should move with the technique, neither getting ahead nor lagging behind.

Ukemi should be reliable, effective, and automatic by the time you reach shodan. As you move on, you have more rank, you are getting older, and it is easy to grow lazy about ukemi. This is disastrous. Conversely, there is nothing so likely to impress your students of the importance of ukemi as seeing their sensei continuing to practice it, and to do it so well they are jealous.

Stages of Ukemi

- I'm so tough (mostly guys)
- Owwww (mostly guys, resisting)
- Please don't hurt me
- This isn't so bad
- Wow, this is fun
- I'm invincible (the best phase, and usually the longest)
- Let's not play too hard
- See, I can still take ukemi

It seems that there is a minimum energy, a stalling speed, for doing ukemi. If nage throws you fast and hard (and correctly), the ukemi pretty much takes care of itself. If nage throws softly and slowly, uke needs to supply enough momentum to make the technique work, or the fall can knock the breath out of him. This is rather strange and I haven't figured out why it is. Uke needs to blend with nage, minimizing the risk should nage decide to change direction or speed. Be careful not to fall too soon, in case nage changes direction. Don't be late, either. In the next figure, uke is reaching down to the mat to convert the fall into an easy roll.

A common criticism of aikido by other martial artists is that it looks too easy, that uke is tanking for nage. It should look easy. After all, it is intended to allow smaller people to throw bigger ones. However, if uke has to tank for nage, there is something wrong.

Don't mistake this for an injunction to always resist taking ukemi. This is quite dangerous to uke if nage knows what he is doing, and frustrating if he doesn't. If nage knows his stuff, resistance will make you hit the mat a lot harder and may well put undue stress on your joints. And you go anyway. If nage is learning, it is frustrating when your uke always resists to the point that nothing works, and nage will not get better that way. Be a generous uke, and give resistance that is reasonable for the rank and ability of nage, but always with a goal of helping him improve. If as uke you are stopping nage more than 10% of the time, you are being too difficult. You might claim to be doing it for uke's benefit, but most likely you are doing it for your own ego. That is not harmonious.

As you progress, ukemi just becomes part of your movement. It isn't separate from an attack or, for that matter, from kaeshi waza or henka waza. You give nage an extension to work with, whether a blow or a grab, and you keep that energy going, ready to flow into whatever comes next.

Ukemi as an opportunity to learn

There is no substitute for feeling a really great technician doing technique, and you need great ukemi to survive the experience comfortably enough to see what he does. As we can't download the details of a technique directly into our brains, we have to use all our senses to see how a skilled technician is doing the technique. We can watch, and miss a lot. We can even videotape a technique, and play it back frame by frame, but video resolution is just not that high and we can see less detail on video than if we are watching in real life. When we are uke, however, we can feel subtle movements that we cannot see. A quite small change in position can have a large effect on uke. Of course, we might not be able to feel much either, unless the technician gives us time to feel it. If the technique is performed quickly enough, we are still likely to miss most of it.

Taking ukemi. Uke should have a strong extension to avoid damaging his shoulder as he hits the mat and to convert a mostly vertical and sudden stop into a more gradual roll.

When we are working with a beginner, it is good to be uke. We can watch him do something, and see it isn't quite right, but not be able to figure out what the problem is until we feel it. One concern with beginners is that they are prone to do surprising things. You do have to be ready for anything, as a beginner might do something quite tricky even without any intention of hurting you. This is good ukemi training.

Dojos do develop their own "agreements". There is a generally unspoken collusion that students will respond in certain ways. That is why it is crucial to work with beginners, who have not become "trained", and also to visit other dojos, even other styles, and experience other ways of doing familiar techniques. Most of the strange variations are viable, and sometimes different people will react in ways that make our favorite techniques not work satisfactorily.

Ukemi and Technique: you can't have one without the other

Ukemi and technique cannot be considered separately. One implies the other. To be a nage you must have an uke. After a time, and in some situations, the roles become somewhat interchangeable. One person might begin as uke, and change roles, and this might happen more than once.

Which of these is yin and which is yang? Male and female, black and white, light and dark, right and wrong, nage and uke, attack and defense?

Doing Technique

As discussed earlier, technique starts before contact is made, even for a grab, and ends after contact is broken. Like two bodies in space interacting through gravitation, as a potential attacker approaches, the strength of the interaction increases. As he moves away, it diminishes. An encounter might result in physical contact, or just result in an interaction at a distance as an attack is forestalled by your attitude.

The most important part of a technique is escaping, evading, or suppressing the attack, whether it is a punch, a grab, or some other attack. Otherwise, the result will likely be ai-uchi. The next most important part is to put uke off balance, mentally and physically (kuzushi). This can also suppress an impending attack. Once I have his balance, I can do any technique I choose. The application of the technique (kake) is the next step. It is important, but quite easy to do if the previous two parts were done well. Some people, especially beginners, think most about kake, applying force to make it work when they get stuck. As a result, they might end up hurting themselves and other people. Typically, they do the technique slowly through the difficult parts, then they see the throw at the end and slam their uke to the ground. This is not a good way to practice. It is far better to work on just the escape and kuzushi than just on the kake. The throw itself should still be crisp and clean, but should be a consequence of the preceding movements.

Finally, there is completion (zanshin). This literally translates as "remaining spirit", when you should remain aware of the technique and of uke for a moment longer than the technique itself lasts, before moving on. This is like the follow-through in western sports. You can have too much zanshin, not letting go of the moment, but most students don't exhibit enough.

Escape and Making the Connection

When you are attacked, you need to escape the intent of the attack. However, to do technique, you also need to connect to uke.

Escape may involve arm movements, but the body movements, getting out of the target zone, are more important. We can escape an attack by using irimi, tenkan, or tenshin. We can also just move sideways off the line of attack.

Irimi is a linear movement towards uke, moving diagonally off the line of attack so that uke's attack misses. It is generally done facing uke, and finishing behind him, even at shikaku (dead point) where uke cannot effectively continue the attack. Irimi can, however, be done with one's back to uke, and in front of as well as behind uke, though nage should not be too far from uke. In any case, irimi results in momentary loss of the target by uke. Uke, if allowed to do so, will turn to reacquire his target, which tends to put him into a technique such as irimi nage.

The timing of irimi is to move as uke attacks. Don't think of avoiding the attack, think of giving uke a good opportunity to hit you and entering past it as he tries. Generally, an irimi breaks the connection uke establishes by attacking. The connection is then re-established by nage from a different place and used to execute the technique.

Unlike irimi, tenkan and tenshin continue uke's connection, though extending it to the point where uke is forced to move or fall. Nage then increases the loss of balance until uke does fall.

Tenkan is a rotary movement with nage's center moving in a similar direction to irimi, and again can be done to the front or behind uke. The rotation can be advantageous by making a punch only a glancing blow, and in providing momentum for the throw.

Tenshin is a step back and off line. It is not a step to the side and a turn, as this could leave nage vulnerable to a blow to the kidney. If well executed against a determined attack, tenshin leads into a technique. If not well executed, if the attack is not committed or if nage's timing is off, tenshin merely re-establishes ma-ai along a different line. Thus, if nage moves in tenshin, and uke lets go and doesn't follow, uke and nage should be about at the same distance as when they started. If uke grabs hold and locks solid, nage must have been a little late. (Nage should then change direction and execute a technique.)

There are other directions for escape than these, but they are less generally applicable. A sideways movement can be made similar to a tenshin escape, increasing the distance between uke and nage. Stepping straight back is generally unwise unless you can run backwards faster than your aite can run forwards. Stepping straight into uke tends to be painful – knees hitting knees – unless you can catch uke in a withdrawing movement. Still, moving in can be better than standing still.

Whatever the escape movement, nage should still be in hanmi, with the focus of the kamae still being where nage needs power. This is often towards uke (in his new position) or where nage plans to take him next. In the case of a yokomen attack, nage should face the danger – uke's arm.

A key concept of Aikido Schools of Ueshiba (ASU) is marubashi. This is the idea of taking the center. Rather than evading uke's attack, nage cuts the attack down and forces uke off balance in so doing. This is different from most of the aikido I'd been taught previously. However, the concept is not that different if we look at a technique relativistically. Instead of nage moving out of the way of uke's attack, nage moves uke's attack off the center, capturing uke's center. There is still no clash of force.

Kuzushi

Kuzushi is an undermining of uke. It can involve taking his balance physically and mentally, and maneuvering him into an awkward and weak position. You can do this by influencing his mind or his body, and should ideally do both. You can take the balance by shifting in time or space. If uke is trying to grab your wrist, and you move it away from him just as he grasps it, he will tend to reach for it, losing his balance a little. You can do this straight back, but usually it is more effective to do it off to the side as well (tenshin). You can do it by moving in, too, generally accompanied by an atemi. If uke is moving in to grab with a set pace and you change the timing at which he will arrive at his destination, this will also mess up the attack. The mechanics were addressed earlier.

There are lots of exercises for manipulating uke at the point of contact (whether a grasp or a blow). Generally you want to draw uke out, because it is easier to then flow from the over-extension into the technique. You can move uke's balance behind him by initially extending to the side, as in tenchi nage. It isn't necessary to take uke's balance so completely he falls over. Even if nage merely disturbs uke's balance, he is then in a better position to apply technique as uke can no longer resist effectively.

Techniques can be classified according to whether the balance is broken to uke's front or back.* The following table shows typical kuzushi for different techniques. While there are many ways to do any technique, a common way to break uke's balance for the beginning of these techniques is identified in the table. If you draw an equilateral triangle with uke's feet at two of the points, the apex can be either in front of or behind uke. In this situation, we can think of uke as a tripod with a missing leg. A tripod is, of course, very stable on three legs, but falls once one of them is removed.

---

* In judo, kuzushi is sometimes analyzed into eight directions. In reality there are an infinite number of directions, but, particularly in kihon, these two are enough to worry about, and encompass the others.

Kuzushi for Some Different Techniques

Front Triangle Point	Back Triangle Point
Ikkyo through gokyo, irimi. Sankyo projection forwards	Ikkyo through gokyo, tenkan. Nikkyo projection. Sankyo projection backwards
Shiho nage irimi	Shiho nage tenkan
Kote gaeshi irimi	Kote gaeshi tenkan
Irimi nage tenkan (one way)	Sokumen irimi nage. Irimi nage tenkan (another way)
Kaiten nage	Tenchi nage
Most forms of koshi nage	Tenchi koshi nage
Ude kimi nage	Aiki otoshi. Sumi otoshi

In some techniques, the direction of kuzushi is predominantly one way. Ikkyo irimi, for example, involves breaking uke's balance to his front (omote), and keeping it there, though moving through different directions of extension to the front and twisting his body somewhat. In other techniques, the kuzushi might change dramatically. For example, in a typical irimi nage, uke is first bent forward, turned around, and then bent backwards. In a more advanced irimi, nage might take uke's balance back right from the start. In a typical sankyo, kuzushi might be taken forward, then backwards, then forwards again. For sankyo nage, a third change in direction might be applied, leading to a forwards throw. If nage fails to take uke's balance in the appropriate direction at the appropriate step of the technique, uke can be quite difficult to throw, and may counter the technique.

Taking uke's balance backwards. Nage should take uke's balance to a point between and behind uke's heels

The feeling with which to take kuzushi is like catching a fish with an artificial lure. The fish comes to grab the lure. If we let him grab it and taste it before striking, he realizes it is artificial, and spits it out. If we strike too soon, we whip it away before he can grab it. If we are too energetic, even if he's taken the lure we can rip the lure out of his mouth. Similarly, with an uke, we want him to grab at the "lure" with the intent to catch it and the belief than he can. We want to present the target in such a way that he grabs it almost by reflex (offering a suki). If we are too obvious in presenting the suki, he may shy away. If we are too subtle, he might miss the opportunity. We want him to think he has us, and to move the lure as he grabs in such a way that we have the advantage, leaving uke off balance.

This is a very nice feeling when it is done right. Nage feels as if uke is not resisting, just flowing nicely. Uke feels as if he has been sucked into a vortex rather than just overpowered. However, it is important not to become too enamored with this feeling. "Flowing" is nice when it works, but it often doesn't on the street or with beginners, and then you have to be ready with kihon: good strong technique executed precisely from a good posture.

Taking uke's balance forwards. Nage should take uke's balance to a point between and in front of uke's toes.

Of course, uke might not "bite". He might have a plan of attack already programmed in his head that is different from what we are expecting. Or he might be leery of grabbing something that seems a little too obvious. If he is preprogrammed and we can slip off line, uke will do the job for us. If uke is not committing, perhaps there is no real threat, and we can just let it go. Perhaps there is a very real threat, but uke is too smart to be taken in by our lure. Then uke might be too close, and we have to stand him off, possibly doing technique in the process, possibly just shoving him away.

The other side of the coin is that nage must keep his own balance. Otherwise, he will not be able to effectively and powerfully apply technique without being countered. All that I have said that nage should do to uke, nage should avoid doing to himself or allowing uke to do to him (until it is his turn to be uke). In particular, nage should not over-extend himself, he should keep his center of gravity within his base area, and he should control his own balance and momentum.

The way nage moves his own hands can contribute vitally to controlling uke, particularly when escaping from a grasp. The hands are an expression of the entire person. If uke holds strongly, nage can manipulate uke entirely through the hands. Thus, nage lifting his hands like a sword (or a beer mug –

hence bieru waza) disturbs not only uke's grip, but his entire body, setting him up for a throw such as sokumen irimi nage. Cutting down can similarly be used to apply ikkyo, nikkyo, sankyo, or yonkyo, or for throwing with shiho nage, irimi nage, and so on. The figure below shows nage controlling uke through moving her arm, taking her balance and eventually throwing her with this connection. Her center of gravity is clearly off to one side and unsupported, and she is running to catch up and avoid falling to the mat.

This discussion has mostly been framed in physical terms. However, balance is as much mental as physical. You can influence one by the other. If somebody thinks you are about to push him, for example, he will often lean into your push. Similarly, if somebody is intimidated, it will be easier to take his balance physically. This influencing of uke's physical balance by taking his mind is the basis of the "no touch" throws sometimes seen in demonstrations.

Nage must take uke's balance while keeping his own

Another aspect of mental/physical kuzushi is the way you try to throw uke. If uke is coming forwards and you try to make him go back, you will feel resistance. This is obvious, yet people often create resistance for themselves by trying to throw uke in a way that creates resistance rather than harmony. You should make uke want to fall. Too strong a grip or too sudden a movement might have the effect of making uke freeze rather than fall.

A more subtle aspect of this is that if uke is resisting, he is using muscles, and muscles have a twitch reflex as discussed earlier. Sometimes you can lightly "bounce" uke in one direction and take his balance in another. Kokyu ho is an excellent opportunity to practice this.

Kake

While often over emphasized in practice, the actual throw or hold is an important part of the exercise. It should be applied crisply and accurately. Nage should feel little or no resistance, but if he does he should cut through it rather than meeting it.

If, for example, nage stops uke's movement and tries to push it in another direction, he will meet resistance. He should avoid this by going around that point, making the corners of the technique circular. On the other hand, nage's movement should not feel tentative. Nage should be quite crisp and definite in all his moves.

We all know aikidoka who can throw us strongly who, nevertheless do not hurt us. We know other people who manage to crank our arms just a little bit too much at the wrong place. The difference is technique, awareness, and attitude.

Zanshin

Nage should complete the technique and move on. The feeling of connectedness, zanshin, is critical to good aikido, and is indispensable to flowing technique. Students are often prone to cutting techniques short. Instead, there should be a mindfulness of uke and nage's connection to uke before (senshin), during (tsushin) and after (zanshin) the technique. In henka waza or multiple attack situations, the mindfulness should flow from one attack to the next, whether the attacks are by one uke or several.

Similarly, uke should feel this connection in doing his part, attacking and taking ukemi. If the roles of uke and nage change (kaeshi waza), connection should be felt as one person attacks, takes ukemi, is attacked, takes the balance, and so on, but control of the connection should change with the role. Whoever controls the connection is nage.

Zanshin. Don't cut the technique short, but don't hold onto it either.

Kaeshi and Henka Waza

Flexibility is life. If uke gets the chance to struggle and won't let you do the initial technique you might need to change to another. Almost any combination of techniques can be used for either kaeshi or henka waza (which are not really different), even going from one technique, adjusting, and going back to the same technique. Thus, you can go from ikkyo to ikkyo, either turning out of the technique or, on meeting resistance, easing up, re-establishing a solid base, and again doing ikkyo in a different direction or with a different timing. Changing from shiho nage to irimi nage would be another example. If uke turns out of the shiho nage, instead of being harsher and applying more power (which would be especially inappropriate with a beginner), follow uke's direction, extend his arm out and draw him into an irimi nage.

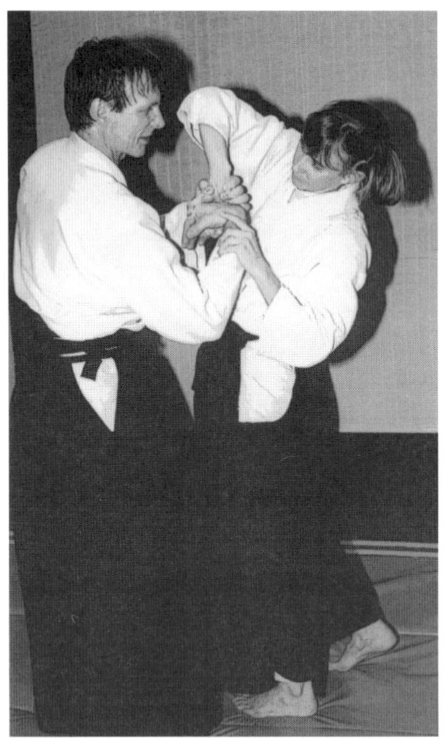

Kaeshi Waza: Nikkyo to Sankyo. Aite must flow with the technique, getting ahead of it in order to apply kaeshi waza.

In this figure, the original uke has flowed with his partner's nikkyo and is turning it into a sankyo. Resistance to the nikkyo would have allowed that technique to succeed. By going with aite's power and pulling his hand off his partner's shoulder, the original uke was able to rotate his hand, capture his partner's balance, and complete the technique.

When you change direction, find another suki and then do a second technique, you must do this smoothly and with conviction (mu shin), or uke can stop you again. The slightest pause in execution will give aite the opportunity to resist. To flow smoothly from one technique to the next, you must be familiar with basic techniques. You don't have time to hesitate, still less to stop and think.

In this sort of situation, the difference between uke and nage is the degree of control of the technique at any instant. Even with two evenly matched people, there is almost no chance that the amount of control will be equal in a given situation. One way to study control, how it shifts, and how to manipulate this shift, is to do a technique repeatedly without releasing uke. This approach works well with either ikkyo or, particularly for henka waza, shiho nage. In one case, repeatedly apply the technique, let uke slip out or do ukemi (which is not that different) and reapply the technique (henka waza). In the other case, allow uke to slip out from under it and let him do the technique to you, then you slip out from under his technique and do it back on him (kaeshi waza). Look for what lets you take back the control. There is something, a feeling, beyond the mere mechanics of the technique: how and when, rather than just what. This is the flow of energy, aiki.

Another good practice for henka waza is to do a series of techniques, letting uke take ukemi and get back to his feet without letting go of him, then doing the next technique on him. For example, start with shiho nage, then do kote gaeshi, then ikkyo, back to kote gaeshi, and finally shiho nage. You must stay ahead of uke, so that before he has recovered his balance from escaping (taking ukemi) from shiho nage, you are already taking his balance for kote gaeshi. This exercise should result in a single flowing movement from start to finish, the tempo and direction being varied so that you can maintain control and do each technique with the feeling of holding uke down, just easing up enough to encourage uke to keep trying. It should be like bouncing a basketball: now holding uke down, now letting him up so that you can knock him back down.

In doing kaeshi waza, on the other hand, you should be escaping from this feeling of being held down and applying the same feeling to your partner. As the one who is trying to change the movement to do kaeshi waza, it is critical that you not indiscriminately settle firmly and resist. If you do, you may or may not succeed in stopping nage but that will depend on relative strength and ability and on how well nage is applying the technique. If you are about the same size, strength, and ability, nage should succeed every time. You should not resist, but neither should you let your partner take total control and do whatever he wants to you. What you should do is to flow with the technique, and divert your partner's power to bring about his downfall. If you leave it too late, just do the ukemi. Too early, and he will do a different technique on you. A slight resistance at the right time followed by a sudden release, may help you control your aite. There should be the same feeling of connection whether you are doing technique or ukemi (though from the other side).

For example, if somebody is doing shiho nage on you and you resist, he will throw harder and you will hit the ground even harder. If, however, as he drives your arm through the initial moves, you flow with it and over-extend his power, you can continue and throw him with a kokyu extension. Alternatively, let him take your hand over the top of his head, but extend as he does so. Then you can turn and bring him into position for you to do an irimi nage. In either case, it is easy to do with a careless or cooperative partner. What is difficult is to give him confidence that he has control of the situation, then to flow with it so well that he doesn't even realize he has lost control until it is too late for him to recover it.

Counter techniques should flow naturally out of your aikido. They can be practiced slowly and carefully, from one known technique to another, from a technique to a counter technique, an expression of the interaction between uke and nage. They should not be an exercise in strength any more than other parts of aikido. Nage should flow out of the technique that uke is attempting to apply, and into a more advantageous position. Using more strength than you can handle, and the rigidity that typically goes with this, will prevent fluidity, and the result may be that somebody gets hurt, the original technique may be applied anyway, or, worse, the whole exercise may stop in deadlock.

In practicing kaeshi waza, the original uke should still attack in a determined fashion, forcing nage to defend himself. The original nage should make a definite attempt to apply the technique. It might be necessary to ease off considerably at first, while both parties learn the techniques, but eventually the entire exchange must take place at normal speed, with fluid movement.

Ukemi is the key to kaeshi waza. With good ukemi, neither party is worried about taking the fall. As the original technique is applied, feel the direction the flow of power is going. Don't try to stop it, just redirect it to where you have a better position and all that goes with it (posture, balance, and opportunity), capture your aite's balance, and apply your technique. This flow will grow out of your ukemi and jiyu waza practice when you become proficient enough.

Free Practice

A free-flowing interplay with nage and uke changing roles can go on for quite a time without either being able to apply a decisive technique. There will be a temptation to use strength or to speed up to beat your aite, but that merely gives a short term satisfaction from throwing uke and you will not be learning the more valuable skill. Strength and speed do have a place, but the important issues are who controls themselves and the other person, who best maintains their center, mentally and physically, and who has superior technical ability. As you age, you will lose strength and speed, and must develop skill and wisdom to replace them.

Getting Ahead of Uke

To maintain effective control of a technique, nage must be ahead of uke and keep this relationship. This is the opposite of allowing kaeshi waza. However, if nage gets ahead of uke and applies technique as hard and fast as he can, it will be difficult for uke to survive in one piece. Instead, nage should allow uke to catch up to the extent that he can do good ukemi, while retaining the ability to get further ahead at any time. Nage should be relaxed, and uke scrambling to keep up.

Classifying Attacks and Techniques

There are two kinds of attacks, grabs and strikes, with some like kata tori men uchi where uke both grabs and strikes. Grabs are somewhat easier to deal with, because uke intends to establish a physical connection with us that we can then manipulate. Strikes are somewhat more intimidating, especially with a weapon, but inherently involve movement, so there is less tendency to stand there and let uke settle into his attack.

A good grabbing attack will involve more than just taking hold of nage's arm or gi. It should establish a connection between centers also, and the intent is to actually put nage into a position where he is controlled by the grab. Katate tori, for example, can be established from shomen uchi, by uke cutting down nage's defense and holding nage off balance.

The arms are the main targets for uke to grab onto, either one hand to one hand, two hands to one hand, or two hands to two hands. If uke grabs with one hand, he is probably going to be trying to hit you with the other. By immediately executing an atemi, you can pre-empt that part of the attack and make the situation a defense from a pure grab. If you are too late, you can apply technique to the striking arm, dealing with the grab at a convenient time.

Kata tori, eri tori, hiji tori and so on are techniques that involve uke grabbing nage's gi. This is feasible on the street when he is wearing a substantial coat, but in warmer climates a tee shirt is commonly the heaviest clothing, and that is often hard to grip and liable to tear anyway. Where I grew up I'd hear stories about people sewing razor blades behind the lapels of their coats to prevent this sort of attack.

Chokes and strangles are a sort of grip where you especially don't want uke to get a good hold. Standing strangles from the front are not much threat unless the attacker is much bigger and stronger than you, or unless they are applied after he gets control of your body, as the attacker is right in front where you can punch, kick, and gouge out his eyes. Chokes from behind are much more serious. In any case, uke must establish some degree of control of nage's body to effectively apply any choke, and nage should prevent this control.

A word of warning about practicing strangles. Strangles flatten the blood vessels in the neck, making the victim unconscious within seconds by starving the brain of oxygen. If this state is continued, brain damage will occur, and finally death will ensue. If a strangle is done to the neck of someone that has some degree of arterial disease – and that is likely to be anybody over the age of forty years old – the vessels might not readily open again, perhaps causing brain damage. Judoka often practice strangles on each other, and there does not seem to be an epidemic of judoka with brain damage, but they are generally young when they are involved in competition. Still, there is an element of risk at any age. You must make up your own mind about the risks.

Chokes involve cutting off the air supply through pressure on the windpipe. This takes longer than a strangle to have an effect, as there is still air in uke's lungs. However, pressure on the windpipe can collapse it permanently, requiring urgent medical intervention if the victim is to survive. Thus, chokes should be avoided.

The strikes typically used in aikido are sometimes criticized as being impractical, that nobody with any knowledge or training would attack that way. However, there is no way to attack that is so dumb that somebody somewhere hasn't used it. Additionally, while they may not be the attacks of choice for a trained boxer or a karateka, they do cover a lot of street possibilities.

Shomen uchi, in particular, is sometimes dismissed as totally impractical, and shuto (knife hand) strikes in karate aren't usually done that way or at that target (the forehead). Shuto strikes may be more akin to a jodan tsuki. Still, I've heard of at least one karateka who used shomen strikes effectively in sparring. In any case, the range from yokomen uchi through shomen uchi to gyaku yokomen uchi covers the range of overhead strikes to the head, such as with a tire iron.

Yokomen uchi covers not only head strikes with a weapon or beer bottle, but also a roundhouse punch, which is perhaps one of the commonest punches thrown in brawls. The danger with these is not that you don't know they're coming. Unless you aren't even looking that way, you see it coming a mile away. However, these punches are extremely powerful, often with the entire weight of the attacker behind them. The key is to move into them or away from them, so that you take care of the problem before it comes close to landing, or after the power has dissipated (and while moving off the line of attack).

Tsuki is typically taught as somewhere between a chudan or gedan tsuki, as a punch to the stomach. It is often done with the hand turned fingers up and the wrist bent, and is often not a serious attack at all. In the street, most people want to punch you in the head. They may well not commit, but might try to crowd you and jab when they think you have let them get too close for you to defend yourself. Karateka might attack with a straight punch as it is fast and powerful. You might have to deal with one or two before you can control the rhythm enough to do something. Some styles have a squarer stance than others. Boxers might jab or hook, trying to get around your defenses.

A backfist should be dealt with something like a jab. In a way, it is easier, as you have a deflection angle. However, a good backfist attack will lead with the elbow, and this can be more difficult to deal with.

Kicks are more and more commonly used on the street, perhaps because of the influence of movies and TV shows like Karate Kid and Power Rangers. Kicks have more range and power, but are usually not executed well in the street. (And if you are attacked by a trained martial artist, it comes down to who is better trained, who can take more punishment, and who is bigger.) Like a backfist leading with an elbow, most kicks should lead with the knee.

Elbows, knees, body, and head can also be used for strikes if the attacker gets close enough. Of course, you should have the attacker controlled before he gets close to you, but this isn't necessarily easy. Probably more concern is that these close-in weapons can be used during a technique. As a common example, students often leave themselves open when doing sankyo, when they let uke get his elbow too close to nage's face. In doing shiho nage, they can leave the back and kidneys open to a strike. Irimi nage can leave nage open to an elbow strike, and so on. You should look for opportunities for atemi, both for nage to use against uke during a technique, and for opportunities for uke to attack nage that you need to prevent.

An attack will usually continue until somebody is out of action, and might be continued until the victim is dead. There might be a quick exchange of attack and defense before the attacker backs off and decides to bother somebody else, but this is probably the exception. A fight might stop when somebody gets too tired to continue. It might result in an eventual stalemate. It might stop when somebody gets too hurt to continue, or when somebody is knocked down. However, you'd best assume that an altercation will continue as long as the attacker is able to continue it. It probably will not be a single attack with a nice crisp finish, except in the dojo. It will probably not be one attacker, either.

Somebody attacks. You defend. Perhaps the first technique doesn't work, so you change to something else. Maybe you throw uke down. If he gets back up and comes in again, you mustn't be fazed by this or dwell on the last technique. Just deal with the current attack. Maybe you start getting something to work and uke sees an opening and tries something different in the middle of what you think is a nice clean movement. You must learn to deal with that too. Maybe uke ends up in sankyo and you think you have him controlled and yet he turns against the movement and tries to get at you again, and you know you're going to hurt him if you complete the technique. In the dojo, of course, you'd let go rather than hurt him. In the street, you slam him down, and if something breaks, well at least you made the attempt to control him without injury and he did it to himself. You must keep going as long as is necessary.

As you become more experienced, you should think about different possible ways you could be attacked, and think what you'd do with them. Perhaps start with what seems the closest traditional attack / technique combination, and play with that. Maybe invite some other martial artists to train with you, if you are sure they are interested in studying together rather than proving their art is better. Eventually, all attacks will seem the same and all techniques will too. At this point, you will be seeing the flow of aggression from the attacker and leading it to where it can dissipate without harm to yourself and, hopefully, to the aggressor: you will be doing aikido rather than just aikido techniques.

Most attacks in the street are premeditated. Attackers will pick easy victims, so if you don't look like a victim and avoid places where you are likely to be attacked, you might go for your entire lifetime and not be attacked. This is good. From what I've heard, bar fights generally start with either a push (one handed or two) or a powerful punch at the head, often when the attacker thinks you are not watching him. You might well get attacked with no warning from behind. Again, it is better not to be alone, and to avoid bad places.

Aikido has been described as a "dynamic sphere" (Westbrook and Ratti), where all attacks and all defenses form part of a continuum. There is some evidence that O Sensei thought this way, and that it was his students who categorized and named the attacks and defenses. However, particularly for students, there is an advantage in naming manageable pieces of the whole, as long as we don't forget it is a whole.

Different teachers and organizations named attacks and techniques differently. Aikido in the Dynamic Sphere numbers them all, as did Noro Sensei in France. In the Institute of Aikido, where I got my first shodan, we numbered the attacks and named the techniques. Unfortunately, the number systems used were not consistent between different organizations, and I think using numbers loses some of the flavor of the art, though ikkyo to gokyo are numbered. Aikikai, Yoshinkan, and Tomiki name the attacks and defenses, but the names are not always the same there either. Aikikai groups seem to name the techniques as attack-technique-variation. In any case, the names used are descriptive or enumerative and do not represent any classification other than that techniques with a common name are similar. However, there are similarities and differences between attacks and between techniques, and I have made an attempt to classify attacks and defenses by similarity.

There are maybe a dozen common attacks in aikido, and another dozen that are less common. However, we can group them according to how we deal with them. We can separate high and low line attacks according to whether the attack is above or below nage's elbow. Mid level attacks can be dealt with either way. We can also distinguish ai hanmi or gyaku hanmi attacks. Subclasses might be blows and grabs. Ushiro techniques are a variation of ai hanmi attacks, as they derive from ai hanmi grabs. This classification is shown in the following table.

Some techniques could fit as either ai or gyaku hanmi techniques, according to how nage reacts. Thus, tsuki can be dealt with by nage using his ai or gyaku hand. However, once nage has made the decision, the relationship still holds in the vast majority of cases.

All of the ai hanmi attacks are related. Thus, ushiro katate tori is a technique that starts as kosa dori (ai hanmi katate tori). It progresses to ushiro as uke moves behind nage. It becomes ushiro ryo katate tori as nage moves and threatens an atemi with his free hand, making uke grab that hand. It is similar to the techniques done in response to mune tsuki by moving inside of uke's striking hand. There are some mune tsuki techniques where uke could start as for kosa dori and then move to the outside, but these are generally a little slower.

Kata tori is also different according to which hand nage does technique on. If it is uke's free hand the attack would be in this group also.

Classification of Attacks

Stance	Height	Grabs	Blows
Ai hanmi	Low	Kosa dori (ai hanmi katate tori), ushiro katate tori.	Mune tsuki inside, kicks, foot sweeps.
	High	Kata tori (free hand), ushiro kata tori, ushiro kubi shime.	Shomen uchi (outside techniques).
Gyaku hanmi	Low	Katate tori, katate tori ryote mochi (morote tori), katate ryote tori (ryote tori).	Shomen uchi (inside techniques), mune tsuki outside, kicks, foot sweeps.
	High	Kata tori, held hand.	Yokomen uchi roundhouse punch, high kick.

All of the gyaku hanmi attacks are similarly related. Most members of this group typically involve being inside of the attack, as in yokomen uchi. The exception is again mune tsuki, where techniques moving to the outside, like irimi nage, are more related to this group.

Most importantly, techniques done from either a grab or a blow are similar. Kosa dori ikkyo and tsuki ikkyo are similar, as are (gyaku hanmi) katate tori and yokomen uchi shiho nage. Techniques from katate ryote tori (ryote tori) can be done as either ai hanmi or gyaku hanmi according to how we move initially, but are generally gyaku. Eri tori where both lapels are grabbed could be made to fit either group according to how nage turned. Ushiro eri or kata tori could similarly fit either group, but would be a high attack.

Really low attacks are not generally practiced in aikido, though sometimes we practice against low kicks and foot sweeps. High kicks are not that likely in the street, but also fit this scheme. Attacks with weapons also generally fit, being mostly shomen, yokomen, or tsuki. Suwari waza does not change this classification. Hanmi handachi would make virtually all attacks high.

Aikido techniques can also be classified by similarity. One way to do this, as shown in the next table, is to group them according to what part of uke's body is manipulated, and how. Thus, ikkyo and related techniques are characterized by rotating the arm up and in ("wax on") to control the shoulder. Shiho nage and related techniques also work on the arm and shoulder, but rotate the arm the other way ("wax off"). Irimi nage involves control of the head. Kaiten nage and related techniques work more on the torso. Trips and sweeps are more common in judo than aikido, but would form a separate group. Analogues of ikkyo and shiho nage would work on the legs and feet.

Aikido – Moving On

There is something of a correlation between the attacks and the techniques. Thus, ikkyo is an ai hanmi technique, with nage's right hand holding uke's right wrist. While we can do ikkyo from a gyaku hanmi attack, we change hands to do so, changing the attack from gyaku hanmi to ai hanmi. I think of irimi nage as also being an ai hanmi technique. Shiho nage is similarly more related in my mind to gyaku hanmi. The "torso" group seems to be mixed.

Classifying the techniques and attacks in this way won't, of course, make the techniques any easier to learn, and the differences are not absolute, but perhaps it will make the inter-relationships somewhat clearer, or just provoke some thought. Generally, if we are attacked in ai hanmi, we should choose one of the ai hanmi techniques when time is critical, such as during technique from punches or sword taking. In this case it is probably best, in general, not to cross the line of attack.

Groups of Techniques

Ikkyo group	**Shiho nage group**	**Head**	**Torso**
Ikkyo, nikkyo, sankyo, yonkyo, gokyo.	Shiho nage, kote gaeshi, ude kimi nage.	Irimi nage, shallow sokumen irimi nage.	Kaiten nage, tenchi nage, koshi nage, deep sokumen irimi nage, aiki otoshi, juji nage.

Variations of techniques can also be classified as irimi/tenkan, omote/ura, or positive/negative. These terms are not identical, and in fact mean very different things, though there is considerable overlap in usage. Irimi is an entering movement. Tenkan is a turning movement. Omote is in front. Ura is behind. Positive is when we enter with a feeling of brushing aside or crushing all opposition. Negative is when we give uke a hole to fall into. The similarity is that we normally do irimi techniques to the front with a positive feeling.

Kokyu Ho: kokyu tanden ho, ryote tori tenchi nage suwari waza

Kokyu ho is an exercise in finding and exploiting suki, in kuzushi. The technique isn't too difficult to do standing, so long as you maintain extension, but when you are sitting it can be difficult to move uke, especially if you are taller but lighter than him. (See the section on physics.) Suwari waza limits your ability to move, and this forces you to find an opening in uke's position.

A good basic approach is to reach out and touch uke's torso with a finger of one hand, and the mat with a finger of the other. If you touch uke's body between the sternum and shoulder, just under the clavicle, it is quite difficult for him to resist. The harder he holds on and resists, the more it pushes him over. Touching the mat at the same time, somewhere off to the side near his knee, will also tend to tip him over. Touching with a finger tends to get away from the idea of using strength. Just reach out and touch uke.

The trick is getting to this position. If you push straight into uke's power and are able to overcome it, you are just using strength. This might be enough to push uke over, but if that happens either you are stronger than uke or uke isn't really trying. That is not what you are seeking. Sometimes the easiest way to get from A to B is not a straight line. There are a number of directions along which you can direct your power so that uke finds it harder to resist. Just by changing your direction so that you are pushing a little off the line of his power and curving around to where you want to be, you will find you have made it much harder for uke to resist your movement. This is a suki. Feel for the suki and push through there.

Changing the tempo – pushing momentarily against uke's strength, letting go, and changing the direction – can also help. There is a twitch reflex in many ukes that can be used productively to get past their power. Perhaps more important, if you reach out towards uke and do so without warning and in a way that is mechanically correct, he will not have time to react until it is too late. Once you have the correct position, the harder he pushes the more he pushes himself off balance.

Everybody has his own idea of how kokyu ho should be done. Unfortunately, people will often try to stop other people from doing it in a different way from what they think is right. This is very disheartening for small people and beginners, as kokyu ho seems to be different for every uke they practice with. Uke's job is not to teach, just to be there for nage to practice with. Uke should give an honest attack, and not think about what technique nage is doing, and certainly not how to stop him doing it.

Common ways to prevent nage from doing kokyu ho are to grasp nage's wrists and bear down with all your strength, or to grasp nage's wrists and lock up, immobile. Or uke can flow with nage's effort, resisting mildly, and redirect his strength away from where it needs to be to affect uke. In general, nage can deal with these games by not waiting for uke to settle. If uke tries to bear down or lock up, keep the hands high and moving. If uke tries to redirect, stay just ahead of him. Kokyu ho is an exercise, so it is perfectly fine to just smile at uke and ask him to attack again if you get stuck. However, if you think about kokyu ho as an exercise in finding suki, you will figure out how to turn the tables on them, and learn something in the process other than how strong you are.

The good ways to practice are the ones that leave you scratching your head. Occasionally, I have done things and do not know how or why it worked. Once when I was out of town at a different dojo, a larger, stronger, younger uke clamped down on my wrists and grinned at me. I didn't figure it would work, but there was nothing to lose, so I moved the only things I could, my hands. I made a circular movement, and uke fell over. He didn't tank for me, because he got angry and grabbed harder, and the same thing happened. Unfortunately, the teacher clapped before we could do it enough times for me to figure it out. If I could figure out how to do this at will, I guess I'd be an aikido master and be able to walk on water too.

Nothing is of any use unless you apply it. You could die as the world expert in something and, unless you have passed on that knowledge, what value is it then? The value in kokyu ho is to learn how to find and exploit suki. There are many suki in any conflict. Some we may see too late to use them. Some we only see after they are gone.

Kokyu ho should not be a test of your strength, but of understanding

As we progress in aikido, we start to see suki and to exploit them without thinking. This is aikido, and also the "void" Musashi was talking about. This is how our aikido must become if it is to work as we get older and less physically strong. This is what aikido is all about and, no doubt, why so many instructors stress the importance of practicing kokyu ho, which is a very good exercise for this.

Kokyu Nage

This is often used as an omnibus term for any technique that doesn't have a name, or a name that can't be brought to mind. I generally use it for any technique where the flow of the technique is manipulated to make it work rather than using specific control techniques such as twisting uke's wrist. It seems to be similar to what Iwama Ryu calls ki no nagare.

Almost any technique can be done as a kokyu technique. For example, yokomen uchi shiho nage can be done without gripping uke's hand. Some techniques are more commonly done as kokyu techniques than others. The distinction between irimi nage, particularly sokumen irimi nage, and kokyu nage is often blurry.

The essence of kokyu nage is to take the flow of uke's power and redirect it so that he falls down. This can sometimes be done with no contact between uke and nage, though this is usually done in demonstrations rather than in the street. However, one student I had who was also a bouncer said that kokyu nage worked very well when trouble broke out, particularly as the people involved were often inebriated and somewhat unsteady on their feet.

The ubiquity and lack of form of kokyu nage makes it difficult to write about. I recommend that you try to do each technique you know without pain compliance, leverage, or atemi. Instead, pay attention to the flow of energy, and see what happens. In a sense, kokyu nage is the highest expression of aikido, as it involves just the manipulation of uke's energy.

Ikkyo: oshi taoshi, ude osae

Ikkyo is a useful technique in itself, as well as being the key to a number of other techniques: nikkyo, sankyo, yonkyo, and gokyo, as well as possibly irimi nage and kaiten nage. Reportedly, it was the one aikido technique taught to the British Army for riot control: ikkyo from every conceivable attack.

Ikkyo is mechanically simple. It does not involve complicated evolutions by nage, nor is any pain applied to ensure uke's compliance. This makes it more difficult to do effectively, but makes the study even more interesting. I went through a phase at about shodan where ikkyo would not work reliably for me on anybody larger than I am (which was most of the people I worked with). I eventually figured out that I needed to get into the technique a bit sooner, and to alter the angle between uke and nage. These kinds of adjustments are especially important in doing ikkyo. It can be a very effective technique or a totally useless one, depending on how you approach it. If you are big enough, you can always make it work by brute force, but if you are that big, who needs aikido anyway.

Mechanics

Mechanically, ikkyo is an arm bar with uke's elbow bent to a greater or lesser extent, and with the whole arm being rotated to lock up uke's shoulder and, through that, his entire body. The initial movement should be like a shomen strike with a sword, executed "with one breath", a single crisp movement to overwhelm uke. Uke's arm is pushed up, rotated over the top, and cut down while nage enters with his body.

Do not make an initial regressive move (towards your own body), as this gives uke an advantage. Rather, extend up and out. To improve this movement, practice ikkyo undo. The more that nage is in a lower position than uke, the stronger the initial part of the technique will be, as he is then pushing uke's arm up by pushing against the floor.

The initial contact is made with the front hand, and this typically provides perhaps 15% of the impetus to uke. The second hand connects with uke's elbow, rotating it forwards and driving it into a bigger, stronger circle, one that intersects with the ground. There is a lag between the two movements, with one hand beginning the movement and then the second following it a fraction of a second later. Also, nage's hands follow somewhat different trajectories. These movements should, of course, be made using the power of nage's entire body, not just his arms. Ideally, there should be little force involved, with nage perhaps moving a little laterally so that he attacks a corner of uke's body rather than bulling through the middle, but there should be power in reserve. Uke should be forced to slap the mat to save his face if ikkyo is done correctly.

Nage might need to adjust his distance relative to uke, particularly if there is a difference in size. I prefer to position the rear foot then slide the front foot forward as I cut uke down. This provides a strong initial move without compromising my balance. My feet should be lined up to push in the direction I want to push uke's arm.

Ikkyo can be completed as a pin or as a throw, according to the direction of the impetus given to uke and uke's action in receiving the technique. The pin results from a more downwards cut, while the throw is more outwards.

If uke is not immediately driven to the mat, the first move of ikkyo irimi as a pin should let nage take a strong position, while holding uke bent over in a weak posture. Nage's weight should be forward over his front leg and his hips can be rotated to generate a lot of power while drawing uke to the side, off center. Nage should have most of his weight over uke's arm, yet not allow uke's arm to touch the front of his thighs (to avoid a big uke picking him up). His nose should be behind his toes. His inside hand (the one on uke's elbow) should be lower than his outside hand. Both arms should be extended, almost straight. The angle between uke's arm and his torso should be about ninety degrees relative to the long axis of his body, and perhaps ten degrees behind his shoulder. Uke's balance should be at his toes. Further forward than this, and he must either fall or step. Further back, and nage is at risk of a counter technique.

From the correct position, nage can drive uke to the mat, pushing uke's shoulder diagonally sideways, forwards, and down with a motion from the hips like pushing a broom through sand. This should knock uke to the mat, in which case nage can proceed to apply the immobilization. If uke resists and pushes back, nage should zag the other way, over-extending uke in the other direction while keeping uke's shoulder down and taking him to the floor. Nage must push from a position of strength for both of these movements, and the final movement especially must not be a pull. Otherwise, nage might have uke collapse across his knee, or uke can enter to counter the technique.

For ikkyo irimi, nage should initially enter to uke's front and cut him down with a sword strike. For ikkyo tenkan, nage's arms should make the same motion, but nage should place his gyaku foot beside uke's front foot, turned to point in the same direction, and then turn his body through 180 degrees (tenkan), while cutting uke down. Ikkyo tenkan is a one-count technique, blending with uke's push, turning, and cutting down. In either variation, nage must push uke to the floor ahead of him, rather than kneeling and pulling.

Timing and Tempo

Ikkyo irimi benefits from an early timing. If you atemi at uke's face, and apply ikkyo when uke puts up a hand to protect his face, this is about the right timing. Some people object that this is too aggressive to be aikido. However, this approach makes perfect sense when done in response to an initial grab (by uke) such as kata tori. It is also perfectly sensible if you are attacked again after the initial attack, or if your wife or child is attacked and you must distract her attacker.

Ikkyo irimi is perhaps a three-count technique. You make the first movement in one breath, all the way to holding uke bent over. You drive him to the mat one way as a second, then zag the other way and pin as a third. A strong ikkyo could short-circuit the second and third counts, but if not, don't try to run the whole technique into one move with the zigzag. In particular, if you drive uke to the mat with the zig, and don't pause, it will be quite difficult to make him reverse direction.

On the other hand, do not pause with your hands high as you enter, making two counts of the initial move. This is a good place for uke to attempt a reversal and your ribs are exposed. Just as a single cylinder engine tends to stop with the piston approaching compression, so ikkyo tends to stall out at top dead center. Drive through this point and pause, if you must, where it is more difficult for uke to perform a counter technique.

Kuzushi

Ikkyo irimi typically relies on imbalancing uke to his front, generally at a right angle to the line between his feet. Some ways of doing it are more to the rear of this line. Some are more to the front. A strong ikkyo irimi, for example, will drive uke's arm back over his head and back foot. A complete tenkan will go as far the other way, taking uke's balance forward and, as he steps to recover his balance, further extending him, all the way to the floor. Intermediate options also work well, such as drawing uke forward so that he is weak then collapsing him to the ground at nage's feet. Uke is also bent over in a weak posture.

Immobilization

The pin usually done from ikkyo is an exercise rather than a combat pin. Accordingly, it should be done from the correct position and uke should push up to test if nage is in fact doing it correctly. Attention should be paid to the relative positions of uke's and nage's bodies. Uke's arm should be pushed high, and his elbow rolled forwards. Nage should have one knee in uke's ribs and the other knee at his wrist. This gives nage a lot of stability. Nage should be sitting down on his heels, leaning forward a little from the hips and extending his arms fully.

Mechanically, uke should be unable to roll away from nage because of the long lever provided by uke's arm. He should be unable to roll towards nage without bending his own shoulder in a new direction. There are some pressure points accessible, but they would not work on somebody sufficiently trained, angry, or drugged and so I am not in favor of depending on them.

After completing the pin, nage should, as for all pins, move away while still controlling uke's ability to attack him, and maintain ma-ai as he stands up.

Ukemi

The main goals for ukemi in receiving ikkyo are to make sure that your elbow does not get hyper-extended, and that, even if ikkyo is applied vigorously, your face does not hit the mat. To avoid the elbow being hyper-extended, keep it somewhat bent so that the technique is applied as a shoulder rotation rather than an arm bar. To avoid a face plant, slap the mat with your free hand as your face is driven towards the mat.

Finer Points

To do an effective ikkyo, nage should drive uke into the technique with a circular motion as if turning a big vertical wheel, accelerating uke's body towards the ground through the impetus applied to his arm. As uke grasps at your arm, start moving it in a trajectory that will lead his power up, over his head, out to the side, and down to the ground. Keep your own arms extended.

Ikkyo. Nage must control uke so that he is off balance and held down. Uke's elbow should be lower than his wrist.

The feeling should be that you are creating a vortex, and sucking uke along, rather than grabbing hold of him and smashing him to the ground. As you do so, you may be depending to an extent on uke's commitment to grab your hand, but not absolutely. You can even go further than this, attacking uke with a shomen strike as he comes to attack you. Then as he puts his hand up to defend his face, you execute ikkyo on that hand. This is more direct, but the feeling should still be up, out, and down.

The motion of the two hands moving in three dimensions as they perform ikkyo is quite complex. At the Brain and Perception Lab at Bristol University we had a nice little tool to draw in three dimensions. Unfortunately I can't reproduce those drawings here. Ikkyo should feel like stepping in with a sword (or two swords one after the other) to perform a shomen strike. The motion should use nage's entire body, or a small nage will have difficulty with a large uke. The position of the suki varies according to the relationship between uke and nage. With a big nage or an early technique (sen sen no sen), ikkyo can be applied almost through uke's head, driving uke's elbow through where his head was. A smaller nage or a larger uke with stiff arms may require nage to move laterally before the downwards cut. However, it may be more viable to try for a direct technique (uke's elbow to uke's head), and turning slightly away when meeting resistance, rather than trying to make a supple uke follow out to the side. Lateral movement should come from nage stepping a little to the side, though a rotation of the hips is also good towards the end of the downwards cut.

Ikkyo: side view, showing hand position to cut down uke. Note that nage's arms are almost straight and in front of his body, and that uke's arm is neither. Uke's elbow should follow a wider trajectory than his wrist.

Variations and Problems

Ikkyo can be done against a straight arm, locking out the joint, and this may be an older way to do it. In fact, some schools of both aikido and aikijutsu practice taking ikkyo in this way, from where a quick jerk would usually finish the fight in the street. Uke should avoid allowing this to happen, as it puts his arm into a vulnerable position and the elbow could easily be damaged accidentally. It is generally better ukemi for uke to keep his arm turned and somewhat flexed so that nage cannot easily hyper-extend his elbow.

A common problem with practicing ikkyo is that uke feels it is safe to resist, and there is no application of pain to deter him from doing so as a new student tries to do the technique slowly and tentatively. If this is a problem, try striking at uke's face with your hand, making him defend himself and giving you the initiative (sente). If uke steps as you attempt to take his balance, turn into tenkan.

More generally, problems with ikkyo irimi result from nage not taking uke's balance, particularly with a big strong uke who doesn't commit to the attack. In this case it is better in the street or during jiyuwaza to change the technique, such as into nikkyo or irimi nage or, if uke is pushing towards nage, to ikkyo tenkan.

If uke grips strongly (as he should), there is a very easy initial movement from kosa dori using a nikkyo, by which nage merely cuts against uke's wrist with his tegatana, lowering his whole arm as if lowering a sword. This movement rotates uke's wrist, arm and body into a better position for the application of ikkyo, as well as being quite painful if uke resists.

Some people do ikkyo as they step forward with the inside foot, perhaps even driving a hip against uke or stepping in and driving the front leg (rear outer side of thigh) against uke's torso to knock him off balance. This step requires better timing than sliding in with the front foot as described above. If you do not get the step almost complete before uke pushes back, you will be in an awkward position. This method does provide more momentum, but is risky for a smaller nage.

These thoughts were primarily directed at ikkyo irimi. If you are a little late and meet resistance when doing ikkyo irimi, do not persist, because uke will be able to hit you while you struggle and you have two arms occupied while he has only one. Instead, turn at once and do another technique, such as ikkyo tenkan. The entire body should still be used to cut uke down. Nage should continue pushing uke down to the ground as he turns. The result should be just as dynamic as the ikkyo irimi, and result in uke's feet flying through the air as he slaps the mat with his free hand.

The commonest problems with ikkyo tenkan are when nage steps backwards rather than turning, when nage allows his hands to drift out of position from in front of his center, and when he loses extension. Nage should place his foot next to uke's foot and turn as if to go back to back, while extending to keep uke in front of him. As he does this, nage's hands should be lowered, as for a shomen uchi sword cut, and remain in front of his hips. The feeling should be a lot like irimi nage tenkan, but with both nage's hands on uke's arm instead of one on his head. Nage must push uke rather than pulling him, whether into irimi or tenkan, and maintain his extension.

Counter Techniques

Ikkyo can be countered by flowing with it and turning out. This typically happens when nage is a little hesitant and does not get uke's balance, especially if uke steps forward as nage rotates his shoulder. To inhibit this counteraction, nage can change the timing or direction. If the change in timing is done well, uke has to slap the mat to prevent a squashed nose, and the technique is over in that one breath. If nage turns away from uke as he steps, the step will put him in a worse position rather than a better one. The extreme example of this is ikkyo tenkan (ura).

As uke turns to flow with the technique, nage can further extend uke so that he loses his center and nage can then still apply ikkyo. This is a good way to study sente. Ikkyo can also be turned into nikkyo, sankyo, etc. by appropriate hand movements.

If uke attempts to fight the technique and stands up (in which case nage did not get uke's balance), the direction of the technique can be reversed and uke's new movement continued into a figure four lock or some derivative of this. Alternatively, as uke stands up, nage can enter in front of uke for a koshi nage or shiho nage.

If uke is successful in turning out of the ikkyo and taking control of the flow, he can then redirect the flow into any of a number of kaeshi waza. He can in turn apply ikkyo or do any of that series of techniques. He can step behind his partner and do irimi nage tenkan. If nage does not take uke's balance and does not extend his arms, uke can step close and pick nage up and throw with aiki otoshi, or he can punch and kick him.

Particular Applications

Kosa Dori (ai hanmi katate tori). Be sure to get your hand above uke's forearm and push across in front of uke's face.

Yokomen Uchi. Do not knock the striking arm down so far that ikkyo is difficult to take. Instead, knock it only a little down and more out and past your head. (If you do knock it down too far, apply kote gaeshi or ude kimi nage instead.) For irimi, take uke's arm across his front. For tenkan, enter deeply past uke's side as you apply the technique.

Tsuki. As for yokomen uchi, do not knock the arm down as much as out. You can do ikkyo with a hand either on top of uke's hand (like nikkyo or gokyo) or underneath.

Ushiro Ryo Katate Tori. Keep your arms extended and take uke's balance in front of your body as he goes behind. Keep uke's arm extended and don't allow him to pull you off balance sideways or backwards. The extension is more important than the details of what you do with your arms and hands.

Nikkyo: kote mawashi, kote maki

Nikkyo is a rotation (in the same direction as ikkyo) of the two bones in the forearm while uke's forearm is held more or less horizontal, typically using uke's hand bent towards the underside of his forearm for leverage. Again, the technique should lock up uke's shoulder. If uke resists, the forearm hurts. Because pain is involved, people tend to forget to take uke's balance, and this nevertheless does generally work. However, the same principles apply to nikkyo as to any other technique: deal with the attack, take uke's balance, and then apply technique. Some people are strong enough to resist, otherwise.

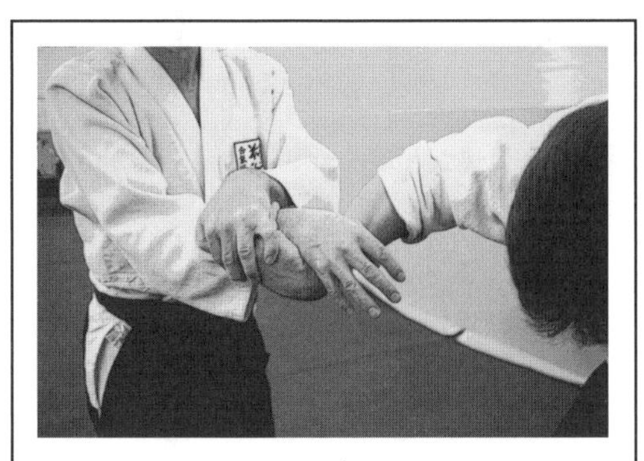

Nikkyo: the bones of the forearm are twisted around each other

I remember as a beginner thinking nikkyo was a rather trivial technique, an "Indian burn". Then Andy Allen grabbed hold of me and I learned how effective it is. There are different schools of thought as to how nikkyo works. One opinion is that a small bone, the pisiform, is brought into an articulation that it does not usually have. Another is that the periostia of the radius and ulna are brought to bear on each other. Both ideas may be valid, but for a good nikkyo the whole of uke's arm, his whole body, even, should be involved. Different practitioners might also apply the technique differently.

There are many ways to apply nikkyo. A basic irimi method is to begin from ikkyo, then bending uke's hand in at the wrist and rotating his hand to twist the forearm as you continue to cut down with an ikkyo-like movement. To maximize the effect, uke's fingers should be rotated towards uke's wrist as vigorously as the hand is rotated downwards. Once the slack is taken out of uke's arm and body, this rotation should be completed by the lowering of nage's arm as in a sword strike rather than by twisting uke's arm with your hands. The leverage obtained by nage locking his wrist and lowering his arm is more effective.

A similar nikkyo, as shown above, can be done by nage using two hands on uke's hand and wrist. The basic direction is shown by pointing at uke's face with a finger and rotating your hand down to point at his feet as you lower your arm and hips. If the hand is rotated in any other plane, uke will most likely not go straight down. With a suitably angled cut uke can be made to move backwards or forwards at will. If you meet resistance, you can also cut down a little in front of uke to get uke's balance out in front, where he is weak, before cutting down. However, uke can use this to your disadvantage if you cut too far out. The movement should be like feeling around the edges of uke's power for a suki (as when doing kokyu ho). Instead, if a strong horizontal cut to uke's rear is used, he can be forced to throw his feet out behind him to save his arm.

In this nikkyo, nage should not grasp uke's forearm. If he does, uke can make the two grips symmetrical and might reverse the technique, particularly if nage did not take uke's balance. Instead, nage's hand should be over uke's forearm, so that if uke puts his hand on nage's fingers (which he shouldn't be given the opportunity to do) and pushes, uke applies nikkyo to himself. If necessary, nage can trap uke's fingers on his forearm using his thumb under the forearm so that uke cannot readily let go.

Nikkyo tenkan uses the same position of uke's arm, but with the back of uke's hand trapped against the front of nage's shoulder to give more power to the technique. Often people try to apply this technique by bowing. This is not really the best way, as it makes it easier for uke to raise their elbow to counter the technique. A stronger technique results when nage squats (lowering his body into jigotai), and drives in on uke. The bow is then incidental to the resulting body mechanics, and the nikkyo is more powerful. Uke's hand must be firmly pressed in to nage's shoulder, bending uke's wrist, taking up the slack in his arm, and rolling uke's hand somewhat down nage's chest. For the strongest result, both of nage's hands should be used to do this. However, one hand is adequate until nage commences the jigotai, and even then may suffice. The other hand can profitably be used to deliver an atemi to uke's face, distracting him and tying up his free hand. This hand is then drawn back to the two-handed nikkyo position with a scraping, rotating motion of the forearm along the top of uke's arm.

Few ukes can remain standing long enough for nage to complete this action, so it usually gets truncated. People frequently see this movement and think nage is pressing down on uke's elbow. Pressing down on uke's elbow with a hand during nikkyo is mechanically unsound, particularly if uke is taller and stronger than nage. Nage's hand is at the end of a third order lever that is twice as long as the lever arm at which uke's elbow is operating, and so has twice the velocity ratio but only half the power, and uke can use his shoulder muscles to resist. Locking uke's hand to nage's body with two hands lets nage apply a lot of torque from his body to uke's forearm. In effect, you're using your body from the waist to the shoulder (maybe 2 ft. long) as the lever to rotate uke's arm, and applying power with the strong muscles of your torso. There is a lot of power, but not much range of movement, so the hands should first take up the slack. As the slack is taken out of the technique, it comes to be applied center to center.

Variations on this nikkyo tenkan may be used when uke resists or is too tall for the basic technique to conveniently work. If uke pushes out, straightening his arm (generally a bad idea for uke, as it makes his elbow vulnerable), and especially if he is a little taller, reach inside with your gyaku hand and push against the elbow to bend it inside to out (the way the elbow normally bends), and pull down on the elbow, while keeping uke's hand fixed on your shoulder. (This is one of the few times a pull is useful in aikido.) Alternatively, rotate the hand more and proceed as if doing the basic nikkyo irimi. If, instead, uke moves in, bending his elbow further, reach out and put a hand on uke's elbow and draw it in closer, pressing his wrist into a still more flexed position (like the immobilization for gokyo, only on nage's shoulder).

Sometimes an uke merely taps but does not move in the desired direction. If this happens in nikkyo or any other technique, do not ease up or uke will be in charge and can apply a kaeshi technique. Tell him what you want him to do while continuing to apply the technique. Criminals have realized that law enforcement officers train in the martial arts and learn to stop when uke taps. You should learn to feel when an uke is faking, but don't abuse your ukes.

Once uke goes to the floor, nage must change his hand position, which is another point at which uke might try to counter the technique. Too avoid this, make uke take a position from which he cannot move quickly – typically with his weight distributed between his knees and his free hand. If the weight is not on the free hand and nage eases off (which he should not do), uke can jump back to his feet. You can also circumvent this by moving quickly into the pin, but it is not good to depend on speed. It is better to move correctly, so that uke remains controlled at all times. You can rotate uke's arm using his hand as a lever, or by the torque between his wrist and elbow.

Once uke is in an acceptable position, the takedown is like ikkyo, either irimi or tenkan. If you drive uke's shoulder to the mat by stepping in, you are doing ikkyo irimi. If you turn and press down, you are doing ikkyo tenkan. In any case, keep the nikkyo on uke's arm with one hand, and the other on his elbow.

Either of these moves should result in nage kneeling close to uke's side, with uke's arm stretched high on the mat as for the ikkyo pin, but with uke's hand flexed and rotated. Compliance can generally be achieved by bending his hand towards the wrist while rotating the hand away from nage. This should involve nage locking his wrist and using his own forearm as a lever, rather than by flexing his wrist.

Uke's arm can then be transferred into a more secure pin. The safest way to do this is to hold uke's shoulder to the mat with the tegatana of nage's inside hand on the back of uke's shoulder, then pick up uke's arm and rotate it into position in the crook of nage's inside arm, while nage maintains extension into uke's shoulder. At this point, nage has a substantial degree of control with that single arm. Nage then turns to get his knees in position, one at uke's short ribs and the other at the back of uke's head. He rotates uke's hand so that the palm is towards nage's biceps, and traps that wrist in the crook of his elbow, thus maintaining the nikkyo on uke's arm. Again, this position is sufficient in most cases to control uke. Nage's other hand is then drawn across the inside of uke's elbow, the tegatana bending uke's arm and pulling it into nage's stomach. All the slack should be out of uke's arm at this point. Nage then turns his whole body towards uke's head, the rotation of nage's torso applying the pin to uke's arm. A small movement of nage's body should be sufficient. The movement should be both applied and released slowly and carefully.

Nikkyo Pin: Trap uke's wrist with his palm against your biceps, draw his elbow against your body and turn your body.

A counter to nikkyo is to flow with it, pulling your hand off your partner's shoulder if it is pinned there, and perhaps rotating your forearm the opposite way to where uke wants to go to reposition his hand so that, for example, you can apply sankyo (see Page 130). To prevent being countered, take uke's balance and begin to apply the nikkyo early with your hands, keeping slack out of uke's arm, and then press his hand firmly against your shoulder.

Sankyo: kote hineri, shibori kime

Sankyo is a rotation of the two bones of uke's forearm around one another, as for nikkyo, but with his forearm held more or less vertical and his hand flexed towards the back of his forearm. The direction of rotation is the same as for nikkyo. Like ikkyo and nikkyo, the technique controls uke's body through his arm, again using uke's fingers and hand as a lever. Sankyo irimi might involve taking uke up on his toes – the "classical" sankyo position – or just cutting him down. If nage has broken uke's balance sufficiently, taking uke up on his toes is unnecessary. If nage tries to cut down directly, and uke resists, then nage should drive uke up on his toes, taking his balance before again cutting down (or changing to another technique).

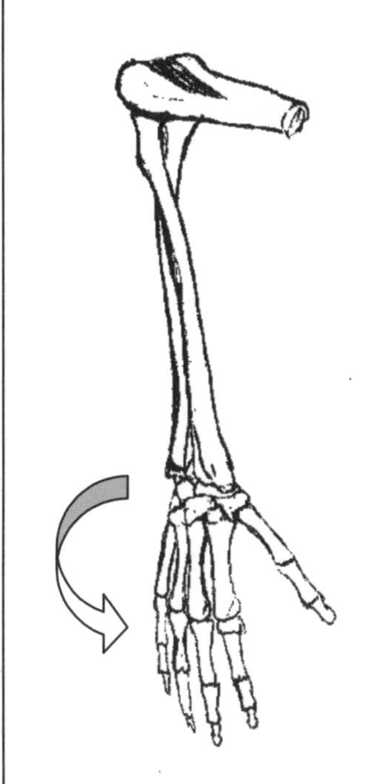

Sankyo: the bones of the forearm are again twisted in pronation. (Right hand.)

Sankyo can involve taking kuzushi several times during the course of a single technique. It can start from ikkyo, breaking uke's balance to the front. The balance can then be driven back and up, then driven forward. Finally, with uke bending forward and nage stepping in front, the balance can be broken further forward, towards the "missing leg" of a tripod so that uke falls to the floor with a minimal effort on nage's part.

Nage must take all the slack out of uke's arm. Slack can actually be dangerous for uke, as the technique then tends to come on more suddenly, but nage also has more control when the slack is removed. This is particularly important with regard to controlling uke's elbow when it is near nage's face. For a sankyo where nage goes under uke's arm, a more effective technique is often possible by locking uke's hand and nage rotating his body about that hand. Then, nage's large and strong body muscles will apply the technique rather than his arm muscles.

It is not necessary to grip uke's hand tightly. Considerable control can be applied just by using the tegatana and cutting towards uke's face, using uke's grip to torque his hand and arm. However, this form of sankyo should be transitioned to the traditional grip as soon as can conveniently be done, as uke can take over if control of the connection falters.

The cut down is a sword strike, where the mechanics involved rotate uke's elbow forward close by the position occupied by uke's head (which forces uke to move and further lose his balance) and down, while maintaining the rotation of uke's forearm. This cut is often made loosely, like casting a fishing rod, and away from uke. This sometimes works, particularly if uke's balance is taken, but is less effective at controlling uke's shoulder than the sword-strike motion shown below.

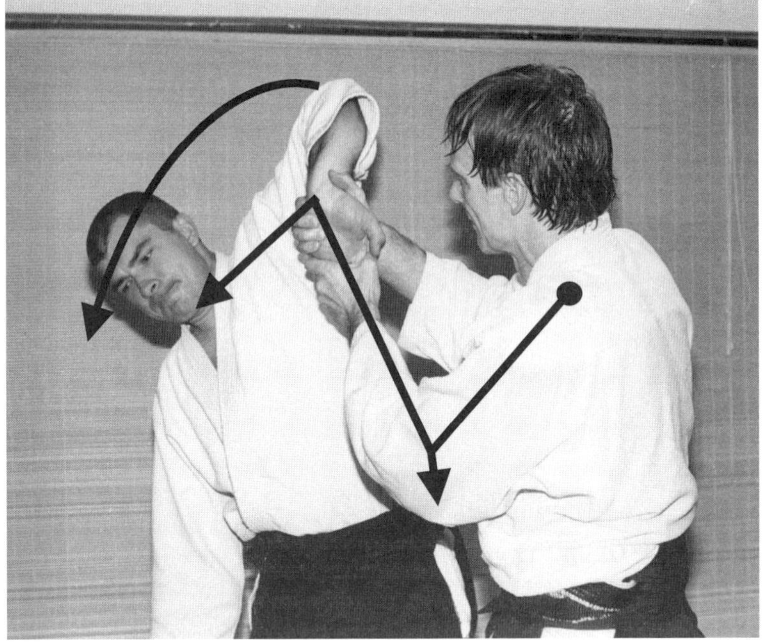

Sankyo: cutting down like a sword.

Nage's nearside hand (the one closer to uke) is the more important one, and he should hold uke's hand with his whole hand, rather than with his fingers and thumb. Nage's thumb, particularly, is vulnerable to being injured if uke struggles. If the web of nage's hand (instead of his thumb) is used to apply pressure to uke's hand, nage's grip is stronger and his thumb is safer. Generally, nage should grasp uke's hand with his fingers hooked around the edge of the blade of uke's hand. A smaller nage, particularly somebody with smaller hands, can usefully slide his hand down to grasp uke's fingers rather than the blade of the hand. This can be quite painful to uke, even damaging, and should be used with discretion. As always, uke should not struggle unreasonably, though nage should be able to still apply the technique if he does.

Once uke is bent over, and while maintaining the torque on uke's arm, nage changes hanmi, stepping to the front of uke's arm. He then puts a hand on uke's elbow and extends him diagonally forwards and sideways (towards where his balance is weakest, which depends on where uke's feet are). The pressure needed on the elbow should be quite light. If a lot of pressure is required, most likely the rotation of the wrist has been lost and uke has regained his balance. Then nage is vulnerable to a kaeshi technique.

Sankyo pin: press uke's palm to your shoulder and control his shoulder with your other arm as necessary. Rotate your torso.

Once uke is on the ground, nage should keep the pressure and rotation on uke's arm to prevent him rising. He should kneel next to uke, kneeling on the gi or hair as opportunity presents itself, with a knee by his head and the other by his ribs as for nikkyo. However, uke's arm is held somewhat differently. Nage should change hands while maintaining the rotation and downwards pressure on uke's arm. Uke's hand should be trapped, again with nage's fingers wrapped around the blade of the hand and with uke's palm towards nage's chest. He controls uke's upper arm as shown in the figure and takes the slack out of uke's arm with his arms. Nage turns his body to apply the pin.

A standing pin can also be applied. After nage cuts down uke, he should not change his grip, but maintain the torque on uke's arm while driving his shoulder into the mat. Nage's hand can be pressed against his thigh, and he can turn his hips if more power is needed.

Sankyo irimi can be turned into sankyo nage simply by being more forceful with the backwards or forwards movements from the initial position, turning the hips and using the whole body to generate impetus for the throw, and continuing the movement further. So long as nage has uke's balance, uke is forced to throw himself back or forwards to protect his arm. (It is, naturally, important during practice for nage to let go so that uke can fall. Uke should flow with the direction nage provides, to protect his arm.) If you have a problem throwing uke one way, reverse the direction and throw the other way, or continue into the immobilization.

As in ikkyo, sankyo tenkan is very like the irimi technique with a turn from the hip. The downwards cut finishes with uke's arm between uke's and nage's bodies. Nage then places his free hand on the inside of uke's elbow and extends uke's arm, still twisting his forearm. This works particularly well when uke steps forwards to resist sankyo irimi. Then when nage cuts down and moves behind uke, uke's legs are twisted awkwardly and he falls down.

Control uke's elbow.

A fault commonly seen with sankyo tenkan is for nage to reach up for uke's elbow to force it down. This feels strong to nage, but makes uke disproportionately stronger and exposes nage to a punch in the ribs. Instead, if you meet resistance use your free hand to strike at uke's face, distracting him and making it easier to perform the technique. Once you cut uke down, then you can safely grasp and push down on his elbow. Uke's hand should describe a descending spiral around his body, but, as for ikkyo tenkan, nage's arms cut vertically down. If nage merely runs around uke without this downwards impetus, a flexible uke can turn and counter the technique when he gets tired of being turned round and round.

The primary counter to sankyo is for uke to raise the elbow a little ahead of nage's expectations and move it along the arc nage intends to follow, round and down, putting nage in sankyo instead. If nage flows with this movement and keeps the pressure on, however, he can make it extremely difficult for uke to escape.

Sankyo can be used for tanto tori. In this case, the rotation of uke's arm can be applied by pressing against the knife blade if it is held in the "ice pick" grip. If it is held in the saber grip, nage will probably need to attempt to drive the knife into uke's body to make him give up his balance by flinching from the blade.

Yonkyo: tekubi osae

Yonkyo involves holding uke's forearm like the handle of a sword and cutting down to make uke's shoulder meet the mat. This may include driving the elbow forwards and down like thrusting with a sword to complete the movement. Once again, the effect is similar to ikkyo in controlling uke's shoulder and body. There is a pressure point on the forearm, more effective than some, but this should not be relied upon as much as getting uke's balance and controlling him by body position. Some ukes apparently do not feel pain from this technique. Uke's balance should be taken away before the hands are in position for yonkyo (typically using an ikkyo motion) and the imbalance maintained by the cutting action with uke's arm. The cut and thrust movement is like the Iwama sixth bokken suburi, though to gedan position.

Yonkyo. Cut down as if uke's arm is a sword.

For tenkan, nage should enter to uke's side, then cut down as for irimi yonkyo while turning his body, so that uke is propelled forwards, around nage, and down. Once again, the rotation should come from nage's hips, not his arms.

Once uke is on the mat, insert your leg between his arm and body and, using your whole body, push his hand further towards his shoulder (which would eventually dislocate the shoulder), and while continuing to apply pressure to the forearm.

The correct hand grip and positioning of uke's elbow and forearm are crucial to this technique. If uke is able to keep his elbow high as you cut down, he can counter you. If you are able to drive the elbow down (controlling the shoulder as for ikkyo), you can continue and drive uke to the floor. Nage's wrists must remain strong (aligned with his forearms) rather than "broken" (flexed). When done correctly, nage should feel that he is lowering a sword to gedan, and the mechanics of that movement should take care of the technique. The cut down should involve the entire bodies, not just the arms – nage using his whole body to apply the technique, and tying up uke's entire body. If you get the technique perfectly, a single cut will be all that is needed. If it does not work quite that well, you might need to cut until uke resists, and then step in and cut again.

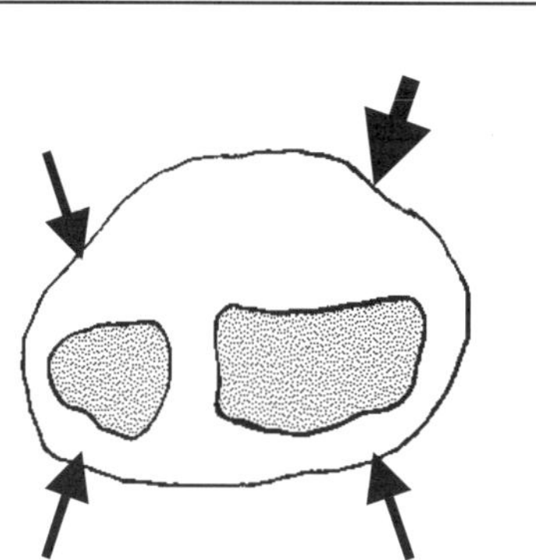

Yonkyo Pressure Points. The forearm is shown in cross section, ventral side up. The main point is shown by the largest arrow. The radius (thumb side) is the larger bone.

As uke, don't struggle unduly against yonkyo, as you will receive severe bruises on the forearm if nage is doing it correctly. You can block the pain, but that won't stop bruising. Years ago, Gary and I used to see who could be most bull headed, and we got bruises that lasted a week. I don't know if you could damage the radial nerve with yonkyo or not. We didn't suffer long-term effects.

You can do yonkyo with similar movements to any of the four sides of the "box" that represents the wrist. The various options for the pressure point are shown in the figure, with the main point being shown larger than the others. You can also do yonkyo on the leg in corresponding ways, though most people have rather bulky legs which, unless you have uke's balance, are too strong to manipulate conveniently. However, the application of technique to the leg can have quite dramatic results, especially if applied with a hard object like a jo. Apparently the anatomical basis for yonkyo is applying pressure to the periosteum. I have heard people claim the pain is, instead, the result of pressure to the radial nerve. However, pressure on a nerve would cause numbness and tingling distal to the point of application, like when you hit your funny bone, whereas yonkyo hurts where the pressure is applied.

Yonkyo can be applied with a jo from a front kick

Gokyo: ude nobashi

Gokyo is very similar to ikkyo, but is modified to make it safer for nage when uke has a knife. With ikkyo, nage has the knuckles of both his hands upwards. For gokyo, nage's outer hand is turned the other way (like nikkyo), with the thumb on the front (palmar side) of uke's wrist. This grip restricts uke's mobility, making it harder for uke to twist his hand so as to cut nage's wrist with the knife. The alternative name (nobashi) implies more of a stretch than a rotation.

Gokyo. Stop uke's attack firmly and without knocking his arm down too far.

Gokyo is typically demonstrated from a yokomen strike, but can also be used for tsuki and shomen attacks. For some reason, people seem to be less familiar with using gokyo from an overhead (shomen) strike. While it is a less effective knife attack, people do attack that way. The key in this case is a strong atemi to the face with the leading hand, while stopping the knife strike and taking uke's balance with the other hand, cupping uke's elbow. Nage can then capture the knife hand, control the knife, and drive uke to the mat as for ikkyo.

For a yokomen strike, nage can move in early with a strong atemi, or can step back for a later timing. In either case, he should control uke's forearm with his forearm, the two impacting about the middle of the forearms. Too far out on uke's forearm, and nage is vulnerable to a slash on the forearm. Too close in towards the elbow, and uke's arm can swing around nage's defending arm to cut his neck. Similarly, if the contact point is too far out on nage's arm, nage's fingers will be too weak to stop the blow. Too close in, and he won't have the necessary range and mobility.

Gokyo is typically done as an irimi technique. If you are a little late, you can grasp uke's arm and enter deeply behind uke to perform the tenkan version. However, timing and position are even more critical. Too late, and there is a good chance uke will strike your ribs, especially if you drive his arm down too far and are too close.

For the immobilization, after driving uke to the mat, nage should lift uke's elbow and flex his wrist against the mat, keeping a firm grasp of uke's wrist to control the knife hand until uke has opened his fingers to release the knife. Sometimes uke will resist allowing nage to bend his arm. In this case, nage can dig the fingers of his hand into the tendon at the base of uke's biceps (under his arm near the elbow) as he pulls up, and he can use his inner knee to strike uke's ribs. When uke's hand opens to release the knife, nage should sweep the knife clear of uke's hand while maintaining pressure on the elbow.

Whenever practicing weapons technique, nage should be rather more assertive then in general practice, as the situation he is practicing for is more serious.

Gokyo. Control the angle of the knife through the thumb on uke's wrist.

Shiho Nage

"Shiho nage" means "four directions throw", implying all directions. It can be done in many ways, also, but a key method is to position uke so that a sword-striking (shomen uchi) motion will bring him to the ground. Uke must be unbalanced, with his hand behind his back as shown in the figure below, rather than on his shoulder. Generally, uke is placed in this position by rotating uke's forearm the opposite way from ikkyo using uke's hand as a lever, twisting his arm, and driving his elbow up and out past his body, making uke raise up to relieve the pressure on his arm, and taking uke's arm over nage's head then cutting down behind uke's back.

Shiho Nage. Uke's hand should be cut down behind his shoulder.

Nage's initial push must be past or away from uke to avoid coming into conflict with him and cramping the technique. If you're strong enough you can drive uke out of the way by pushing directly towards uke, but directly over-powering uke isn't really aikido. For shiho nage irimi, the direction of the push should extend uke's balance to his front, towards the weak point that makes an equilateral triangle with uke's feet. This should inhibit any attempt by uke to turn so that he can strike or kick nage. For shiho nage tenkan, the direction of nage's push should be along uke's original line of attack, nage turning to take the direction of the throw behind uke's body (towards uke's rear triangle weak point) and moving out of his line of attack. Irimi should be done when uke pulls. Tenkan is done when uke pushes strongly.

To begin, uke's arm should be held securely but not too tightly. There should be no space between nage's hands and uke's hand, but if nage grips too tightly it can be hard for nage to move freely. Nage's power must come all the way from the ground. Nage must not duck under uke's arm, as uke can then counter quite easily. Instead, nage should take uke's arm over his head. Uke's arm is swung up, nage turns his hips, and uke's arm is swung down. The overall motion is to take uke's arm over nage's head as if cutting with a sword in shiho giri. It must be a single movement up, over, and down. Pausing at the top will allow uke to counteract the technique. Leaning back (towards uke) during the turn will allow uke to pull nage backwards and off balance. It is better to lean the other way a little, keeping your hands where you can see them without raising your head.

The angle of uke's elbow varies widely from one nage to another, from almost straight to more than 90 degrees of flexion. The position depends on the relative size of uke and nage, among other things. In general, the more bent the arm the safer the technique is for uke.

If nage does not have uke's balance and loses the initiative, uke can rotate out of the technique. There are various ways to prevent this, but the main one is to extend uke so that he can't turn so readily.

The direction of the final cut should be down uke's back, as shown below. A diagonal cut outwards (relative to uke) towards nage's feet will work but risks injuring uke's elbow. Shiho nage should be done with a single movement, sweeping uke off his feet and dashing him to the mat.

Shiho Nage. Nage should cut down in line with uke's forearm rather than outwards, which could damage his elbow.

Sometimes uke will resist. This is dangerous with any technique, but particularly with shiho nage as a struggle could result in uke's elbow being damaged. However, if uke resists the initial movement, change the direction of the extension. If he pulls his hand down onto his shoulder, lock your arms and bow. If you almost get the technique but he locks up, maintain the pressure, adjust your distance and angle, and cut again.

Generally, uke should take an easy, backwards fall (ushiro ukemi). However, sometimes people will make this difficult and even dangerous by cranking on uke's arm, cutting to the side as well as down, perhaps with the arm almost straight. Accordingly, uke should learn how to take a breakfall over the top from shiho nage. This breakfall is achieved by uke aligning his body with the direction of the throw to avoid undue stress on the elbow. The necessary movement is sometimes described as bringing the head to the hand, but the whole body needs to be turned to avoid an unfair strain on the elbow. Uke can then follow the technique over the top, or (somewhat more difficult) he can just follow it backwards. In either case, he should land in a slapping breakfall with minimal stress on the arm and elbow. You can land without slapping, but it tends to knock the wind out of you even on a soft mat.

The ukemi can be learned quite easily and with minimal risk if nage holds uke's arm in the correct position without applying any torque. By nage bending his knees and bowing slowly, uke can take the fall in his own time. Once uke has done the ukemi a few times, nage can walk through shiho nage while holding softly, and gradually working up to a full intensity throw.

Shiho Nage Ukemi: uke should move his head towards his hand, and align his body to avoid letting the technique twist his elbow.

Shiho nage accounts for a large fraction of aikido injuries, mostly "shiho nage elbow". To my mind, this is often due to an unforgiving or even malicious attitude on nage's part. However, uke can survive quite vigorous throws by being neither early nor late in the ukemi, and staying with nage as he executes the throw. It is quite an exhilarating throw when done in one breath, whether you are uke or nage.

Shiho nage, as the name implies, can be done to any direction. The deciding factor is how nage turns his hips. However, nage must turn his hips in a fashion that also controls uke. This is only possible if he has taken uke's balance in the correct direction.

The Barbarella Technique. There is an excellent practice for shiho nage* where uke and nage press their palms together and nage manipulates this contact so that uke cannot readily maintain his balance, but falls in shiho nage. When you can do this reliably with various ukes, you understand the mechanics of shiho nage. It is then much easier and safer to execute the entire throw.

Kaeshi waza for shiho nage usually depends on finding a suki at one of two points: the initial movement or with nage's hands overhead. If uke blends with the initial movement he can sometimes over-extend nage, step forward, and throw. As nage turns to cut overhead, if he is hesitant or off balance, uke can turn with the movement, extend, and cut nage down into an irimi nage. The common beginner escape, turning as nage turns, is only part of this movement, and leaves uke vulnerable. Of course, if nage does the technique correctly, these suki don't exist.

* I first saw this practice demonstrated by Chuck Clark, head of Jiyushinkan, Tempe, Arizona. This approach can be used for other techniques also.

Kote Gaeshi

Kote gaeshi is a quite versatile technique, being useful against an empty hand attack or a knife. It can be a big technique or a small one. It can be done tenkan or irimi, using uke’s hand for leverage or open handed. It involves both a strong kuzushi and strong pain compliance. Nage should flow in a smooth wide movement, taking uke along with him. The technique typically flows in a horizontal circle then a vertical one. The movement as uke falls is similar to shiho nage, but uke generally rotates about his arm rather than about his center as in shiho nage.

Kote Gaeshi

Mechanics: wrist turn out

This technique resembles a reverse nikkyo, applying a twisting motion to the bones in uke's forearm but in the opposite direction to nikkyo. Different people like to apply the technique in different ways, and many of these work. The keys are to prevent uke from straightening out his wrist, and to use his flexed hand as a lever to apply the technique.

Some people use two thumbs on the back of uke’s hand to apply the technique. This is only useful if your uke is smaller or if they are not resisting. It is better to either grasp uke’s hand with both your hands, as shown in the figure below, or grasp above the wrist with one hand and apply the technique on uke's hand with the other, curling uke's fingers in, beginning with his little finger. Kote gaeshi can also be very effectively applied by striking uke's flexed hand and driving through from the hips, though this is rather drastic for normal practice. To see if your way is effective, have uke extend his hand in a tight fist. Grasp his fist and throw uke from there.

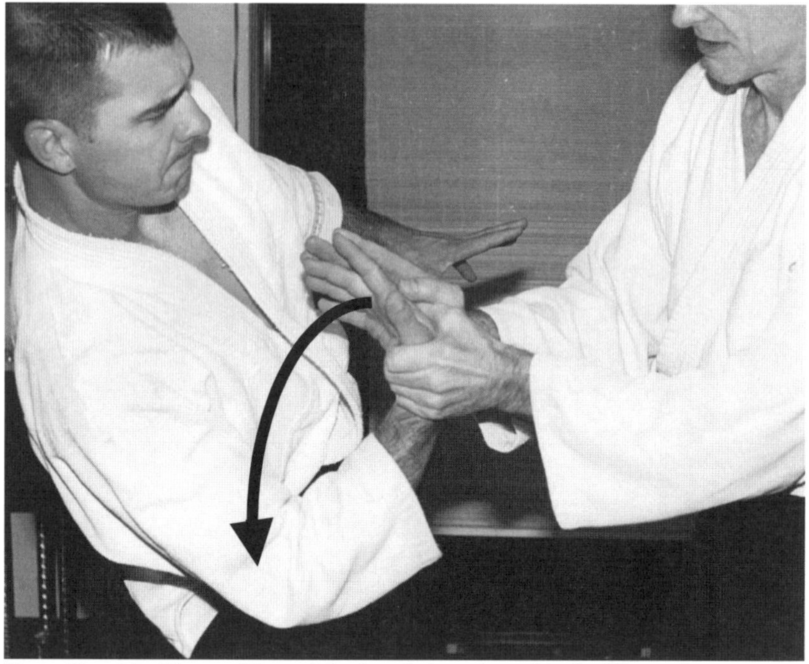

Kote Gaeshi. The position of the hands is quite critical. Uke and nage should only be this close for an attack such as kata dori.

Mechanics: body movement

The movement of nage's body as it relates to uke's body movement is more important than the technical details of how you catch the hand and twist the arm. As Saito Sensei describes in a kumi tachi with two aites, think of turning to cut down the attacker behind you with a horizontal slice, then reverse direction to cut down the one in front with shomen uchi. This may seem difficult to relate to kote gaeshi with a real uke, and indeed the details of the movements are not identical, but if you have practiced kote gaeshi long enough and think about how to move your body to cut with the sword rather than about throwing uke, eventually the two will become one and you will throw uke effectively and effortlessly.

Typically, nage turns his hips one way to get uke moving, then turns back the other way to throw. (However, this is not needed in all versions of the technique.) Nage should blend with uke, sweep him off his feet one way, then, as he recovers his balance, sweep him off the other way, making this a two-count technique. Another way to think of this hip movement is that it is like katate hachi no ji gaeshi with a jo.

Initially, uke might be moving or still, and nage moves strongly off the line of attack, building up momentum. He uses this momentum to get uke moving faster, while stopping himself. As uke recovers, nage does the same movement again in the opposite direction. If you try to reverse uke's movement too early, the technique will be difficult. If you wait too long, he will have time to recover his balance and counter you.

Kuzushi

The initial movement of kote gaeshi should be to blend with uke, extending his balance to the front and perhaps a little across his line of advance. The throw should not focus on the hand rotation any more than yonkyo should focus on the pressure point. In both cases, the pain compliance should be there, but balance should also be broken.

When practicing kihon from a grab, an uke will sometimes lock up, and it will be hard to start the technique. I remember being rather frustrated by this as a beginner. To take uke's balance in this situation, step behind uke and cut away from and behind him, rather like ikkyo tenkan. Nage should be positioned to cut strongly, but uke's arm should be out to the side or even behind his shoulders where he is weak. (See the figure.) Thus, uke is not positioned so that he can effectively pull back and is forced to move to regain his balance.

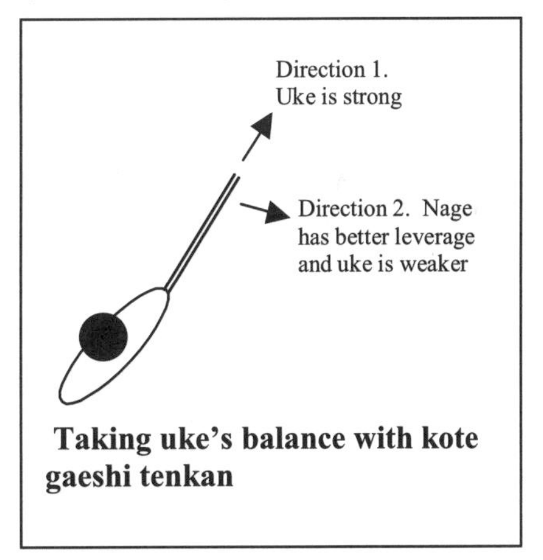

Taking uke's balance with kote gaeshi tenkan

Nage must not quite mirror uke's position (back to back), or he will also be weak and ineffectual. Instead, nage should have his arm in front of his shoulders, so that he can push uke around to nage's front rather than pulling him. The movement should feel like cutting with a sword to nage's front (behind uke). This approach is very different from the way kote gaeshi is often taught to beginners: turn back to back then step away and turn to face uke to throw.

The cutting movement should bring uke around in front of you, perhaps even throwing him to the ground in a sort of kokyu technique. Keep him moving around you rather than you turning back towards him as he moves to recover his balance. Turn and push down to keep uke's balance in front of him as he moves. When uke finally catches up, lift his hand a little to begin the vertical circle, and turn your hips, step, and cut to throw, settling your hips firmly.

Ukemi

The breakfall from a full kote gaeshi is quite important, as it requires uke to fly through the air and slap on landing, after rotating around his own arm. You can often take an easier backwards roll from kote gaeshi, but this can result in more load being taken by your wrist, and it may end up with you frustrating your partners and developing chronically bad wrists.

In a high breakfall, uke should aim to land neither flat on his back nor on his side. Landing flat may hurt his spine. Landing on his side may hurt his hip joint. Landing between these positions should set you on the big muscles of your body, cushioning your bones and vital organs. Uke should slap strongly with his free arm to absorb some of the momentum. The legs can take some of the shock, but there is a risk to uke's knees if they are at an awkward angle. It can be quite unpleasant for guys to cross their legs on impact.

Kote Gaeshi Pin. Nage should control uke's shoulder.

Immobilization

Kote gaeshi is usually finished with a pin, particularly for tanto waza. If you throw uke strongly it is easy to turn him over for the pin: just step around his head as he bounces. If the throw is not quite as crisp, it is important to maintain control of uke as you turn him over. By stepping around uke's head and keeping the same hold on his hand, you can turn the kote gaeshi into a nikkyo, sliding your free hand to uke's elbow to reinforce this with a push down past uke's face and forcing him to turn over. A flexible uke will need more downwards pressure to prevent him wiggling out. A stiff uke will need more room to turn over.

For the standing pin, uke's arm is rotated at the shoulder and held upright while his wrist is flexed so that thc fingcrs movc towards his wrist. You should push down on uke's hand, driving down through your shoulder, your arm straight, pressing on the first two knuckles of his hand. This is like the mechanics to throw uke, but if the pressure is on uke's little finger knuckle instead of the first two, uke will tend to roll over instead of having his shoulder pressed into the mat. This pin can be difficult to execute securely with a stiff uke unless you press down on his shoulder to keep it close to the mat. It can also be difficult to get a flexible uke to tap unless you move his hand towards his head (at the end of his stiff arm with the elbow locked out) until the shoulder locks up. Once that happens, it tightens up the wrist and hand. Again, the shoulder should be kept pressed into the mat: this time by pushing down along uke's arm. If uke has flexible shoulders, you might have to rotate his arm all the way over until his hand is above his head as shown in the figure. With other ukes, their arm will not even be able to reach 45 degrees off the mat. After uke taps, move away before releasing his arm.

Variations and Problems

There are many variations of kote gaeshi from teacher to teacher. The final movement can be a quite small sharp rotation of uke's arm or a bigger movement. It can involve a big step (as in Saito Sensei's third bokken suburi) or just a turn of the hips. Some aikidoka like to cut towards uke's elbow. This applies more stress to the wrist and forearm, but limits nage's ability to use his hips so it tends to be favored by larger people. Some people pull strongly on uke's arm and fling them impressive distances across the mat, but they risk getting whacked on the head by an arm or leg as uke flies past. To my mind, the best compromise is to cut almost at right angles to uke's arm, perhaps a little towards uke (an angle of maybe 80 degrees), with uke's arm almost fully extended. Sometimes people throw so that uke's feet come close to their head. This is not too good. It happens when uke's arm is thrust strongly forward, rotating uke's body away from nage, and his legs towards him – which is not an effective direction. Instead, uke's center should move faster than uke's hand, so that his legs fly outwards and away from nage. Throw too early, and the technique will be hard to do. Throw too late, and uke will swing the other way, and can hit nage whether on purpose or accidentally.

Nage should keep his wrists straight and bend uke's. Bending your wrist weakens it. Nage's wrists should be strong, uke's weak.

There is a variation of kote gaeshi where nage grasps uke's hand from underneath and rotates it. This is almost a shiho nage – if the grip is slipped a little and nage turns his hips, uke will be in shiho nage.

A nice open-hand practice for the flow of kote gaeshi can be derived from the basic technique when uke attacks with a tsuki. As uke strikes, turn off line facing his arm, brush it past you and down with the hand nearer uke, taking his balance forward, and pass his arm to your other hand, working at uke's elbow rather than his wrist.. Make a circular movement continuing up, back towards uke, and down. If done smartly with a small radius and small but forceful hip movement, uke should fly into the air and land on his back – a rather abbreviated kote gaeshi.

Counters

The main counters from kote gaeshi involve keeping a little ahead of nage, and taking over the technique. This is easy to do if nage is sloppy, but difficult to do if uke's wrist is torqued strongly. In this case, uke must relax and go with the technique rather than trying to resist. Counters might include changing from kote gaeshi to shiho nage or irimi nage.

Particular Applications

Kote gaeshi seems to be done most from tsuki, especially with a knife. It is tempting to grab at uke's wrist, but hard to succeed. Furthermore, you could get punched in the thumb, which would be painful for a long time. Instead, blend forearm or hand to forearm. This gives nage a broader target and his arm can be conveniently rotated to bring his hand to uke's wrist while maintaining contact.

If uke resists, making a fist to prevent the flexion of his wrist (not very practical but frustrating to beginners), the technique can still be performed quite effectively by treating the fist as a ball to be rotated with both hands. A great way to practice the actual wrist manipulation is to have uke extend his arm as if punching, but to stiffen his wrist. Nage takes hold of the fist like a ball with one hand, and lays his other hand over uke's fist so that it matches, little finger to little finger, ring finger to ring finger. Nage then rotates the fist towards uke's elbow while turning it outwards. The action must come from nage's hips rather than just his arms unless nage is stronger than uke, but it works amazingly well for a static technique. A variant on this shown by Hans Goto is to look at the effect of either pushing uke's fist into their center or drawing it out. Pushing it in solidifies uke's position and makes the kote gaeshi hard to do. Drawing it out, even just an inch or two, makes the technique much easier.

For any kote gaeshi, but particularly when dealing with a knife, do not let uke push you into an uncomfortable position. Consciously drive the knife away from your face and towards his. In kote gaeshi with a knife, there is a moment as uke bounces on the mat at which it is very easy to disarm uke with a quick rotary movement.

If uke attacks kata tori and holds on to your shoulder as you attempt to do kote gaeshi on his other hand with a large sweeping movement, you can be stopped by the arm gripping your shoulder. You can still perform kote gaeshi if you use a small rotation. Just turn his hand over with a hip movement, and he will fall.

If uke grabs both lapels of your gi with one hand (eri tori), turn your body, grasp his forearm, drive his fist into your chest so that the wrist flexes, and apply kote gaeshi with the other hand through your gi, turning your body to supply power.

Irimi Nage

My enemy attacks
But behind him
I am already standing
O Sensei

To perform irimi nage, typically nage enters past uke's attack, traps uke's head, and uses it to throw him. Nage should blend with uke. If he is too ponderous, uke will turn and hit him. Because of the importance of blending, irimi nage is one of the most critical techniques for practicing aikido.

The quotation above encapsulates the timing for irimi nage. The key is to move as uke attacks and enter behind him, from which position you can throw him. The best practice for this timing is probably in kumi tachi, for example where nage moves off the line of uke's attack and cuts uke's wrist at the same time as uke strikes.

There are many varieties of irimi nage. In the more aggressive versions, nage enters as uke attacks and throws him back where he started. Less aggressive versions capture the head and then lead it round in half a circle before throwing. The difference is in timing, not in mindset. Nage should have the same mindset in both cases, whether an early or late irimi nage, merely redirecting the throw when the contact occurs later.

Irimi nage is sometimes done by taking uke almost to the floor and then letting him stand up, helping him up and back down in another direction. The way most people do this misses the point a little. If you take kuzushi well enough, you can just push uke to the floor. As you take uke's balance, if you just keep pushing down, he will generally fall on his face. If he resists a direct push, often "weighting" him down with the elbow relaxed will take him the rest of the way.

If you do that, it is enough. The technique is over. The fall is not spectacular, but you should have definite control. If he struggles back up, then, of course, you blend with this new direction of movement and as he stands up you throw him down. If uke is bent over you certainly don't fight to pull him back up. A more abbreviated version of this relies on the immediate response of uke. As nage tries to push the head down, uke pushes back and nage flows with this new direction, stepping in to throw uke down.

Irimi nage can be related to Saito's third bokken suburi. As uke attacks, nage blends with the attack in the same manner as laying back the sword and establishes a connection with uke. As nage goes to throw, he steps in and cuts strongly. In this way, the power of the throw comes from the hips and body rather than from the arms. By striking as for a shomen uchi, the arms make a strong movement that comes from nage's center. Control of uke's head and body allow nage's power and momentum to be transferred to uke's body.

Irimi Nage. Control the head and the body will generally follow.

It is generally important to control uke's head, bringing it down onto nage's shoulder and keeping it there while throwing uke by moving his head with your body. Smaller people can have a problem with this, and it may prove easier to capture uke's head if you put your hand on uke's head above the ear rather than on the neck. This gives nage more leverage on uke's neck. You must be behind uke's shoulder, so that he can't turn and hit you.

Sokumen irimi nage is a variation of irimi nage where nage faces the same way as uke and throws with a backwards sweep of his arm. This can be done as a hip throw, nage stepping in close to uke and throwing with a large body movement, like koshi nage done the opposite way. The arm movement then becomes more of a sweep and less of a strike. With this approach, it is helpful to step in behind uke as you drive his head back, taking his space. Your body must blend with uke's body. Instead, it can be done as an atemi to uke's face. This atemi should be done fast enough to make uke flinch, and slow enough to give him time to flinch. As he flinches, follow through and knock him down. An even smaller movement can be used from katate tori (gyaku), especially if uke holds on strongly. The head is then not even involved, and the technique comes close to being kote gaeshi.

Sokumen Irimi Nage

The final push must follow uke's head down. Sometimes I see it done with a horizontal swing of nage's arm or, even less effectively, with nage's arm continuing up towards the ceiling. If the technique is done this way, uke can duck under the movement and turn in to punch nage in the floating ribs. If you follow uke's head, maintaining the connection, even if he tries to duck you can push him to the mat.

Some ukes flinch forward instead of away from the atemi. The logic is to shorten the distance for the arm to build up speed and power, and this is generally a learned reflex of practiced fighters. If this happens, you need to use this new direction of movement to throw them, or just pause and follow his head back after the flinch.

A common problem with this atemi is for uke to raise his arm to protect his face, and perhaps push back. When this happens, the attack becomes a lot like kata tori, and nage can either redirect uke's force back over his head, or turn away from it and direct it down and round. Either of these movements can end up with irimi nage again, or you can move into another technique such as ikkyo. If you take uke's balance as for kote gaeshi tenkan (pivoting and stepping away from uke, though facing uke's back rather than almost back to back), while pushing uke's head up and backwards (spreading your own arms), uke's power to resist generally goes away.

A counter technique from the normal irimi nage would be for uke to follow nage's hand as nage steps behind uke and cuts down uke's hand. Uke then grips nage's hand and escapes under his arm to apply sankyo. If this happens, step more broadly, taking uke's balance better and staying ahead of him to prevent him applying sankyo, then throwing as before, or simply hold him closer.

Irimi Nage. Nage must get uke's head behind his hips.

Kaiten Nage

This technique compromises uke's posture, bending him over (in the same position as ikkyo) so that he is open to further attack while nage retains an upright position. Typically, this is done from an ikkyo entrance, changing hands to hold uke's head down and swinging uke's arm up and over in a circular motion to throw.

Nage's initial cut should be deep, going all the way down so that his fingers touch the floor and uke's head is well ahead of his toes and his back is almost horizontal: otherwise uke will not be far enough off balance. If uke does stand up at this point, even partially, change techniques or throw him tenkan.

Having cut uke down, at the lowest point of its trajectory nage should hold down uke's head. The arm doing this should be straight, with nage's weight over the head. Nage's hand should be placed between the crown and the back of uke's head. It should not be placed on uke's neck, as he can push harder against a hand in that position.

Kaiten Nage

Kaiten nage irimi consists of keeping uke's head down and swinging his arm up across his back, his elbow locked out and his arm forward as far towards his head as it will go, and using his stiff arm to rotate his body and throw him. The direction of the throw should be across uke's body, along the line through his shoulders. If uke's arm tends to collapse, either the arm position or the direction is wrong. As nage throws he should step through so that he can strike uke's head or ribs with his knee. The action of stepping provides momentum to the throw. The ukemi is a straightforward front roll.

We sometimes see nage reach up for uke's head while uke is still standing erect. This is possible if you have uke's balance well enough (in which case anything works) but (as for sankyo tenkan) this approach puts nage in a mechanically weak position and exposes his ribs to a punch. Rather, nage should cut uke down so that he can push his head all the way down to the floor if necessary.

By holding uke's head in place or even pulling it back and thrusting hard on the arm you can flip him in the air. This takes more strength to do, and makes the ukemi harder, but you should learn to deal with this fall also. The ukemi is easiest if you do not resist, but flow with the throw and away from nage.

The tenkan throw results from nage moving towards uke's hips, taking uke's head with him and bringing it down towards his thigh. Uke's arm should be allowed to fall almost parallel to, but still above, his back. (Thus becoming ineffective for the irimi throw but better positioned for the tenkan.) Nage continues moving circularly around behind uke, keeping uke's head close to nage's thigh, rotating with uke, then continuing the rotation from the hips to throw using both uke's arm and head. The technique should start with nage moving around uke, but finish with uke moving around nage. The ukemi is somewhat more difficult than the irimi variation, as uke tends to underestimate how far away the optimal point of impact is, and may then arch his back, taking a heavy fall. Uke needs to reach a little further than expected.

Kaiten Nage Irimi – over uke's back. Control his head.

Kaiten Nage Tenkan – step around behind uke.

Kaiten nage is perhaps most easily practiced from (gyaku hanmi) katate tori, when no hand change is necessary. It can be performed as a single complex movement (in one breath) that ends by spinning uke off into an ukemi. The tempo is like a wave: you cut down hard, then at the bottom of the cut you almost relax while you change position and bring the arm up, then you extend to throw (or atemi).

Kaiten nage can be avoided by uke flowing with the technique and escaping under nage's arm (the one holding uke's wrist rather than the one on his head). This is generally due to nage not adequately breaking uke's balance. If it does happen, nage can grasp uke's collar using the hand on his head, and overbalance him backwards. If uke should attempt to close with nage to grasp his legs (as a wrestler might do), nage can stop him by using an atemi with the knee to uke's head or body, or just by pushing uke's head to the floor. For the latter, nage must maintain his extension and ma-ai.

Tenchi Nage

To perform tenchi nage, nage enters between uke's arms and throws with either arm or body contact. When I was a beginner, I thought this looked similar to irimi nage. What I now see as being different is that for irimi nage, nage is outside uke's arms (ura), while for tenchi nage he is inside (omote), and uke's body is controlled through uke's arms or body contact rather than through his head or body contact. Katate ryote tori (ryote tori) tenchi nage is ideal for experimenting with timing: uke attacking at the same speed and nage either matching his timing, being early, or being late. However you do it, the keys are to upset uke's balance backwards and throwing him where he is weak. The technique relies a lot on the arms at first, but should get to the point where it becomes a body technique. There are always people out there who are bigger and stronger, and if you rely on arm strength one of these people will be able to hold you down and prevent you throwing.

Tenchi Nage. Nage must maintain his extension and keep his arms in front of his body.

As always, nage should avoid direct conflict with uke's strength. To prevent being held down, nage must set up the technique so that he brings much of his weight and strength to bear on uke in such a way that uke has only a small part of his strength to resist with. Thus, when uke tries to clamp down on your arms, move them and your center so that your position becomes better and his worse. An inch or two will suffice. When nage is pushing from his center and uke is trying to resist being rotated rather than also pushing from his center, the technique is half over.

Nage should push along his "chi" (earth) hand by moving his center (hips) towards uke and off line, pushing so that his force acts sideways against uke's chi (earth) arm, giving nage better leverage. Nage's "ten" (heaven) arm should execute an atemi to uke's face. This will encourage uke to hold on to that hand

and move his head back. The direction should collapse uke's "ten" arm by bending his elbow. If this sounds a lot like the kokyu ho exercise, it should. That exercise as generally done is ryote tori tenchi nage suwari waza. The same lessons about suki apply to tachi waza.

Kuzushi for tenchi nage irimi is towards the back, to the apex of an equilateral triangle from uke's heels. This is where nage should push uke's chi hand. Uke will respond either by falling, or by stepping back with the front foot. If nage then steps behind uke, he will throw him anyway, towards uke's new weak point.

Sometimes an uke will lean forwards to prevent being thrown backwards. They will generally only do this when they know what is coming, and it can be countered in two ways. You can use a strong atemi to the face. If uke believes you are going to hit his face, almost always he will jerk it back out of the way and you can continue on. This may be the only way to deal with this if the sensei wants an irimi tenchi nage. However, when the situation is more fluid, if uke is leaning forward to prevent tenchi nage, it is perhaps more satisfying to help uke move in the direction he wants to go, and perhaps either throwing in that direction with a tenchi nage tenkan, or to break away from the ten hand (the one going to go to the face) and turn the technique into kaiten nage.

Tenchi Nage. Nage must maintain good extension.

Common problems for nage include entering with the arms spread too wide apart, and inadequate extension. The angle between nage's arms should not be more than 90 degrees. Besides being ineffective, too wide an angle can put an excessive stress on nage's shoulder joints, possibly leading to a torn rotator cuff. Nage must extend both hands to his front and step to one side to enter past uke's legs. Without the extension, uke will be able to keep coming towards nage. A strong nage can allow uke to enter, flexing his arms, then push out strongly to throw uke. However, this does require a lot of arm strength relative to uke's body mass and inertia and I can rarely do it that way.

Tenchi nage tenkan is done by turning as uke attacks, so that nage pushes him in almost the direction he was going rather than turning his momentum back on him. This requires better timing, though less strength. Often, it is better to switch hand positions, so that the initial ten (heaven) hand becomes the final chi (earth) hand. In any case, nage must not collapse and let uke too close. Instead, he should maintain unbendable arms and turn.

If nage leans forward too much as he throws, uke can perform a sacrifice throw by holding on to nage's arms and dropping in front of his feet, throwing nage over the top. Nage can prevent this by maintaining good posture at the end of the throw, with his back straight and his weight behind his front foot. If uke is still able to hold on and nage is in danger of being thrown, he should bend his knees and move to suwari waza, still controlling uke.

Ude Kimi Nage

This is a takedown or throw from the initial movement of shiho nage, and is good for practicing taking the balance for that throw. It can be applied as a throw with nage's hand on uke's elbow or under uke's arm. Uke's arm must be extended so that his elbow and head are ahead of his big toe (in which case he should be off balance). Otherwise, when nage pushes down on the elbow, a strong uke can just stand up and look at him.

Nage's initial motion is like drawing a katana, with uke's arm as the sword, while he moves in to uke's side. His second movement is to drive his tegatana into uke's elbow, bending it the normal way, with a direction mostly down, but turning his hips to impart a forward motion to uke also. Nage continues this motion, pushing down and rotating until uke is lying face down on the mat with nage kneeling just behind the arm. An immobilization can be applied by rotating uke's hand outwards, while preventing him rolling over by using an elbow in his ribs (but not allowing the grip to slip nor changing hands).

Ude Kimi Nage - takedown. Uke's elbow and head (balance) must be in front of his toes, while nage keeps his center.

To throw, nage just extends further, stepping as needed to maintain the connection to uke. Uke's arm must be extended to get him off balance as before, so that when downwards pressure is applied near the elbow, it further extends uke forwards. Nage can use uke's hand to apply a shiho-nage-like rotation to uke's arm also. This is actually safer for uke's elbow, setting it up for the next movement, and tends to further break uke's balance. (A similar application of force, in which nage is centered but the force is applied off-center to uke, can also be used to advantage for applying ikkyo to a stiff uke.)

The force must not be directed too close to uke's body or a solid uke can resist. On the other hand, it must not be too far from being at a right angle to uke's arm, or the force slips down uke's arm and is ineffective. Thus, the more uke is rotated so that his arm is at an angle behind his body (as, for example, with ikkyo irimi), the stronger the technique.

To throw, nage's arm is usually applied under uke's upper arm. Nage should throw by stepping forwards with the inside leg (the one closer to uke). Using a smooth motion rather than jerking uke's arm, nage should make contact with uke's arm just above the elbow towards the outside, using his own arm just above the elbow on the inside. (Nage's forearm isn't generally strong enough and his shoulder is too high unless uke is really tall.) Nage can throw with his whole body, rotating his inside hip and arm forward to throw, while pulling uke's arm back and down with the other one, as if using a pump handle. Nage should also rotate his extended arm as he throws, finishing with his palm down. Alternatively, nage can pivot uke around nage's inside foot and arm, using uke's arm as a lever and rotating his (nage's) whole body to provide the motive force.

Uke Kimi Nage - throw. From this point, nage should extend and rotate her left arm, and push down with her right.

One alternative way to throw would be to grip uke's arm as for the takedown, but stepping and extending forward so that uke has to fall. Another way would be to apply the same technique from in front of uke's arm. From katate tori (gyaku hanmi) for example, nage can take uke's balance out to the side, hook uke's arm near the elbow, and step back, pulling uke into the throw.

Uke should, as part of his ukemi, avoid letting his arm become fully straight, or his elbow might get hyperextended. Generally, uke can achieve this by rotating his arm so that his elbow is either up or down rather than towards nage, in the event that nage does not apply this rotation. If uke's arm does get straightened, he must not let his body lag in the ukemi, or his arm will get hurt. The elbow joint itself might be damaged, or the biceps insertion might tear loose as uke tries to protect the joint.

Koshi Nage

Koshi nage is a hip throw. Judo has many more hip techniques than aikido and it can be useful to look at these. The hip may be inserted only a little (uki goshi - floating hip) or a lot (o goshi – major hip). A leg may be used to aid the technique (harai goshi - sweeping hip, hane goshi – spring hip throw, or uchi mata – inner thigh). If uke is loaded higher on nage's body, the result is more of a shoulder throw (seoi nage or kata guruma). The commonest variety of koshi nage in aikido requires a deep hip insertion as shown in the figure.

Koshi Nage. Nage must keep uke extended and with her weight forwards.

For koshi nage, you should take uke's balance and, as he steps forwards to recover it, leave your hips in the way for him to fall over. It should not require a lot of strength: Anita at 100 lbs. can throw Karl at 230 lbs. The heaviest guy I've thrown claimed to be 450 lbs.

The ukemi can be the softest and easiest fall possible with uke's feet off the ground – unless he is quite large, you should be able to wrap an arm around uke and lay him softly on the mat in front of your feet.

Many people dislike koshi nage because they have been thrown hard from it, and because they find it a difficult throw to perform. A common problem while learning koshi nage is that uke is afraid of the fall, and resists (often unknowingly) by pushing his hips forward and leaning back. Done intentionally, this is, in fact, one of the commonest counters to a hip throw in judo. The way to deal with it in aikido is to talk softly to your uke and convince him you are not going to throw him hard or hurt him. Once you are reasonably proficient at koshi nage you can work on taking his balance more completely.

Uke's balance is taken in koshi nage by drawing him forward so that his weight is on his toes, but not so far that he has to step. If you maintain this position as you step in, uke will find it very difficult to resist. Alternatively, if you pull harder, forcing uke to step and moving into position just as he steps, the effect will be quite dramatic.

It is not necessary to slam your uke in performing koshi nage, though some people do teach this way. Some people have poor balance and rush through the technique so that they don't fall over themselves, slamming their ukes to the ground to recover their own balance. This is an indication that their technique needs to be improved. If koshi nage is learned precisely, nage will have control enough to do the technique with less effort, uke will stop resisting during practice, and everybody will be happy.

Koshi Nage Ukemi can be quite gentle and undramatic

To practice a classical koshi nage, nage should enter crosswise in front of uke with his knees slightly bent and his hips turned so that one hip is against uke's belly. The point of contact should be below uke's center. Nage's hip that is nearer to uke should be lower than the other one. (The position is like in downhill snow skiing, when the knees are pushed into the hill - in which case, uke would be coming from downhill.) By tipping the hips the other way, nage should be able to float uke off the mat, over the top, and back onto the mat. If you practice lifting uke in the way described but not completing the throw (uchi komi), you will become comfortable with picking uke up, and he will get comfortable with being picked up gently and will lose his fear of the technique. You should be able to pick up your uke with little effort and hold him there indefinitely, not straining and perfectly able to talk. Then you can float him over and, with an arm around his waist, lay him on the mat. (Unless he is really big.)

As uke, don't try to "help" nage. In particular, don't flop onto his back. This can strain his back muscles and ligaments. Instead, just stand there, not leaning backwards or forwards, and let them load you up and tip you over.

Generally, the ukemi should involve catching hold of nage's gi or sleeve with one hand (the one that naturally reaches over nage), watching nage's face so that you don't land twisted, and breathing out and slapping with the other hand as you fall to the mat. You can sometimes float over nage and into a front roll if nage is being generous. As nage, the lower you can catch uke the easier it is to tip him over your body. However, there are practical limits to how much you can carry: your ability to carry weight diminishes the more you bend your knees, and you do carry a part of uke's weight. (Hopefully not a large part of it.) Fortunately, short people are generally lighter too, though it can be a challenge to lift a short heavy uke.

As nage, you can do various things with your arms. Generally, one arm will extend uke up and forward. The other may be deployed around uke's waist, pulling uke into contact with nage. If nage's arm is higher on uke's body it can pull uke down, so that the point of contact is higher and the technique requires more muscle to do. However, this is less of an issue if you push uke in the right direction (up and over) rather than pulling him in and down.

Generally, nage controls one of uke's arms. The other arm can be a problem, especially if the particular technique leaves uke's elbow close to nage's

Koshi Nage. Float uke onto your hips.

face so that nage can take a nasty whack in the face purely by accident as uke swings his arm to slap the mat. In some techniques, nage might want to grasp both of uke's arms, though this might make the ukemi a little more difficult (particularly if nage forgets to let go.) This control can take the form of another technique, but with your body a little too close. Thus, you can readily turn sankyo or kote gaeshi into a koshi nage. Shiho nage can also be turned into one, but you need to relax your grip on uke's hand as you enter, or the pressure on his arm might turn him into an awkward position. With juyi nage you control both of uke's arms, but again if you don't hold on too tightly you can insert the hips for koshi nage.

Mechanically, it is important to keep your feet under your hips. Beginners often straddle their legs for stability, but this is neither necessary nor safe. If your legs are wide, uke could fall down your leg and damage your knee. If you rotate your hips to execute the technique (as you should do), the angle, and risk of injury, will be greater.

If you have your legs straight under your hips, this is your strongest position and you can carry the greatest weight. While the goal is to carry as little weight as possible, you will still carry some, especially when doing the technique slowly.

Koshi nage is a nice technique, but would you want to do it in the street? Uke's elbow can get close to your face, and you might worry about getting kneed as you enter. These are serious concerns. If you find yourself in the range for being kneed, either move out of the way (in which case you can't do koshi nage) or move in so close you are jamming the knee, in which case you're about at the right place for the technique. To prevent being elbowed, you need to control that elbow, typically by putting a hand on it and guiding it past your face.

I find that koshi nage is really great for two situations. One is when you get tangled up and neither you nor uke has a hand free to strike with and neither can let go: then by inserting the hips and rolling uke over them, you can throw very nicely. The other is when you enter as for tenchi nage but end up too close. You can then pick up uke and throw him back where he came from.

Weapons

Weapons can be studied in their own right and as training tools for aikido. I've studied aiki-ken and aiki-jo a little, and use these to improve my understanding of aikido. That is what I am going to talk about here, not how to kill somebody with a sword or stick.

Aikido involves practicing with an uke, to study how to deal with attacks. However, ukes are not perfect, they can only do what they can do, and they are not always available. A jo or bokken can, however, almost always be available and you don't need a mat to practice with one, just a high ceiling.

These practice tools are not toys. They are real weapons and should be treated with respect. A bokken is a wooden sword, and quite capable of breaking somebody's skull. Musashi reputedly fought his most famous duel using a cut-down wooden oar as a sword (perhaps because his opponent Sasaki Kojiro favored a long katana). He killed him with a single blow to the head. A jo is also a weapon in its own right, and there are traditional martial arts styles devoted to studying it (jodo).

Many of the movements of aikido come from the actions of cutting with a Japanese long sword (tachi, katana) – a heavy two-handed weapon capable of cutting a human body into pieces. It was not wielded lightly and quickly: Musashi, one of the most revered swordsmen in Japanese history, warned against "short sword chopping" with a katana. It wasn't that you couldn't kill somebody that way, just that it wasn't the best way to use a katana. Similarly, with aikido, you should practice with big flowing movements, at least until you understand aikido well enough to make the techniques smaller while still controlling uke.

Practicing with two attackers

The power of cutting with a katana comes from the legs. Similarly, the power for doing aikido techniques comes from the legs. Regular practice with a suburito and a bundle of bamboo will develop good cutting power and good aikido power.

However, particularly as you progress, it is better if you can also do cutting practice with a live blade. Cutting will teach that force isn't enough, and subtle things like the angle of the hands make a big difference, just as for taijutsu. The sword should be swung in a relaxed fashion, letting it do the cutting rather than trying to hammer it through the target. You must cut so that the blade is aligned with the direction of the cut. You should aim to cut through the target, rather than at it – which tends to happen with a bokken and a fixed target. The ideal movement will let the sword flow through the target and leave a clean-cut surface behind.

Weapons teach more about distance and timing than only practicing empty-handed with an uke. I expect the same things can be taught either way, but the weapons give us a different perspective on these aspects of aikido. The Japanese have been fighting with swords for hundreds of years, and have studied that art more than they studied the unarmed arts. Thus, they may have a predisposition to teach the finer points of fighting with swords.

With a sword, the primary part of the weapon is the last six inches of the blade, though other parts can be used in a pinch, even the pommel. This makes the ma-ai very precise. Only the last few inches of the blades are crossed. This is enough to engage the opponent's sword and feel what he is doing. Your arms should be somewhat extended, though you can sometimes sucker in your opponent by letting them pull back a little.

Jo Suburi – Toma Katate Uchi

Kumi tachi and kumi jo provide tools for learning movement, distance (ma-ai) and timing. In each case, they are a stylized set of simple techniques. The two partners learn how to make aggressive moves and defensive moves that are generally similar to tai jutsu movements. Thus, for example, with these stylized movements we can study the kamae, the defenses, and the body movements involved in applying techniques.

There are a set series of moves, and even set variations. Sometimes these feel unnatural at first. You should work at them and study them until they feel natural, then you can study the variations that arise when the situation changes from the ideal one. The exact sequences used are not so important. Different styles and different schools often teach these a little differently. However, each move should be performed crisply and efficiently.

The Sword and Body

Aikido is derived from the sword. We often hear this said, but what does it mean? There are probably deeper meanings, but many of the movements used in aikido techniques are taken from movements with the sword. Doing these same movements with a sword and an uke can help us to understand those aikido techniques.

In the first figure, uke took hold of nage in migi hanmi (right handed) kosa dori (ai hanmi katate tori). Nage lifted the sword to jodan, turned so that the sword would cut down in front of uke's face, and lowered the sword to chudan. This applies a form of nikkyo to uke's arm, forcing him into the position shown. A similar motion would also be the start of ikkyo and related techniques, rolling uke's shoulder and bending him at the waist. As in tai jutsu ikkyo, the cut can be more towards the face or more towards the wrist, depending on how strongly uke is holding and how stiff he is. Generally, it should follow the periphery of his center.

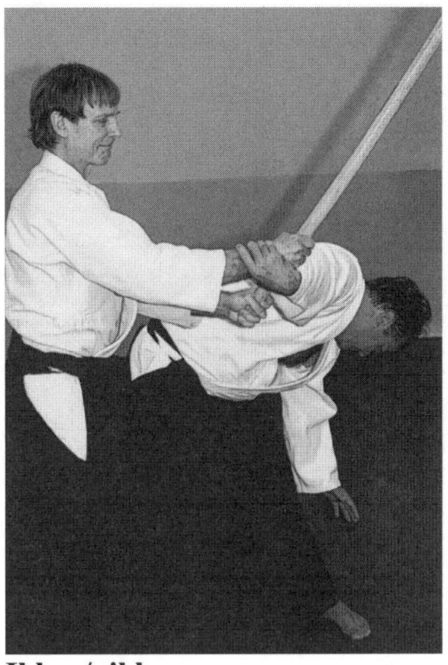
Ikkyo/nikkyo

Shiho Nage – taking uke's balance.

In the next figure, uke was again holding in migi hanmi kosa dori. Nage has made a cut from left to right as if to cut through uke's torso. This extends uke is a fashion appropriate for shiho nage. If, from this position, nage then follows the sword, stepping in, turns and cuts behind uke, uke will fall as for shiho nage irimi. If nage turns without stepping in, this will result in shiho nage tenkan. The target for the final cut can be thought of as a second attacker coming from any direction, or nage can continue to turn until he can cut uke again, depending on how you want to do shiho nage.

If nage extends uke in the same way as for shiho nage, maintains the tension and inserts his other arm under uke's arm,

Shiho Nage – throwing

Ude Kimi Nage

he can step forward to throw uke in ude kimi nage.

If nage steps behind uke, maintaining this extension and cutting behind uke, uke will lose his balance and have to step in front of nage or fall. Nage then has several options. He might again perform ude kimi nage, either a throw or an immobilization. If uke lets go of nage's arm, after nage turns a greater or lesser degree, nage can turn back and cut uke down with an irimi nage. If uke holds on but recovers and stands back up, and nage turns to cut across uke's forearm, this will result in kote gaeshi. The difference between these techniques depends on how uke responds. This, in turn depends at least to some extent on how nage sets up uke.

If uke grasps nage's forearm with both hands as in katate tori ryote mochi (morote tori), nage might sometimes find it difficult to raise his sword. However, by turning so that the sword is about at a right angle to uke's arms, raising the sword becomes much easier. Nage can then turn either towards or away from uke to throw. If nage turns away, he can cut down and throw with kokyu nage (next page). If nage turns towards uke, his arms will be in a position to push back uke's head, allowing him to perform a kokyu nage (sokumen irimi nage) as shown in the figure on the next page.

Kote Gaeshi – taking uke's balance out and behind his body.

Kote Gaeshi – throwing

Tanto

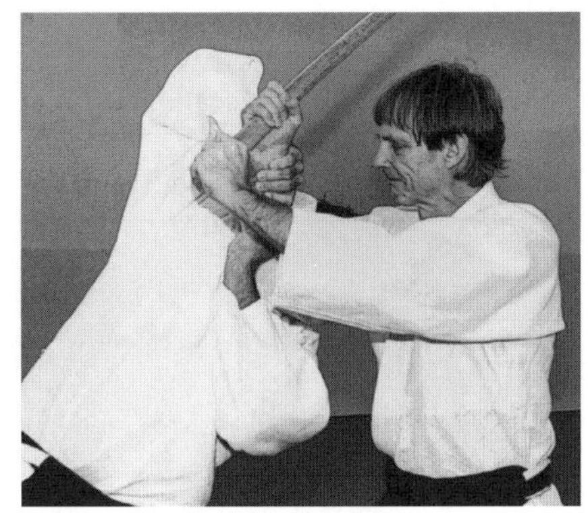

Kokyu Nage - throwing

Knife technique (tanto waza) is dangerous when performed on the street. You are so likely to get cut that many teachers tell their students they will get cut. However, I feel this is setting them up for failure. Go in knowing it is likely, but don't assume the worst.

Cuts can be dangerous or trivial, depending on how deep and where on the body they are. Bad places to be cut are the neck, the inside of the forearm, or the hands. However, cuts are less likely to kill you than are stab wounds. Stab wounds are particularly dangerous to the heart, neck, brachial plexus, and the kidney.

In aikido, we generally practice knife techniques with wooden or rubber knives. However, there is no substitute for a real, metal knife for practicing knife technique. It doesn't have to be needle pointed or razor sharp, but the risk of being cut and the reality of a metal blade are worth some risk. In any case, this is a decision you must make for yourself, with due consideration of the legal issues. Don't sue me if you use a metal knife and get hurt.

On the other hand, most ukes will be reluctant to really try to cut or stab you with a real knife. They will most likely attack a bit slower and more carefully. Thus, it is probably good to practice with both metal and substitute knives.

Whatever weapon you use for practicing, it should be robust enough that it will not come apart or break to make it more dangerous. You should always treat even a blunt knife as if it was real and razor sharp. You can put your hand on the blade of a knife with little risk of being cut, but only on the back of a one-edged knife or on the side of the blade. You can grasp the edge, but a slight slicing movement will result in a severe cut and it should only be done if there is no safer option.[*]

The knife is more dangerous than the rest of uke, so you should get a hand on uke's knife hand, gripping his fingers so that he can not readily switch the knife from hand to hand, and keep your hand on his until you have removed the knife from his grip. You do still have to beware of his other hand, his feet, his head, other people, and so on, but there is a high priority on holding onto the knife.

---

[*] There are European martial art texts that show grasping the blade of a knife. However, the knife may not have had sharp edges – such as a knife used for dispatching armored opponents – or the combatants may have worn gloves.

Aikido – Moving On

The same basic rules apply to tanto waza as to other techniques – evasion, taking the balance, and applying technique – but the stakes are higher. Still, don't tense up and make it easy for your attacker. Remain relaxed and move correctly.

Suppose uke attacks with a strong thrust (tsuki). He is probably not a great knife fighter or else he thinks you are an easy target. Get off line, blend with his

Gokyo Irimi: block must be firm and early. Don't knock the knife down to where uke can cut your body.

arm, and perhaps perform kote gaeshi. You can usefully drive the knife towards his face as an atemi. In any case, control the position of the blade so that it is more danger to him than to you.

If he flies through the air, you can usually remove the knife as you turn him over after he hits the mat, his mind being momentarily elsewhere. If not, or if he takes a back roll, keep both hands on the knife hand and use that to roll him over, applying nikkyo. (Releasing one hand to take his elbow as we usually do for kote gaeshi gives him more chance to get the knife free to slash at you.) Pin him face down, and rotate the knife out of his grip using leverage on his hand, the handle, the knife guard, or, if the knife is in a position that you can do this without getting cut, on the knife blade.

Take the knife and move back. Sometimes people act as if they would cut up an attacker after immobilizing him. This does not seem to me to be in the spirit of aikido, and if there are witnesses you will certainly go to jail for doing this on the street unless, possibly, there is more than one attacker and you can argue that you had to do it to keep the downed attacker out of the fight.

Sometimes people will sweep the knife off to the side. This might look good in a demo, but I want to keep control of that knife.

Knife attacks – like any other strikes – can be thrusts (tsuki) or cuts (yokomen or shomen). What is different is that what would be a touch with an

Gokyo: control the knife with your thumb on his pulse.

empty-handed attack becomes serious and possibly deadly. Thus, somebody attacking with a knife can use short, quick slashes instead of more committed strikes. A knife can be held like a saber or an ice pick. From an "ice pick" grip, the knife might be hidden in the hand and laid along the forearm. Then you cannot safely grasp uke's forearm. The pommel can be used to strike a hard target (like your ribs or head). Uke might strike this way, then flex his wrist to slash and then stab on the return stroke. Uke might trap your arm with the knife and cut it as you try to pull away. Uke might change the grip from time to time, even switching hands.

Slashing attacks can be dealt with by evading the slashes, but you will need to get inside the arc of the knife to deal with the attacker. Generally, it is best to allow the first one or two slashes to go past, and then to block the next one. You must be careful of the risk that uke will pull the knife back in, cutting your hand or arm on the way. You might have to take a cut to get past the knife to uke. If you have to, use the backs of your forearms, as they are less vulnerable.

It is somewhat safer to block the back slash, preferably near the elbow. Uke can still pull back and try to cut you, but it is more difficult, especially if (in the street) you strike hard at the elbow and hyper-extend it. You can then move in and apply a technique.

Knife attacks are harder to deal with than empty-handed ones. The best option is to run away if you can, or get a weapon – a broomstick has longer reach and should allow you to deal with a knife attack relatively safely. A gun is better than a knife if it can be brought to bear rapidly enough. However, while you might use aikido in these defenses, they are not really aikido and will not be addressed further.

If you think you are good at dealing with knife attacks, have an uke attack you with a magic marker – preferably one that washes out. Each mark he gets on you is a cut or stab wound.

As knife attacks are somewhat more serious than unarmed attacks, you and your uke should be prepared to be rather more rigorous. It is all very well to say that aikido is the art of peace and harmony, but if you are attacked your first duty is to yourself and your family, not to an attacker.

Kote Gaeshi – make sure the knife is closer to uke than to your own body.

Jiyu Waza: dealing with uncertainty

Jiyu waza is a free flowing practice where there are basically no rules, other than not to hurt one another. It is difficult for many students because it is so free flowing, but it should be practiced until students have no problem dealing with whatever comes. In particular, it is important that students practice it enough that they don't have to think about technique, and spontaneously generate techniques that they might not have seen before but which are viable and within the limits of what we think of as aikido.

Students should start practicing slowly with one uke and with a limited set of attacks, so that they get used to moving correctly and taking uke's balance. It is a good idea to use a wide range of techniques rather than one or two.

As students improve, more attacks can be added, and additional people (addressed further below). Uke might attack, then as nage tries to throw, perhaps he will change roles, turning the technique into an opportunity to throw his original nage, perhaps this change of roles continues for a time.

What is important is that the student keeps his center. It is also good practice to keep erect, so that your head does not accidentally bang into uke's. There is little that is right and wrong in this format. There is no set attack that uke should be doing. There is no set technique that nage should be doing. Nage must learn to respond spontaneously to whatever comes his way. To do that, you simply have to practice doing it, and practice a lot.

There are some guidelines that can be followed. First of all, do a range of techniques. It is a bad idea to do the same technique twice running. It is also a bad idea to even have a set sequence of techniques, though not as bad as always doing the same one.

Think about what attack is coming. Rather than thinking about a technique, think about how you can evade and take uke's balance. By the time you have his balance, the appropriate technique will probably be obvious. As he will not attack exactly the same way each time, you will do different techniques.

See everything around you. It is a bad idea to fixate on one attacker. Certainly in the street, and perhaps on the mat, somebody else might get in on the action. You must be ready for it and not be surprised.

Pay attention to what you are doing at the moment. Finish each technique crisply and let go of it in your mind. Don't cut a technique short, but don't hold onto it once it has been done.

If something goes wrong with a technique, keep moving, flow into something else. At the least, take care of the attack and move on. Don't stop and think about what went wrong. Don't keep going with part of your mind worrying about something that is past.

Pace yourself. If you try to move too fast, you will make more mistakes. Speed on the mat is attained through proficiency and not wasting time, rather than by rushing. Give each movement its due weight, neither too much nor too little.

There is a natural rhythm. If you rush it, you'll be ineffective and tire rapidly because you have to put more into the technique. If you're too slow, your techniques will only work on a really good uke. Give yourself time, but keep moving and keep your techniques crisp. Position yourself so that your uke's attacks fit this rhythm. Offer the suki you want uke to use.

Multiple Attacks: taninsugake

Aikido is designed to deal with multiple attacks. The basic approach was presented in "Doing Aikido". Most people will have had to deal with multiple attacks in order to get their shodan. Multiple attacks are not very different from what is already learned, though with a greater emphasis on orchestrating everybody's movement rather than just yours and your uke's. Nage must take charge.

As uke in taninsugake, you should attack firmly and at every opportunity, but you are not trying to kill nage, you are trying to give him something to learn with. You should not fight taking the falls either. Do what is necessary to give nage a good practice while protecting yourself. When you are thrown, do not forget where everyone is. Bounce back to your feet. If you continue to lie on the mat you may get stepped on or have another uke fall on top of you. Pay attention to what is going on.

Perhaps the most important aspect of multiple attacks is that nage must control the mat. This involves a number of things, including the way nage moves in relationship to the mat, the way he moves relative to the mob of ukes, and the way he throws in this situation.

It might seem too obvious to mention, but nage should keep away from corners and edges of the mat. If he gets next to an edge, he's restricted, as if there were twice as many ukes. If he gets in a corner it's like having four times as many. If he does get trapped through not paying attention to where he's going, he must burst through the line of attackers and get some space. Less of a problem in most practice situations, but vital in the street, are other obstructions. If there is a slippery wet patch on a plastic mat, avoid it. If there is a gap between two mats, avoid that too. It is vital to be aware of your physical surroundings and where your ukes are.

Multiple attacks require orchestrating the movements of the entire group of attackers, not just having a string of individual encounters one at a time. You must deal with the immediate problems one at a time, of course, but you can't focus on that immediate attacker to the point where you forget the others. You deal with that attacker while moving in a direction that decides who will reach you next, and where they will be coming from, and where you will be at the time.

Nage is like a magnet, attracting ukes. Typically the nearest ones will attack fastest and soonest. The further ones will generally start moving towards you slowly, picking up the pace as they get closer. So if you stay in the same place you will get overwhelmed. This "magnetic" effect means that it is better not to back away from ukes. If nage retreats, this draws all the ukes towards him (and one might be close behind), while moving forward tends to scatter those in his path. Thus it is better to move forward, off line of any one of them, through the line of attackers, or to go through where one of them is coming from and throwing him out of the way.

Just as in the case of an attack by an individual uke, nage must evade the attack of all the ukes. The difference with multiple attackers is that nage's options are more limited. He almost never wants to back up, as I said, not even with a tenshin movement. He wants to irimi past his attackers, slipping between two of them. He can use a tenkan movement for this, but it makes him a bigger target and is most appropriate when he is not too crowded.

Nage can just evade, but it is better if he can also take the uke he is closest to and use him to clear a space. Almost all aikido techniques can involve large horizontal circular movements. This is ideal for clearing space: not many aites will walk in through another uke. Also, throwing each uke slows down his next attack by a second or two longer than if you just evade him.

When an attacker is close, nage can use him as an obstacle, scooting around behind him. This limits other uke's options. However, it also means that you have an uke close, and he can turn in an unexpected direction and get a shot at you.

What happens when things go wrong with multiple attacks is that, more often than a dramatic failure, nage will get slowed down progressively, and the ukes get closer and closer until nage is hemmed in with no room to maneuver and they bear him to the ground. This is especially evident with many ukes at once. To avoid this, if nage starts to feel oppressed and boxed in, he must change the situation. He must actively burst out of the ring of attackers and start throwing more vigorously with bigger and more sweeping movements.

In a multiple attack situation, you must be sufficiently comfortable with your techniques to not need to think about what you are doing, just when, where, and how. The more positive your techniques, the easier the other ukes will fall. We don't want to be too rough, but if we don't throw the first uke firmly and crisply, the next one will be harder to throw and the exercise will go downhill.

You should do techniques that either are over with quickly, or which allow you to keep contact with one uke while using them to clear the space around you.

You can practice throwing freely by starting with an easy situation, with one uke attacking slowly. As you find that you are not having to think about what technique to do next (other than generalities like not repeating the same throw again and again), your uke can attack harder and harder. You can move up to two ukes when you are comfortable with one, and another, and another. After three or four ukes, it makes little difference how many there are, except that the one nage might get tired before all the ukes, particularly if he works hard physically to throw them.

There is a rhythm to multiple attacks. Nage must orchestrate that rhythm to his benefit. If all the ukes rush in at the start, nage must move to prevent them arriving at the same time. Nage should pick one uke and throw him decisively, then move again to an advantageous position. Nage should move, turn, breathing all the time, and keep going. Staying in one place is bad. Getting cornered is bad. Forgetting to breathe is bad. Forgetting to turn is bad. Think positively and actively, orchestrating the movements of everybody on the mat. As the ukes and nage get tired, there is a tendency to fall into a comfortable rhythm. This is not a good way to practice. There is a tendency for nage to let his spirit drop as he gets tired. He must throw off the feeling and keep moving vigorously.

You can get too attached to the situation with multiple attackers. Do not set yourself on the mat and wait for an attack. If you do, most likely it will come from a surprising direction. Instead, remain relaxed and move constantly, both turning and moving across the mat to new positions. Throw one attacker and move on towards the next. Forget the last technique. Focus on the current attacker and let yourself throw him without thinking about it. Keep the entire picture in the mind of where people are, how fast they are coming, but try to keep your distance from the situation, focusing on your center.

Taninsugake is vitally important to aikido. Students should begin practicing it as soon as their ukemi is adequate. They can practice slowly, they can limit their initial practice to open-handed techniques, but it is important to start early and keep doing it.

Part 4. Concluding Thoughts

As I said at the beginning, this is my understanding of aikido at this point in my life. My aikido has changed since I wrote "Doing Aikido", having grown to include more than that world view. It will probably keep changing.

Really Doing Aikido

Aikido is a self-defense art, so there is a tendency to think that we must get meaner and nastier than our attackers. This is incorrect and shallow thinking. While the ability to be mean and nasty might sometimes be useful, this is not aikido.

When somebody attacks you, there is a reason. The reason does not have to be good, but there has to be one. Schoolyard fights used to be about who was biggest and best. These days, even schoolyard fights can be lethal. Fights outside always had that possibility. Perhaps the attacker wants something you have. Perhaps he doesn't like how you look. Perhaps he is afraid of you. If you can figure out the reason why he is acting aggressively towards you, perhaps you can avoid the need to do anything physical.

To my mind, aikido is to avoid fighting if possible. It isn't worth fighting over little things. But sometimes we have to fight. If somebody wants your wife, of course you have to stop him or die trying. We can avoid most fights by not going to obviously dangerous places. We can avoid returning rude gestures and words when we have a problem while driving.

But if you do have to fight, and you do win, what then? Our moral code is written into the law. As I understand it, and I am not a lawyer, it is both immoral and illegal to keep beating on somebody after you win. As I write this, a man recently got six to ten years for killing a man who attacked him first, because he kept beating on the guy. If you knock the wind out of somebody and then pick up his head and pound it into the pavement, or take a knife away from somebody and then cut them up, it has gone from attempted battery on you, to you committing battery, and maybe worse, on them.

If you do have a physical problem, you should do all in your power to resolve it in your favor. Getting tense and angry and swinging wildly at your opponent is not the most effective way to do this. You should stay calm and centered. How you deal with the opponent depends on your level of training. At the lowest level, you might be simply overwhelmed and fail to do anything effective. Almost as bad, you might try to apply particular techniques as your opponent attacks and not succeed. At a higher level, techniques appear on their own, while your conscious mind manages the strategy, looks for other attackers or weapons, and so on. At a still higher level, you manipulate your attacker to attack in the way you want him to and at your timing.

At the highest level, of course, your attacker decides he doesn't want to attack you and he goes away. This might not feel like a win. You might want to beat up your attacker. However, this is immature and risky as well as illegal.

In doing technique, how much is determined by your attacker and how much by you? If you give your attacker complete freedom to attack, it is quite difficult to protect yourself. The first part of a technique is to come together. You should avoid the attack but establish contact and use that contact for the second part – breaking balance. Without the thought of establishing contact, it is difficult to break balance, and without that it is difficult to do a technique. As addressed above, you can do technique in a variety of ways. You can be reactive, take what an attacker gives you, and connect to that. You can be proactive, and reach out and meet him. If you are too early, he will see what you are doing and could use it to your disadvantage. But being proactive is the better way – to actively blend with his attack, making use of whatever openings you can find or make.

Similarly, with a technique, you should be doing what is appropriate, neither letting an attacker dictate nor setting your mind on where you want to go and trying to force an attacker to go there. If you find yourself doing ikkyo and an attacker freezes up, that means part of the connection has gone. Perhaps he has got ahead of you and moved to stop you. A change in direction and timing will get things moving again, possibly as ikkyo, perhaps changing to nikkyo, perhaps totally changing the technique.

At the highest level of practice in the dojo, we can play with these changes forever, allowing the lead to change back and forth between partners (uke and nage being only temporary labels in these cases). This is a good exercise to develop sensitivity to what your partner is doing. In the street, you should be somewhat more in control of the situation. Though still blending with your attacker, you should not be giving him the opportunity to reverse the situation on you, even if he should know how and sees an opening. In any case, do what you have to do both decisively and on purpose.

So, in aikido you should maintain a calm attitude, not sweat the small stuff, and keep things in perspective. Yet you should be able to take care of problems decisively when absolutely necessary. There is aikido in all things. The dojo is part of the real world.

Just Do It

There is a tendency in aikido, and maybe in western society in general, to work too hard. I've seen people working physically hard at aikido and feeling great about it. They muscle their way through the technique, and finish with a great feeling of accomplishment. Perhaps it is part of our culture to value things most that we work hardest to get.

This approach to aikido is okay for beginners, almost inevitable, in fact. But is not what aikido is really about. The less effort you expend on doing aikido the better. Aikido is not about strength training, nor about aerobics. There are plenty of other avenues for doing these sorts of things if you want to. The best aikido is effortless. You get attacked. You deal with it. It doesn't take much effort.

This sort of effortless technique will not happen often at first. Eventually, somebody will grab you, you move and they go flying. You wonder what happened. You might even feel uncomfortable, wondering if uke is just falling for you. That does happen, but usually has a different feeling.

Resistance in uke is something that we soon learn to expect as we are coming up through the ranks. We have to learn to deal with it while we are learning and it can be frustrating. It is easy for uke to shut us down when we are fumbling our way through a technique that is not yet familiar. We might even be stiff, fighting ourselves. All they have to do is clamp down and we can't do our technique.

So we develop good posture, we learn to extend from our legs, through our centers, and to move them by correct physics and timing. But there is another aspect to this. We are practicing with human beings, with all the hopes and fears, thoughts and reactions that go with it.

I sometimes tell people having difficulty doing kokyu ho to just reach out and touch the other person. Amazingly, this almost always works. If they touch the other person just right, their uke just falls over, pushes themselves over, in fact. The same thought will work in doing other techniques. Just reach out and throw the other person. Don't fight yourself or your uke.

This is not a secret. My first aikido instructor told me aikido is easy. It is of course, after a few decades of practice. This is, I believe, what Musashi was meaning when he talked about the void. The void is not naiveté, but the lack of conscious thought that comes through practice, when you do things without thinking, but do them correctly.

Thoughts on Teaching – Doing aikido with lots of ukes

Teaching is another tool that can help your progress as a martial artist, as well as promulgating the art. Unless you can explain to a beginner what you are doing, you probably don't understand it. You might have a technique that works very well, and that looks nice, but you will not be able to improve it past a certain point unless you do understand it. Teaching will tell you what you have not formulated about a technique well enough to pass it on, as well as pushing you to come up with a way to explain it, first to yourself then to others.

Teaching is an honor, but it doesn't make you any different from the students other than in being further along the road. It's nice to have a student offer to fold your hakama after class, but it's probably better for your spirit to do it yourself. It is certainly not right to expect your students to "volunteer" to cut your grass and wash your car unless you do the same for them. Respect has to go both ways.

People come to class for a variety of reasons: to learn self defense, to get some exercise, to socialize, to improve their mind and body, and so on. These are all respectable reasons. If you have enough students, you might specialize, but I don't know any such dojos. People generally do not come to be abused, mentally or physically. They generally don't come to get hurt, though a few seem to come to hurt other people in the guise of practicing or teaching.

What should you teach? Teach what you know. Sometimes teachers will try to teach techniques that look flashy, because they think people like flash. Some people do, but these sorts of techniques will not give students a solid grounding in aikido, even if you can demonstrate them effectively.

Teaching is like dancing with the entire class. You have to know what is happening, and control it. If people are confused, demonstrate again, slower, with more detail and explanation. Show it from a different angle. If people are frustrated, back up to something similar but easier. One way to decide what to teach next is to watch people do a technique, then developing an exercise to fix the problems you see in how they do that technique.

When you change techniques, don't go to something totally new and unrelated. That would be much harder for the class to follow. (This is a general rule, but advanced students also need to learn to deal with novelty. In that case, you will be going from one technique to something totally different, but make sure the class knows why.) To keep to a theme, you might do techniques from one particular attack, or a particular technique from different attacks. You might take a single technique and work on that, piece by piece, either forward chaining or backwards chaining. You might teach the techniques for a test.

Feedback is important, so you should encourage students to tell you what they like and what they don't like. The class is for them, and if you are not being effective in communicating, they should feel free to let you know.

How do you decide what to teach on a particular night? I fantasize that I'll be able to develop a syllabus and figure out the best way to teach aikido, and get a perfect class who will be fit, strong, flexible, always come, and who do what I tell them to do. It will never happen. I can never even guess how many people will be in class on any one night to better than a factor of two. One class I might have twenty students; the next, only six. I never know if they will be beginners or advanced. Sometimes I'll have a few yudansha, maybe as high as sandan, and all the way down to beginners. I can have an idea what I want to teach that night, but nine times out of ten I'll end up doing something different because what I wanted to teach isn't appropriate for who is there, or that it just doesn't communicate to the class that night.

I like to start a class with ukemi, and work up from easy techniques to difficult ones, then do some randori, cool down, and stop. This generally works. If it gets derailed because I thought the class would be able to do something and they couldn't, then I'll change course and take care of that problem. This can be more valuable for them than if I keep to my plan.

What I almost never do is to teach something because I want to practice it myself. If I can't do the technique well myself, I shouldn't be trying to teach it. Sure, I get rusty on some of the techniques on the syllabus. I might have to try them a couple of times before showing somebody, but by and large, the teacher should be teaching techniques that he is comfortable with. Then he will be ready for problems, whether caused by accident or somebody trying to do something they shouldn't. He'll be able to see exactly what a student is doing that is causing him to fail at the technique and help fix the problem.

Should you give praise in class? Of course you should, especially for beginners or for students going through a difficult time. You can't praise beginners too often or too much, as long as it is earned. It should only be merited praise, naturally, and it should be appropriate. You can wean students off praise as they approach shodan, but even after that, exceptionally good performance should be acknowledged.

Feedback is important to most Americans. Don't give praise unless it is earned, but for some people just showing up is difficult. I got little feedback during my early training, mostly negative at that, and was often confused. Hopefully, by the time they reach black belt, students will be pretty well impervious to adversity, particularly if you wean them from the need for continual feedback, but few students start out that way.

When I started teaching, long ago and far away as a new ikkyu in Bristol, my instructor told me never to let a student throw you in class. There is some value in this advice, particularly for new teachers. However, I find it restrictive. I will work in with the class when there's an odd number, or let somebody throw me when I want to feel what a student is doing, to see if his techniques feel right. It does mean that you are not paying as much attention to the entire class as you could otherwise, but you can give much better feedback to that student.

Finally, test people. I used to hear that yudansha can test up to two ranks below their own rank, but different organizations have different rules. Testing shouldn't be important to an advanced student, but it is for a beginner. It should be an opportunity for people to demonstrate what they've learned, to show off a bit, to show why they are where they are in the dojo. Importantly, it reminds you to teach all of the syllabus rather than just the techniques you like.

It is quite important as a teacher to be on time, both at the beginning and end of class. Start beginners out easily. Begin with easy stretches, explaining that you want them to go as far as they are comfortable, not to try to do as much as the more experienced people, or even as much as the more flexible beginners. While you're doing that, explain about posture, about kamae, about the way we practice. Work up to breakfalls, nice easy ones, and then into nice easy techniques. Don't take anything for granted.

You can see more of a person's aikido by watching his students than by watching him. Your students are your mirror, in which both you and anybody else can see your strengths and weaknesses.

How do you know how you are doing as a teacher? Attendance is your most reliable barometer. If most of the students are coming most of the time, and enrollment is increasing or at least holding steady at close to what the mat can accommodate, the dojo is probably doing okay. In any case, attendance will fluctuate from class to class. It might fall over the summer, when people are on vacation. It might increase early in the year when people are looking to burn off some weight acquired over Xmas. It might fall when there is something else happening, like Bike Week or Spring Break. Beyond that, you have to consider what your goals are for the dojo. It is not easy to make a living teaching martial arts. Most of us teach part time.

Practicality is important in some situations – when you have two hours to teach a class of policemen how to be safer on the street, for example. In a typical beginner's class, or any class with beginners, whether it works on the street is way back in importance. Having the students feel they are succeeding is the most important single thing to make happen in a class. Few beginning students will return if they don't feel they are succeeding. As they progress, they will get more resilient when things are not going well.

Ukemi is very important in teaching. If a student feels comfortable with the ukemi, he will learn the techniques easily and quickly. If he is terrified, even if he survives without injury (which is less likely than for a confident uke of the same ability), he will learn slowly or nor at all. Thus, when teaching it is a good idea to spend a lot of time on ukemi, so that students become proficient. With some students, you will need to start with simple stuff, like sitting down and rolling back and forwards (the rocking chair exercise), then progress to back rolls, front rolls, and slapping ukemi. Others might already know ukemi or will learn them faster. Some students – especially kids – take to ukemi like a duck to water. It is important to identify the ones having trouble and help them. Also identify the ones who need to be stretched more, and give them more advanced things to practice. Let students progress at a rate they are comfortable with, and this will differ from student to student, while encouraging them to move along, stretching them a little.

It is good to challenge the students, but few people will feel the class is worthwhile if they are constantly being asked to do more than they are comfortable doing. More important ultimately, constantly practicing techniques you are not ready for will develop bad habits and poor techniques. Ten to one is probably a good rule here also: ten easy ones for every difficult one.

Classes should not always be in a formal setting wearing traditional clothes.

Nobody can see everything that goes on in a class. Still, keep alert. (This is also good practice for street situations.) If you don't actually see problems in class, you should pick up on the resulting tensions. If somebody is being difficult and obnoxious, it shows in his body language and that of the victims and the people who see it happen. Watch the entire class, rather than focusing on one or two people.

Thoughts on Running a Dojo

I avoided having to run a dojo for some time, but eventually did open Enmei Dojo. It has been open in some form for several years now, and I am learning these things first hand. There are lots of details. You need to be competent at business and at "office" politics, both in the school and among schools. It's easy to get bogged down in the details or to get too attached to the perks. Moving forward requires continuing dedication to the art.

Enmei: Clear Circle

Physical	– clear away your opponents	円
Mental	– clear your mind of the confusion of thinking too much, too narrowly, and of the wrong things	明
Spiritual	– be calm, centered, and not overly concerned	

Moving On

Where do we practice? It would be nice if we had our own dojo, purpose built, designed to be just the way we would like it to be. A few schools can do this. More often, we share space because it is cheaper. Thus, we have to practice our art off the mat as well as on it. Part of keeping our place is keeping people happy with us, by being good neighbors.

The facility might have to be whatever we can find, but the mats do need to be adequate. The surface should be firm enough to move briskly on, not slippery or unduly rough. There should be no gaps, and the edge should not be too hard. The mat should provide adequate padding. You can practice rolls on thick carpet (or even without that if you are tough or well padded). Beginners can learn best on a fairly soft mat, but this can make them lazy as they get on in rank. Also, the surface should be firm, not so soft people can't move their feet freely.

Finances are always a problem unless you are independently wealthy. I'd advise being somewhere in the middle for fees. Too low, and some students will question your ability as a teacher. Too high and you may drive good students away.

You do need to keep track of income and outgoing, at least to satisfy the IRS and the local taxing authorities. You need to make sure that students are up to date with dues if you are in somebody else's facility. They have bills to pay also.

You do need liability insurance unless you have nothing that can be taken away from you in a court of law. Sometimes the facility will include this in the rent. Otherwise, you need to get it for yourself. It is not cheap, unless you have a large operation, but the alternative is unattractive also.

It seems to be a facet of human nature that whenever there is more than one person, there will be politics. It can be benign or traumatic, it can be minimal or virulent, it can be dominated by one person or factions can arise that tear a dojo apart, but it will always be there. As we look beyond individual dojos, organizations have politics also. It is important to our dojos and students that we not let them down by ignoring the politics, but hopefully we can follow the aikido ideal of harmony in our political dealings.

To be successful, a dojo has to be popular enough to continue in existence. The degree of success depends on the reasons the teacher is teaching, which might include because he was told to, because he has the urge to spread the art to others, and because that is the only way he can get somebody to practice with. A school might have to be seen to use the facility effectively – generally when there is competition for the space from other activities such as aerobics or yoga. The sensei might have to bring in money in order to keep the dojo open. Few people make much profit teaching aikido, but the rent has to be paid, the electric bill has to be paid, repairs need to be made.

For people to come, you have to attract them. The most effective way to get people to come seems to be word of mouth. (And, conversely, that is the most effective way to chase people away.) But that is only adequate if you meet a lot of new people during the week or for an established school. In addition, you can do demonstrations at local events, at schools, and other places. You can advertise in the papers, in the yellow pages, on the radio, on TV, but these can get costly and be less than successful. Websites can be cheaper. I don't know how effective they are.

From the demonstrations I've seen, there are two approaches. One is to get as many people out there as possible, even if all they can do is demonstrate back rolls. This has the advantage of showing the audience both what they can expect to do at first as well as what they can learn to do eventually. Another approach is for one person to do the whole demo, showing how good his technique is. This is impressive, but can scare off prospective students who can't see themselves doing what is being shown as either uke or nage.

When a new person walks into the dojo, it is important that somebody talks

Teaching is a skill separate from the ability to do good aikido.

to them, asks them if they are interested in taking class. Even if they are not, be polite, because they may know somebody who is a potential student. Encourage them to watch a class. Get them on the mat. Make it easy and non-threatening for them to start. Even the most macho guy is apprehensive when he walks into a dojo: he just hides it better. (They are the ones that are likely to get carried away and hurt somebody else by doing something that they don't really understand, too fast and hard.) Show them what to do, when to bow, how to do breakfalls, how to attack. Don't assume they know anything, but get them doing something, and keep them having fun.

The first things to ask a new prospect are whether they have done other martial arts, and whether they have any physical problems that would make them more likely to get hurt. Make sure they know what they are going to be doing – preferably, as I said, by watching a class. Have them sign a consent form. This won't stop you being sued, but a good consent form makes the case a whole lot easier to win if you are in the right. If they have any physical limitations, make sure they have discussed aikido with their physician.

Safety is crucial. People will not continue coming if they keep getting hurt. This is particularly true when working on breakfalls. Very often all that keeps somebody from doing difficult breakfalls is their perception. How often have you seen ukes bending away from nage when he is trying to do koshi nage? The result is often frustration on the part of nage, and uke is actually more likely to get hurt. When demonstrating a technique, remember to draw attention to the ukemi, especially if it is different or at all complicated.

How much space is needed? Fifty square feet per person seems to be about the practical minimum for the full repertoire of aikido techniques, even with carpet around the mat. A hundred square feet is a lot better, especially for bigger techniques. More is, of course, even better. Most dojos seem to be in the range of 1,000 to 2,000 square feet. Thus, they can comfortably accommodate 10 to 40 students.

It seems to be inevitable that if more than one pair of people are practicing aikido in a single space, they will run into each other no matter how large the space is. A teacher can minimize the chance of injury by encouraging people to practice so as to reduce the chance of collision. Generally it is best to throw outwards, towards the edge of the mat. Sometimes, it is better to have students work in groups.

Rules such as throwing to the outside of the mat can reduce the chance of injury. However, there is no substitute for awareness, and maintaining awareness is an important discipline for everyday life as well as for practicing self defense. Working on the mat is an opportunity for developing awareness, not just of your partner and yourself, but of your surroundings also.

People do get injured, though hopefully not often. I've only seen a couple of serious medical problems in four decades of martial arts practice. Still, you should have a first aid kit for minor scrapes, some first aid training, and ready access to a phone.

Where to go from here?

The main thing is to keep practicing, and one day you'll look at how far you have progressed and be amazed. As Dennis Hooker says when asked how to get good: "don't die, and don't quit". When you really can't practice any more, from injury or age, you can get some of the benefits of aikido by teaching, but I believe that most of the benefits of aikido accrue through regular and vigorous practice. Not everyone agrees. I've had senior teachers tell me that I should just teach and not practice any more. This might suit them, but not me. As I get older, I don't heal as well. I have to be more careful. But so far I have had no major injuries. I encourage everyone to take care of their bodies so that they can continue practicing for a long time also. It helps that the better you become, the less effort it is to do technique.

Life is not easy – things inherently go bad more easily than they go well. Life is about struggling against the second law of thermodynamics, in human affairs just as much as in getting enough to eat. It is our responsibility not to let the morally deficient have a free run. We can't always stop them, but we can make them aware we are watching, and that we will intervene as we can.

As I said in my first book, "Doing Aikido", aikido is a process, not a destination. This book takes another step along the road, but what then? In "Doing Aikido", I suggested, tongue in cheek, that to become a master, you have to be able to walk on water. What does it really take?

I think you are a master in martial arts when you have gone beyond your teachers and become self-determined. Life is easy when you have a sensei. Training can be rigorous, you can take a few lumps, but he is there to tell you where to go next, either verbally or by example. When you have progressed beyond where your sensei can lead, particularly when he is no longer there to guide you, you might be able to move on towards where he was pointing. When you no longer have a sensei, you eventually will have to figure out for yourself where your path goes. You might not even want to go there, but know that is the right way for you and your students. In any case, the responsibility is yours, no matter how good or bad a master you are.

I have been on my own, and have since joined Aikido Schools of Ueshiba. This has given me new goals and aspirations. I can now see further down the road I want to go. Striving is what I think aikido is about, striving to become better. That is what I am trying to do.

Where should you go? Hopefully, you will take what your various sensei have given you, what you will find in this book and other books and videotapes, and, most importantly, from your own experience. Build on these, taking the art another few steps along the road, and train a new generation to carry the art still further.

Glossary

ai hanmi	mutual oblique stance
aiki	flow of energy
aikidoka	an aikido practitioner
aiki ken	method of the sword related to aikido
aiki otoshi	backwards hip throw
aite	practice partner
atemi	strikes
ayumi ashi	normal walking: left foot, right foot
bokken	wooden sword
breakfall	anything uke does to avoid being hurt (same as ukemi)
chudan	middle position
dan	black belt
dori	alternative spelling of tori
eri tori	lapel grab
fune kogi undo	rowing exercise
gedan	low position
gi	uniform
godan	fifth degree black belt
gokyo	fifth principle
gyaku hanmi	opposite (mirror image) oblique stance
gyaku	against the joint
hanmi	oblique stance
hanmi handachi	uke standing, nage kneeling
hara	center of the body
happo giri	eight direction cut
hasso no kamae	defensive sword posture with the sword pointed upwards and the handle by the ear
henka waza	changing techniques
hiji tori	elbow grab
ikkyo	first principle (oshi taoshi, ude osae)
ikkyo undo	exercise for ikkyo
irimi	entering movement
jigotai	posture with the knees bent but the back fairly upright
jiyu waza	free practice
jo	four-foot staff
jo tori	techniques when uke grabs nage's jo
jodan	high position
ju jutsu	Japanese unarmed combat
juji nage	technique involving crossing uke's arms in the form of a letter "X"
kaeshi waza	counter techniques

kaiten nage	rotary throw
kake	actual execution of the technique, after kuzushi
kamae	stance (any stance)
katate tori ryote mochi	morote tori, uke grabs one of uke's arms with both his hands
katate ryote tori	ryote tori, uke grabs both of nage's wrists with his hands
kata tori	grab to the shoulder
kata tori men uchi	grab to the shoulder with a strike to the head
katate tori	wrist grab, sometimes gyaku hanmi
ki	spirit (many other meanings also, depending on the kanji used)
kihon	basic practice
kohei	junior
koho ukemi	backwards rolling fall
kokyu nage	breath throw
kosa dori	ai hanmi katate tori: uke grasps right hand with right hand, or left with left
koshi nage	hip throw
kote gaeshi	wrist turnout throw
kuchi waza	Literally "mouth technique" – talking, generally used pejoratively
kumi jo	pairs practice with a jo
kumi tachi	pairs practice with swords (bokken)
kuzushi	balance
kyu	rank below a black belt
ma-ai	fighting distance
mae geri	front kick
marubashi	taking the center
mitori geiko	learning by watching
morote tori	uke grabs nage's arm with both hands
mudansha	student below the rank of black belt (kyu rank)
mune tsuki	middle punch
mu shin	calm (empty) mind
nage	throw, thrower, shite, tori
nidan	second degree black belt
nikkyo	second principle: wrist turn in (kote mawashi, kote maki)
omote	in front
randori	unstructured practice, often multiple attackers
ryote tori	both wrists held
sandan	third degree black belt
sankyo	third principle (kote hineri, shibori kime)
sempai	senior
sensei	teacher
senshin	state of mind during a technique
sente	strategic advantage

shiho giri	four direction cut
shikaku	uke's blind spot: behind and to the side
shinai	bamboo practice sword used in kendo
shodan	first degree black belt
shomen	"high position" or tokonoma
shomen uchi	vertical strike to the head
sokumen irimi nage	an irimi nage with nage facing the same way as uke, the throw being done by sweeping the back of the arm through their face (also kokyu nage)
soto	outside
suburi	individual practice with a sword or jo
suburito	sword for doing suburi, usually heavy
suki	an opening for attack (see tsuki)
suwari waza	practicing techniques when kneeling
tachi waza	standing techniques
tai jutsu	body techniques (without weapons)
taninsugake	multiple attackers
tanren uchi	practicing striking a target with a bokken
tanto	knife
tachi waza	standing technique
tegatana	literally "sword hand"
tenkan	rotary escape
tenchi nage	"heaven and earth throw"
ten shin	corner step back
tokonoma	"high position" or shomen
tsugi ashi	shuffling movement where the feet do not cross one another
tsuki	punch or thrust
tsushin	state of mind during a technique
uchi	inside
uchi komi	lifting practice (vs. throwing)
ukemi	anything uke does to avoid being hurt (same as the word "breakfall")
undo	exercise
ura	behind
ushiro	behind
ushiro tekubi tori	both wrists grabbed from behind the back (also ushiro ryokata tori)
yokomen uchi	strike to the side of the head or neck; 45° downwards
yondan	fourth degree black belt
yonkyo	fourth principle: forearm hold (tekubi osae)
yudansha	people with a black belt, dan ranks
zanshin	a short pause at the end of a technique to re-settle your mind, state of mind during practice
zempo ukemi	forward rolling ukemi

Index